PORSCHE
THE ULTIMATE GUIDE

EVERYTHING YOU NEED TO KNOW ABOUT EVERY PORSCHE EVER BUILT

SCOTT FARAGHER

©2005 Scott Faragher
Published by

kp books
An Imprint of F+W Publications
700 East State Street • Iola, WI 54990-0001
715-445-2214 • 888-457-2873

Our toll-free number to place an order or obtain
a free catalog is (800) 258-0929.

All rights reserved. No portion of this publication may be reproduced or transmitted in any form or by any means, electronic or mechanical, including photocopy, recording, or any information storage and retrieval system, without permission in writing from the publisher, except by a reviewer who may quote brief passages in a critical article or review to be printed in a magazine or newspaper, or electronically transmitted on radio, television, or the Internet.

Library of Congress Catalog Number: 2005922626

ISBN:0-87349-720-1

Designed by: Jamie Griffin
Edited by: Brian Earnest and Tom Collins

Printed in United States of America

Front cover: 2005 911 (Porsche North America)
Back cover: 1960 356B (Dan Lyons); 2004 911 GT2 (Porsche North America); 2003 Carrera GT (Porsche North America)

EDITOR'S NOTE: The Porsche name, Porsche Crest, Tiptronic, 911, 928, Boxter and other Porsche products are all registered trademarks of Dr. Ing h.c. F Porsche A.G. These are used for identification purposes only. All information herein is believed to be accurate at the time of publication. Production numbers, especially for the older cars, are not certain in many instances, especially with the Pre-A and other 356 cars. The same applies to certain other models as well. Part of the problem results from the fact that in the early days of Porsche, car bodies were provided by a variety of coach builders. At some point in the future, as more of the older cars come to light, hopefully truly accurate figures can be obtained. The author makes no warranty for the accuracy of production figures for any specific model.

The new models were generally introduced in August of the preceding year and ran through July of the following year. For example, a 1975 model was usually manufactured from August 1974 to July 1975.

Acknowledgments

I wish to express my gratitude to Katye Harrington for putting up with my often fluctuating moods. Thanks especially to Klaus Parr, Historical Archives, Porsche AG; Mrs. Reinhardt, Legal Department, Porsche AG; Bob Carlson, Publicity director, Porsche NA; Tony Lapine, former chief of design, Porsche Studios; Mark Anderson, 928 International; Sonja Jordan, Maisto International; Thoroughbred Motors in Nashville, the authorized Porsche and Jaguar dealership; and, last but not least, Auto Zone. Where else can you get a fuel pump for a 1988 V-12 Jaguar off the shelf?

— Scott Faragher

Contents

Introduction 6

356 8
    1950-55 11
    1951 356 14
    1952 356 14
  1952 America Roadster 15
    1953 356 16
    1954 356 16
  Speedster 1954-58 17
    1955 356 19
  356A 1956-1959 20
    1957 356A 21
    1958 356A 22
    1959 356A 22
  356B 1960-1963 23
    1961 356B 25
    1962 356B 25
    1963 356B 26
  356C 1963-65 27
    1964 356C 27
    1965 356C 28
  356 Carrera 1955-1965 28

911 34

901 1964-1967 36
    1965 911 40
    1966 911 40
    1967 911S, Targa 41
    1968 911, 911L 43
    1969 911S, 911T, 911E 43
    1970 911S, 911T, 911E 44
    1971 911S, 911T, 911E 45
    1972 911T, 911S, 911E 46
    1973 911T, 911S, 911E 46
    1974 911S, Carrera 47
    1976 911S, Turbo 49
    1977 911S, Turbo Carrera 51
    1978 911SC, Turbo 51
    1979 911SC, Turbo 52
    1980 911SC 53
    1981 911SC 53
    1982 911SC 54
    1983 911SC, Targa, Cabriolet 56
    1984 911 Carrera 58
    1985 911 Carrera 58
    1986 911 Carrera, 911 Turbo 58
    1987 911 Carrera, 911 Turbo 59
    1988 911 Turbo, Carrera 2, Carrera 3.2 59
    1989 Carrera 2, Carrera 4 (964), Speedster, 911 Turbo 59

1990 Carrera 2, Carrera 4 63	928S4 132
1991 911 Carrera 2, 4, Turbo 64	928S4, 928 GT, and 928 GTS 133
1992 Carrera 2, 4, Turbo, America Roadster 65	**944 .... 136**
1993 Carrera 2, 4, Turbo, America Roadster, RS America 66	944 Turbo 149
1994 Carrera 2, 4, Speedster, America Roadster, RS America 67	944S 151
1995 Carrera 2, 4, Turbo 69	Turbo S 152
1996 Carrera 2, 4, 4S, Turbo 69	944S2 Cabriolet 152
1997 911 71	944S2 153
1998 Carrera S, 2, 4, 4S, Targa 72	944SE 153
1999 Carrera S, 2, 4 72	**959 .... 156**
2000 Carrera 2, 4 76	**968 .... 162**
2001-2004 Carrera 2, 4, Turbo 76	Turbo S 173
40th Anniversary 911 79	Sport 173
GT2 80	**Boxster 174**
GT3 81	1997 Boxster 188
2005 82	1998 Boxster 191
912 86	1999 Boxster 191
1976 912E 89	2003 Boxster 191
914 & 914/6 90	2004 Boxster 193
914/6 99	2005 Boxster 194
916 103	Conclusion 195
924 104	**Cayenne 196**
924 Turbo 114	The six-cylinder Cayenne 206
924S 114	Cayenne Turbo 207
928 116	**Carrera GT 210**

Porsche Price Guide 216

Introduction

The Porsche story began with the birth of Ferdinand Porsche in 1875 at Maffersdorf, Bohemia. Porsche was fascinated with all things mechanical from a very early age and experimented extensively with electricity. By the age of 16 he was reported to have installed electric lights in his father's house.

His first automotive work was with wagon maker Jacob Lohner beginning in 1899 on a front-wheel-drive electric car with motors in the wheel hubs. He soon joined the Austrian division of the German Daimler Company, which ultimately became known as Austro-Daimler. During his time there Porsche began working with others at the company in the development of the company's Prinz Heinrich model, named for the 1910 Prince Henry Trials where Daimler cars won first, second, and third places. Porsche subsequently took a position in Stuttgart as technical cirector at Daimler's headquarters in 1923. He remained there for 6 years before being transferred to Austria to work at the Steyr plant. Before departing for the Steyr plant Porsche was instrumental in the designs of the Mercedes-Benz S and SSK models—two of the most desirable cars ever made. The Steyr company was taken over by a bank in 1930 due to financial difficulties and Porsche was dismissed.

At that point Dr. Porsche struck out on his own, aided by the financial assistance of a successful racing driver, German Alfred Rosenberger, and established his own company in April, 1931. His new engineering and design studio opened in Stuttgart, staffed with a dozen engineers and designers, including his son Ferry Porsche (born 1909), Erwin Komenda and Karl Rabe. Ultimately, this team would be responsible for the launch of the Porsche 356 and established the Porsche company as an automobile manufacturer, rather than strictly as a for-hire design studio.

At the Porsche design studio in Stuttgart, Dr. Porsche was hired to develop a racing car for the Auto Union company. The plan was for 16-cylinder rear-engine car designed to compete on the Grand Prix circuit. This car, despite its large size, was the first in a line of mid/rear engine cars that would eventually be Porsche's trademark. Porsche and his team designed and built a variety of engines, including a water-cooled V-10. Other cars and technical improvements were designed for various manufacturers, largely riding the rising tide of new German nationalism under the influence of Adolph Hitler, who had reawakened German pride following World War I.

While Porsche had been associated with many cars since his first work with the electric car, the first of many cars for which he would become personally famous was the Volkswagen "Beetle." Porsche was directed by Adolph Hitler to design a "people's" car, something which would be available to the working-class German citizen. It was intended to be priced at below 1,000 marks—a figure which that was considered within reach of an average working German family at the time. Porsche designed the car as a four-seat passenger vehicle with an air-cooled rear engine.

Porsche decided to start up a totally new, or almost new, project for a people's car. That name, which later met with the good fortune we know about, was officially used for the first time by Porsche on January, 17 1934, when he decided to begin a detailed study of this concept. On April 27 of the same year, only 3 months later, the complete drawings of the prototype were ready. *

Three prototypes were built in the garage of

Dr. Ferry Porsche stands with some 356 series Porsches, a proud automotive heritage.
Porsche NA

Porsche's house in Stuttgart. The plans proved acceptable, and 30 additional cars were made and tested. The original V series cars as they were known were built on a metal spine-type chassis with wooden floorboards and a separate body. Several engines were used in these first cars, including both flat two- and four-cylinder models. A four-cylinder became the ultimate choice. The first car, dubbed V-1, was a coupe, while the second was a roadster. The hardtop versions had horizontal louvers rather than a rear window for the purpose of maintaining structural rigidity.*

Although these cars would change considerably before becoming the Volkswagen Beetle, that car which was manufactured for more than 50 years was clearly influenced by the early V series cars. Hitler was pleased and directed Porsche to manufacture the VW. At this point it was more of an order than a request. Porsche suggested that in order to accomplish this he needed to visit the USA, which he did in 1936, meeting with Henry Ford in an effort to learn some of the requirements for manufacturing large numbers of cars. While in America, Porsche and his traveling companions visited General Motors, Chrysler, and other major manufacturers, taking notes and preparing for their return to Germany.

A site for the VW factory was sought that had rail access and adequate water. The city of Wolfsburg was selected and the VW factory was started, with Hitler himself placing the cornerstone in May, 1938. By 1941 the first VW Beetles were produced. Hitler was also thoroughly committed to automobile racing and technological development in all fields, and devised a race that would highlight the technical advances of German manufacturing. This race would run from Berlin to Rome in late 1939. Porsche set to work on three aerodynamic coupes (Type 60K10) designed for the planned race and based upon the VW Beetle, which had more or less reached its basic appearance by 1936. Meanwhile, the Porsche company had moved to a part of Stuttgart called Zuffenhausen and Porsche, in addition to his title of "Automotive Designer for the Reich," was placed in charge of armaments by Hitler and ordered to design tanks. The tide turned against the Third Reich, however. By 1944, to escape Allied bombing, Porsche and crew moved to remote Gmund, Austria, and set up shop in a converted sawmill. The much-anticipated Berlin to Rome race of 1939 never happened, but the cars Porsche built for that race heavily influenced the 356 coupe, which was the forerunner of the 911.

Ferdinand Porsche was imprisoned by the French in Dijon after the war for nearly 2 years due to his wartime work for the Nazis, but the Porsche company continued under the direction of his son, Ferry, and his sister, Louise Piech. It was after Ferdinand Porsche's hard-won release from French prison in 1947 that things really began to take off for Porsche as a company. The time in prison had taken its toll on the aging Porsche, but the success of the projects that had been started under his hand would soon reach fruition. In the meantime, production of the VW continued and sales increased.

(Porsche) was paid a royalty of 5 marks per unit produced. In addition to this, there was the rent for the buildings at Zuffenhausen, which the American occupants had unilaterally decided to pay him, and the earnings, meager though they were, from the activities in Gmund. It was in part to reinvest these sums of money, otherwise taxed heavily by the government, that Porsche decided to begin producing his new sports car on German soil.*

*Porsche Catalogue Raisonne 1947-1987. Stefano Pasini. Copyright 1987 by Automobilia International Publishing Group, Milano.

Porsche 7

After World War II, Porsche returned to the basic design of the cars planned for the 1939 race. 1948 saw the first Porsche 356, number 1, an open mid-/rear-engine roadster engineered by Karl Rabe and produced under the supervision of Ferry Porsche at Gmund, Austria. It had an 1131cc air-cooled Volkswagen mid-/rear-engine (Motor No. 356-2-034969), tubular frame, an open-top body designed by Erwin Komenda, and was the first to bear the Porsche name, in elongated lettering presented the same as it is today. This car, while mid-engined, unlike the 356 series which it spawned, is clearly visually related to the 356 production cars that followed. The mechanical components, including suspension and steering, were taken directly from Volkswagen.

The 356-2 series that followed differed in that the cars were built on a metal platform, not unlike those of the Volkswagen, rather than with a tubular frame as with 356-1. They also had a rear engine, rather than a mid-engine. Like the 356-1, however, the 356-2 had an aluminum body. The new Porsche made its public debut at the Geneva Auto Show in March 1949 in the form of a two-door coupe and a Beutler-bodied roadster. Production was extremely limited at the Gmund shop, with a total of four cars produced in 1948. In 1949 25 were produced, and 18 in 1950. It is believed that only 51 cars were manufactured and sold from Gmund, but Pasini indicates that chassis numbers 055 and 057 have been found and authenticated. While production numbers of the Gmund 356-2 seem not to be absolutely certain, it is accurate to say that numbers were small, mainly due to the fact that the bodies of the Gmund coupes were literally hand made.

At this point coach builders were literally a holdover from the horse and carriage days. As the term applied to the automotive industry, especially in its infancy, coach-built cars were made to order. A client would select a body style or work with a designer to create one that would then be constructed and affixed to the chassis of whatever brand car he'd purchased.

There were many famous coach builders, especially in France, Germany and the UK. The tradition continued in the U.S. through the 1930s with coachbuilders like Fleetwood. Thus, a James Young-bodied Rolls Royce, for example, had a body designed and fitted to the chassis by the company of coach builder James Young. Usually these custom made car bodies were constructed of aluminum, hand hammered and fitted over a wooden mold, then welded and attached over a wooden frame on the actual car. Some of the famous names among coach builders were: Vanden Plas, Hooper, James Young, Fernandez & Darrin, Freestone & Webb, Pininfarina, H.J. Mulliner, Park Ward, Offord, Fleetwood, Barker, Brewster, Thrupp & Maberly, Compton, and Drauz. Most of these companies were either bought by automotive manufacturers, merged, or went out of business altogether as car manufacturers began making their own bodies in house. In other cases, the term coach builder has been replaced by the more contemporary designation "design studio."

The Swiss company Beutler built six of the eight original cabriolet (convertible/drophead) bodies used on the Gmund 356-2s. Porsche began ordering bodies from the Reutter Company in Stuttgart beginning in 1949 with an initial purchase of 500—the initial projection of sales for the 356. The bodies, steel rather than aluminum, were to be delivered in a staggered manner with an anticipated delivery of less than 10 per month. By the end of 1950, a total of 298 cars had been built and sold, which was far more than anticipated. Later, in 1963-64, Porsche bought Reutter and used it to make the bodies for the 356. Porsche ordered bodies from other companies because in the early years it did not have the facilities to manufacture car bodies in house on the scale required. Porsche did make car bodies in house, but they were hand made, which made the process expensive and time consuming.

The 356 was similar, indeed, to the Volkswagen from which it was spawned, which provided ammunition for its detractors. The essential criticism, one which lingered at least through the 1960s, was that a Porsche was nothing more than a "glorified Volkswagen." It was an observation not meant to be particularly flattering. Comments of this nature were not without some merit, at least in the early years. The basic configuration of a pressed steel body pan-chassis, cable-operated VW brakes, rear swing axle, what was essentially a VW engine, and an outright VW gearbox added to the criticism.

When compared to other sports cars of the era, especially cars like the Jaguar XK-120, the early Porsches looked "bug-like." And while the XK-120 was long, low-slung, and rakish, the Porsche 356 was short, squatty and, as far as most American motorists were concerned, somewhat unusual in appearance. First of all, American motorists, particularly automotive enthusiasts, were not generally used to "small cars." Prior to 1945, a "performance car" meant cars like the Auburn Speedster, a supercharged Cord, a Packard Darrin, a Duesenberg SJ, or possibly a V-16 Cadillac. Americans, with few exceptions during the years preceding World War

This 1949 Porsche 356SL roadster is skirted for racing.
Bob Harrington

II, stuck with American brands. There was really no such thing as a sports car in America, at least prior to the end of the war. That which would have been considered such, had the concept existed at the time, would have been a large, expensive, high-powered car, with an open top. This is not to deny the existence of cars like the 1930s Jaguar SS, or some of the open Mercedes cars that were actually raced on the beach at Daytona before World War II. These cars were for the super rich of the time and seldom seen by the average man in the street.

It was not until after the war that the American psyche was even ready for a sports car. It should be remembered that the American automotive market was in a constant design flux, decade to decade, since the automobile's inception. By the beginning of World War II, American car manufacturers were starting to take bolder design steps. The revolutionary "coffin-nose" American Cord of the late 1930s, for example, was a far cry from the formal and elegant Cord L-29 of the late 1920s. While some American cars had been small up through the late 1930s, compared to, say a V-12 Lincoln Zephyr, the most desirable American cars remained the larger, more expensive models. And for the average working man who could not afford a luxury car, Fords and Chevys dominated the field.

1950-55

During the war years in America, the automobile factories, indeed all manufacturing concerns were focused on the war effort, to the extent that production of passenger cars for the American motoring public was curtailed for several years during that period as car manufacturers began making tanks, airplanes, and other military vehicles instead. At the end of the war, much had changed worldwide. Americans who, for the most part, had stayed within 100 miles of their birthplace, returned home, having been literally all over the world. They had been exposed to people, places and things they never would have imagined.

The suspension of automobile production during the war had resulted in an extreme shortage of cars of all kinds on the home front. Regrettably, many early U.S. cars that might have otherwise been saved were melted down for military use during the war effort on the homefront. The need for new cars after the war was immediate and almost unlimited. Older pre-war cars in good condition still brought high prices due to the immediate postwar shortage, while ex-soldiers had the first shot at new cars. It was out of this milieu that the sports car was born.

Several important automotive trends were happening at the same time in the postwar era. Stock car racing, which had always existed prior to the war in the U.S., mainly as dirt track racing, was on the verge of becoming extremely popular. Ferrari, another major player, was coming into existence, and the world was ready to put the war years behind and move into the modern era. The new America was wide open for something new and different. Within scarcely more than a decade after the end of the war, Porsche, Jaguar, and Ferrari would become major players as the U.S. and the world became fascinated with speed.

A sports car, as the concept developed, should by definition be an open car, should probably have wire wheels, should be exotic in appearance, and should have performance capabilities beyond that of a normal passenger car. Perhaps above all, a sports car should project a certain image for its owner. With the exception of wire wheels, which for some reason were never used, the Porsche 356 met these criteria.

Basically, European as well as American and English postwar car manufacturers resumed production essentially where they had left off prior to the war. This meant that the first postwar cars were not much different than their prewar predecessors. Porsche, on the other hand, was more or less starting from scratch, unencumbered by any preexisting concepts, save the VW that had been designed by Porsche.

The Porsche postwar aerodynamic shape, while not entirely unique (the late 1930s Chrysler Airflow had it, for example), was particularly unusual in that it lacked the vertical grille that had

Dr. Ferry Porsche emphasizes the importance of Porsche engine performance.
Porsche NA

characterized nearly every automobile up to that time. The upright grille had evolved over time from a decorative but functional radiator housing to an expected design element. Even the air-cooled American Franklin had a false radiator shell in its day. The grille and front-end treatment could have been the most significant design aspect of any car of the time. Porsche was able to dispense with the radiator and grille altogether by having an air-cooled, rather than water-cooled, engine. Its placement at the rear of the car, while again not unique, would ultimately become one of the defining elements of Porsche, and Porsche, except for Volkswagen, would become the only company to survive with a strictly rear engine configuration.

The 356 also had an independent four-wheel suspension and a unitized steel body. While the rear suspension, a swing axle type, was primitive by modern standards, it represented the state of the art at the time. The unitized steel body provided a superior rigidity over the standard body-on-frame construction of most manufacturers of the time.

The development of the American market for Porsche rested on the 356 and the changes from its original specifications, which made it more palatable to Americans. These changes included increasing the engine size, reworking of the cable-operated braking system, and proper instrumentation. Sales duties in America beginning in 1950 were granted to Max Hoffman, an Austrian who would become one of the most important figures in the sports car world. Within 10 years after World War II, he would be importing Jaguars, Mercedes, and Porsches into the U.S. market, and would largely be responsible for the Porsche 356 America and Speedster.

While there had been criticisms of the early Porsche cars for a number of reasons, their initial successes in the racing world could not be denied. Though Ferdinand Porsche had not sought to build racing cars per se, they were quickly adapted to racing and their many victories in the most important races of the world did not escape the notice of the American buyer.

The early cars were difficult to drive in that they had a majority of their weight in the rear, which meant that the tail could suddenly swing out violently and without warning if a curve was approached too fast. This trait, rather than being negatively perceived, instead became a source of amusement to Porsche owners, something of an inside joke. It was a fact that the rear-engine cars required a breaking-in period for the new owner. This is still true today, especially of the earlier cars. To the purist, the oversteer and raw noise of an early 356 can never be replaced by a modern hi-tech car.

356 Engines

The Porsche company's use of such a wide variety of four-cylinder engines in what was essentially the same car over the 356's 15-year run seems peculiar in retrospect. Jaguar, by comparison, produced three sports cars similar to each other during roughly the same 15-year period as Porsche (XK-120, XK-140, and XK-150). The Jaguars were comparable to the 356 in that they were similar to each other in appearance with the same front engine and rear-wheel drive.

All of the Jaguar engines featured a cast-iron block, a traditional oil pan at the bottom of the engine, and aluminum heads. The only significant change in the Jaguar engine was its increase in displacement from 3.4 liters to 3.8 liters, and finally to 4.2 liters beginning with the 1965 Jaguar E-Type. Why, then, so many different engines for the Porsche 356? The first Porsche engines were basically Volkswagen power plants—a source of derision for many detractors of the early cars. While this subject was, and still is at times, a source of embarrassment to some Porsche owners, it should be remembered that while it may have essentially been a Volkswagen engine, it was an engine which had been designed by Porsche.

While many are inclined even now to dismiss the earlier Porsche engines due to their paltry horsepower ratings, there is much to be said for their peculiar design both aesthetically and practically. Originally the two-piece block was cast alloy, while the separate individual cylinders were of cast iron with fins for cooling. While cast-iron cylinders were not uncommon, the vertical halves of the Porsche's alloy engine block were. The engine lacked an oil pan as such and retained the oil in the bottom of the crankcase where it was channeled via a camshaft-driven pump to the engine's internal components and then to a vertical oil cooler before recirculation. The engine was also air-cooled, and consequently loud, but designed in such a way that the outside air was directed to the cylinders via a crankshaft-belt driven fan at the end of the generator's main shaft. The air was pulled into a specially designed housing that kept the air focused on the cylinders. Engine changes followed both in construction, displacement, and materials, with the cast-iron cylinders replaced by alloy cylinders. The strange two-piece magnesium alloy vertical engine

The profile of the first 356 is shown in this 1992 car insurance ad.

A 1952 356, with bumpers removed, still is a competitive racer today.
Bob Harrington

block was replaced by a three-section aluminum block beginning with production of the 1955 models, and all subsequent pushrod engines featured the three-piece engine block. The four-cam engines retained the two-piece crankcase throughout production of the 356.

By the end of 1954, a total of six engines had been offered for the year. Again, why? The 356 would ultimately end the way it started, with a flat four-cylinder engine. It is true that during the years since the original modified 40-hp VW engine had been offered, much had changed, but by the conclusion of the 356's successful run in 1965, it still only offered 95 hp at 5800 rpm. This was probably more significant in the U.S. market than elsewhere, due to the beginning of the U.S. muscle car era, where nothing was considered more desirable than an American V-8, the larger the better.

1951 356

Changes in the early cars were frequent, and often involved engines. Engine bore was increased to 80mm bringing engine size to 1286cc and 44 hp, although the 1100 was still offered. In October 1951 the 1500cc debuted with the introduction of the optional Type 527 engine. This engine featured roller bearings, larger Solex carburetors, aluminum heads, and developed 60 brake horsepower (bhp). Side front vent windows were temporarily replaced by one-piece glass. In August 1951, the 1,000th car was produced.

1951 production total: 1,069 cars (900 coupes, 169 cabriolets)

1952 356

1952 saw the introduction of a fully synchronized Porsche gearbox, rather than a Volkswagen transmission. Early cars had no synchronization and it was very easy to grind gears. Some early sports cars were synchronized later, but as with the Jaguar XK 120, not in first gear. The 55-hp 1500 engine and 70-hp roller bearing 1500S engine were available by the end of the year. A one-piece, but still V-shaped, front windshield was introduced as well as a rear folding seat. The spare tire located in the front storage section was repositioned from horizontal to nearly vertical to allow for increased luggage space. Nonetheless, considering the additional presence of the fuel tank, luggage space was minimal. Bumpers were also extended slightly from the coachwork to reduce the damage to the body in a minor incident involving a bumper. Beginning in autumn, a two-arm steering wheel with the Porsche Crest replaced the earlier three-spoke banjo-style wheel similar to those found on many American cars of the 1940s.

1952 Production totals: 1,297 cars (1,057 coupes, 240 cabriolets).

1952 America Roadster

While Porsche was a relatively expensive car even in the early days, some people were not so happy with the pricing, particularly importer Max Hoffman, who wanted lower-priced cars for the American market. Many of the first Porsche buyers were doing everything possible to lighten the cars for racing anyway, especially West Coast owners, including one racer who actually cut the top off one of the three aluminum-bodied 356 SLs. Hoffman consequently suggested a stripped-down version at a lesser cost, a suggestion he felt which would increase sales in the American market. To this end the "America" was devised. It was a lighter-weight car with an even more minimal interior created solely for export to the American market. It was hoped that the American buyer would be more likely to buy this lower-priced version, especially racers for whom it was mainly designed.

Production of an aluminum-bodied America roadster began in 1952 with bodies made by Heuer. The America came with a 90.77-cubic inch 1488cc pushrod engine that produced 75 bhp. Most of these cars entered the U.S. via New York importer Hoffman. According to Laurence Meredith in his book *Original Porsche 356*, "Just 16 examples of the alloy-bodied America Roadster were built by Heuer during 1952, and were intended for competition. Its hump-backed styling and minimal equipment provided inspiration for the Speedster, introduced in 1954." Of the 16 known to have been built by Heuer, 14 are thought to have come to the U.S. Heuer's production only lasted a few months before the company went out of business.

The exact number of America Roadsters built remains uncertain. Pasini offers different numbers. As he says in *Porsche Catalogue Raisonne 1947-1987*: "Production began on the Roadster America in March of 1952, with an all-aluminum body by Glaser; almost all the cars were bought by Max Hoffman, and Briggs Cunningham was naturally one of the first purchasers. But no one knows how many were built, partly because some bodies other than Glaser were produced by Drauz for John von Neumann. The complete list of Roadster Americas by Glaser is confused by the fact that accounts of the period speak of twenty cars built, others of at least fifty or even sixty, and in any case these were actually produced in two distinct series, one in 1952, and the other in 1953."

While the America is especially desirable today due to its extreme rarity, it was significant at the time because in the early days of sports car racing and rally events in the U.S. (and probably elsewhere), many entrants drove to events in the cars they intended to race. As Laurence Meredith observes in his book *Original Porsche 356*: "Competition-minded owners particularly liked the Roadster's talent for being able to shed weight quickly. The glass windscreen, secured by two wing nuts and one bolt, could be removed and substituted for a Perspex one, saving 20 lbs. (9kg). Aluminium bucket seats and leather bonnet straps also saved weight. In true amateur tradition, the Roadster could be driven to a sporting event, stripped of its hubcaps, hood, jack, tools, boot lining and other superfluous trim, take part in a race, and be driven home on the public

This 1953 Cooper-Porsche racer is nicknamed the "Pooper."
Bob Harrington

roads afterwards. In all, as much as 115 lb (51kg) could be saved by the removal of these bits and pieces."

1953 356

1953 356 production: 1,941 cars (1,547 coupes, 394 cabriolets)

1954 356

A total of six engines were available for Porsche cars in 1954, but only the 1,500 and 1,500S were sold in the U.S. As the late Dean Batchelor related in his *Illustrated Porsche Buyer's Guide:* "American importer Max Hoffman didn't accept the smaller displacement models for sale in the United States. He thought, and was probably right, that Americans wouldn't buy the smaller engine sizes at the price the cars would have to be sold for in the United States." One still can't help but wonder, in retrospect, what the point was in having that many engines available for basically the same car.

The 1500S was introduced with a 70-bhp engine, top speed of 105 mph, and acceleration from 0 to 60 mph in 10 seconds. Engine production of the 1100cc engines ended in 1954 altogether. The 5000 car was produced in March 1954. The steering wheel was provided with a horn ring and offered in three colors. Most significantly for the body, horn grilles were incorporated with the turn indicator lights at each side of the front end—a feature that would become a characteristic of all subsequent 356 series cars.

1954 356 production: 1,891 cars (1,363 coupes, 328 cabriolets, 200 Speedsters)

Speedster 1954-58

The first Porsche Speedsters were offered in 356 form in September 1954 as the result of Hoffman's continuing desire for a less-expensive, sportier car for the American market. The Speedster was initially a lighter, stripped-down version of the pre-A series cars. Among its distinctive features were its lower, fully curved windscreen, unlined convertible top, and removable side curtains, rather than roll up windows. Removable side curtain windows were common on most sports cars of the time including Jaguar, MG, and other open cars. They were often difficult to fit and provided extremely poor visibility in rain. The clear plastic windows tended to turn cloudy or brown over time, and became brittle as well, further diminishing their effectiveness.

The Cabriolet, with its higher roofline and padded headliner, was much more effective at keeping the weather out, and was similar to that found on the Jaguar XK-120, and later 140, and 150 "Dropheads." The Jaguar roadsters, like the Porsche Speedster, had minimal tops with side curtain windows, rather than roll-ups. Be that as it may, the lower-profile windscreen and side windows give the Speedster a rakish appearance that is generally considered more attractive than that of the higher profile Cabriolet.

The interior appointments were minimal as expected, with no door pockets or even a glove box. The original Speedster seats were true bucket seats as opposed to the more comfortable seats of the other Porsche cars. The instrument panel was minimal as well, consisting of two large gauges (speedometer and tachometer) and one smaller one (oil and temperature) placed between the two, but slightly higher. By the 1956 model year,

356 Technical Specifications (1950-1955)

Engine:	Opposed air-cooled, four-cylinder, rear-mounted
Body:	Pressed-steel, unibody
Wheelbase:	82.7 inches
Track:	Front: 50.8 in.
	Rear: 49.2 in.

The 356A cabriolet—with its top removed and leaning on the nearby fence.

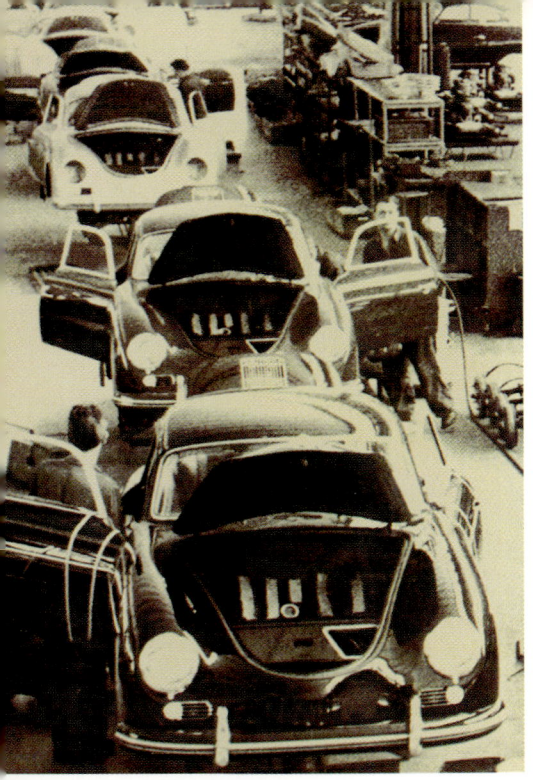

356 coupes come down the assembly line at Stuttgart.
Porsche NA

the three instrument dials were all the same size. The instruments were shaded by a vinyl-covered binnacle the same color as the dashboard cover, but placed within a metal dashboard color coded to match the body color. A similar, though much modernized, instrument binnacle would be incorporated on the new front engine 928 beginning in 1977.

A total of 200 Speedsters were made the first year, and are identified immediately by their unique appearance as well as by the gold "Speedster" script located on each front fender above the beltline. Many people consider the 356 Speedster to be the ultimate Porsche due to its low, rakish lines and classic air-cooled rear-engine configuration. This having been said, the Speedster was unflatteringly referred to by some detractors

1956 356A coupe
Dan Lyons

1956 356A Speedster
Dan Lyons

as resembling an "inverted bathtub." The Speedster was replaced by the Convertible D in August, 1958.

Speedster production: 3,991 cars: (200 in 1954, 1,800 in 1955, 850 in 1956, 575 in 1957, and 566 in 1958)

1955 356

For 1955, Porsche 356 cars destined for the U.S., other than Speedsters, bore the designation "Continental" in gold script. This was apparently a concession to importer Max Hoffman, who felt that the American motorist identified more with a series name than a numerical designation of the type widely used in Europe. The name Continental was not unique to Porsche and had already been used by Ford, Rolls Royce, and Bentley, and would be used again by Ford for its Lincoln brand, beginning the following year with the prestigious Lincoln Continental MK II. However, most imports, such as Mercedes and Jaguar, kept the numerical designations.

The Porsche Continentals were available with two engines: the 1500 and the 1500S. External changes included the addition of a chrome accent strip under each door as well as a longer hood chrome strip featuring a crest and handle. An anti-roll bar was added to front suspension, and heater controls moved from dash to floor tunnel. Porsche dispensed with

1956 356A coupe in blue
Dan Lyons

1956 356A cabriolet
McLellan's Automotive History

1956 356A coupe
McLellan's Automotive History

1956 356A Speedster
McLellan's Automotive History

1958 356A Speedster

the Continental name the following year due to its re-use by Ford in the 1956 Lincoln Continental MK II.

1955 356 production: 4,529 cars (2,382 coupes, 347 cabriolets, and 1,800 Speedsters)

356A 1956-1959

The early 356 cars can be divided into two categories: the Pre-A Series cars produced prior to the debut of the 356A at the Frankfurt Auto Show in September 1955 (as a 1956 model), and the 356A Series cars. The newer cars, the A Series, were similar in appearance to the earlier cars but generally considered to be more comfortable and somewhat easier to handle than their predecessors.

The introduction of the 356A in America for the 1956 year produced some significant changes over the initial 356. Among them were the installation of a one-piece curved windshield, rather than the one-piece windshield with two flat panels. The instrument panel of the Cabriolet and coupe contained three side-by-side gauges, all of the same size.

The Carrera name debuted for a Porsche model in honor of the Carrera Panamericana, a grueling Mexican road race that Porsche had won in 1954 (the last year of the race) in the 1,600cc class. On March 16, 1956, the 10,000th Porsche, a 356A, was produced and appeared with great fanfare and was driven off the line by Ferry Porsche. The 356A was offered in three body styles, the cabriolet, speedster and coupe.

Total production 4,201: (2,921 coupes, 430 cabriolets, 850 Speedsters)

20 Porsche

The 1957 Porsche 550 Spyder is a classic beauty.

1957 356A

The most significant changes to the body for 1957 were the replacement of the twin small rear tail lights, which had been fitted since 1952, with a single horizontal "tear drop" lens on each side, and the placement of the exhaust outlets in the rear bumper ends at each side. The reason for routing the exhaust ports through the rear bumper ends was supposedly to increase the car's ground clearance, and yet there was probably a cosmetic consideration as well since cars as various as some Cadillacs, the 1956 and 1957 Lincoln Continental MK II, and the mid-1950s Ford Thunderbirds had done the same thing, again, primarily for cosmetic reasons. The idea, while good in theory resulted in frequent rust through of the bumper ends on all of these cars. Additionally, replacing original exhaust pipes by aftermarket pipes requires great skill. The license plate light was moved from the top of the plate to underneath in mid-year. The standard, unadorned, Moon-style hubcaps were replaced with chrome hubcaps with a protruding center featuring the Porsche crest on the Carrera and 1600S. Padded sunvisors became standard, replacing the colored plastic ones. The striker plate for the door latch, mounted at

A 1957 Porsche 550 Spyder in racing form
Bob Harrington

356A Technical Specifications (1956-1959)

Engine:	Opposed four-cylinder, air-cooled, rear-mounted.
Body:	Pressed-steel, unibody
Wheelbase:	82.7 in.
Track:	Front: 51.4 in. Rear: 50.1 in.
Front suspension:	Independent with torsion bars, anti-roll bar, trailing arms, and telescopic shock absorbers
Rear suspension:	Independent swing axle, with torsion bars and telescopic shock absorbers
Brakes:	Drum type

the top of the door jamb was lowered in mid-1957 to the center of the door jamb, and remained there for the rest of the 356 series. Another minor interior nuance was the interchanging of the floor-mounted heater control with the shift lever in mid-1957, with the shift lever placed behind the heater control. 1300cc engine production ceased at the end of the year. Zenith carburetors were replaced by Solex carburetors on the 1600 engine.

1957 356 production: 5,240 cars (3,282 coupes, 542 cabriolets, 1,416 Speedsters)

1958 356A

The significance of racing for Porsche could not be denied. Private owners of the RSK racing cars in 1957 and 1958 scored successes on a variety of tracks both in Europe and the U.S. While the 356 was not an RSK, it still was visually similar and was powered by an air-cooled engine. Many Americans did not fully understand the 356 in comparison to other more conventional, and perhaps, more attractive sports cars of the period, but for those who did, the Porsche was in a league of its own. The effects of its racing successes on its marketability cannot be denied.

The excitement of racing or even watching sports car racing during the postwar years of the 1950s will probably never be equaled again. During the 1950s, just about anyone could buy a racing car, or a nearly identical street version of a racing car right off the showroom floor in larger American and European cities. The Jaguar XK-120 and XK-140 again come to mind due to the plaque mounted on the instrument panel proclaiming the street version to be certified as an "exact replica" of the Le Mans winning car.

1958 production: 5,994 cars (3,670 coupes, 1382 cabriolets, 556 Speedsters, and 386 Convertible D's)

1959 356A

The Speedster in its original form had been dropped, but was replaced in August 1958, for the 1959 model year with what was initially known as the Speedster D, so named for Drauz, its body builder. It became known as the Convertible D by the time it reached the market and, unlike the Speedster, had roll-up windows and a higher windscreen. It retained the longitudinal chrome strip side molding found on the earlier Speedster. Unlike the Speedster, which had unadorned interior door panels, the Convertible D featured a lockable fold-over flap for minimal storage of maps and other thin or flat items.

1959 356A Speedster
Dan Lyons

Although the Convertible D was never offered with the four-cam engine, 25 Carrera Speedsters were built with the four-cam 1600 engine in 1959. Production ended for the 356A in September 1959 with the introduction of the 356B.

1959 356 production: 6,735 total (3,793 coupes, including 1,320 B coupes), 944 cabriolets (including 468 B cabriolets), 1,412 Convertible D's, 25 Speedsters, 561 roadsters

356B 1960-1963

The 356B was introduced in Frankfurt at the 1959 show in September with the T-5 body and featured higher front (3.7 inches) and rear (4.1 inches) bumpers, a raised front fender line and higher-placed headlights. The reasoning for the higher bumpers was to protect the bodywork in parking situations, and to this end larger vertical bumper guards were fitted. The license plate lamp was removed from the rear of the body and placed in the rear bumper upper surface with small dual directional lamps. Small air intake grilles similar to those for the horns were placed in line with the horn grilles beneath the bumper at each end of the car. Opening front vent windows, not available since the Gmund cars (except as optional), became standard on the 356B for 1962.

Body styles consisted of the coupe, roadster, and cabriolet, with the Carrera continuing as well. Many felt that the new car had been somewhat "Americanized" over the previous car, but as Pasini relates

1960 356B Super 90
Dan Lyons

1960 56B Super 90 engine
Dan Lyons

1960 356B Super 90 interior
Dan Lyons

in *Porsche Catalogue Raisonne: 1947-1987* "After all, the U.S. market, which absorbed over 40% of production, could not be overlooked."

The Karmann hardtop was introduced in 1960 as a 1961 model based on the cabriolet, and was similar in appearance to the Speedster with its removable fiberglass hardtop in place. The Karmann hardtop had a higher top and windshield and therefore lacked the more fluid shape of the Speedster. The slightly curved "B" pillar posts, such as they were, curved slightly to fit the glass of the roll-up front windows. These cars are reportedly less valuable today than the coupe or roadsters of

Porsche

the same period, but again, that's a matter of personal preference. The hardtop offered considerably better vision for the driver due to its larger glass area. In any case, it is a rarer car in its T-5 or T-6 configuration than the coupe of the corresponding year.

1960 356 production: 7,559 cars (4,413 coupes, 1,617 cabriolets, 1,529 roadsters)

1961 356B

The 1962 356B debuted at the Frankfurt Auto Show in September 1961 as a 1962 model. Collaboration with body builder Drauz ended with the open body being subsequently built by Belgian firm D'Ieteren, while Karmann built the hardtop and Reutter built both the coupe and convertible.

1961 356 production: 7,996 cars (4,176 coupes, 1,648 Karmann hardtops, 1,609 cabriolets, and 563 roadsters)

1962 356B

The changes to the 1962 356B in its T-6 form over the previous year were substantial. The single rear engine hatch grille was replaced by twin grilles of equal size, similar to those found on the 1952 Heuer-bodied America roadster. The rear engine hatch cover was also widened and its lower end was moved down, closer to the bumper. The front hatch cover

1961 356B cabriolet
Dan Lyons

was similarly widened and squared off at the leading edges. The body was also altered to incorporate larger front and rear windows.

Two-thirds of the coupes for the 1962 model year were built by Reutter, while the remainder were built by Karmann. In all, three body styles were available for 1962: the coupe, the Karmann coupe (having replaced the Karmann hardtop), and the cabriolet, which replaced the roadster.

The minimal but effective instruments and controls offered on the early models had advanced steadily, and by 1962 featured three equally large gauges, plus a radio, a clock, and a locking glove compartment. The Carrera 2, with its double overhead camshafts, appeared as a 1962 model with a 1966cc engine, while the slow-selling Karmann hardtop was discontinued mid-year.

1962 356 production: 8,029 cars (6,362 coupes, 99 Karmann hardtop coupes, and 1,568 cabriolets)

1963 356B

For 1963, body styles consisted of the coupe, the cabriolet, and the Karmann coupe.

1963 356 production: 9,692 cars.

1962 356B roadster

356C 1963-65

The 356C, the last of the series differed little visually from its T-6 bodied predecessor of the previous year. Beneath the surface, however, Porsche acquired four-wheel disc brakes. Disc brakes, which had been under development in house at Porsche, were at the time basically the province of Dunlap, which supplied brakes for most disc brake cars of the time, either directly or by allowing other companies to make them under license. Porsche decided to purchase Dunlap brakes as supplied under license by Ate. The application of disc brakes required different wheels from those found on the 356B. To this end, the hubcaps with protruding crest were replaced by flat hubcaps, some of which had no crest, while others had either a chrome or enameled crest.

By this time only two production engines were offered for the 356: the 75-hp 1582cc engine for the 356C, and the 95-hp mill for the 356SC.

Behind the scenes, Reutter was supposed to be preparing for full production of the 901/911 cars. Reutter, however, seemed unwilling to invest in the necessary upgrades, leaving Porsche with the necessity of buying the company, which it did between July 1963 and May 1964 in order to be able to fully produce the 911.

1964 356C

With the 901/911 debuting in late 1963, sales of the 356C should have diminished quickly with buyers wanting the newer body and larger, six-cylinder engine. As it turned out, 1964 was a record year for sales of the last edition of the 356.

356B Technical Specifications (1959-1963)

Engine:	Opposed four-cylinder, air-cooled, rear mounted
Body:	Pressed steel unibody
Wheelbase:	82.7 inches
Track:	Front: 51.4 in.
	Rear: 50.1 in.
Front suspension:	Independent with torsion bars, anti-roll bar, trailing arms, and telescopic shock absorbers
Rear suspension:	Independent swing axle, with torsion bars and telescopic shock absorbers
Brakes:	Drum type

1964 356SC coupe

356C Technical Specifications (1963-1965)

Engine	Opposed four-cylinder, air-cooled, rear-mounted
Chassis:	Pressed steel, unibody
Wheelbase:	82.7 in.
Track:	Front: 51.4 in.
	Rear: 50.1 in.
Front suspension:	Independent with torsion bars, anti-roll bar, trailing arms, and telescopic shock absorbers
Rear suspension:	Independent swing axle, with torsion bars and telescopic shock absorbers
Brakes:	Four-wheel discs

1964 production: 10,312 cars (3,823 Reutter-bodied coupes, 1,745 cabriolets, and 4,744 Karmann-bodied coupes)

1965 356C

1965 production: 1,688 cars (1,100 coupes, 588 cabriolets)

356 Carrera 1955-1965

The first Porsche Carrera, named in honor of the famous Mexican road race, was introduced to the world in September 1955 at the Frankfurt Auto Show, and the Carrera name would become synonymous with high

1965 Porsche 356C cabriolet

1965 356C coupe, in racing form
Bob Harrington

28 *Porsche*

1965 356SC coupe
Dan Lyons

1965 356C cabriolet
Dan Lyons

performance from that point forward. The body was essentially the same as that of the new 356A (except for the distinctive Carrera script), belying the power lurking beneath.

The most significant aspect of the first Carrera was its four-cam engine. The basic engine was essentially a VW opposed flat four-cylinder engine. The difference in the Carrera engine was its unique cylinder heads with two cams per cylinder head, with twin distributors and two spark plugs per cylinder. It also had dry sump lubrication with the oil tank positioned behind a screen stone guard behind the left rear wheel.

Two generations of Porsche Carreras, a 911 (bottom) and a 356 (top) on the road for a 1984 Porsche ad.

The silver Carrera coupe, as first presented in Frankfurt, was fitted with the 100-DIN horsepower 547/1 engine designed by Ernst Fuhrmann. It was essentially the same engine found on the 550 Spyder. The Carrera was 25 percent more expensive than the 356 coupe, a fact which was a deterrent in itself. It was also discovered fairly early that the Carrera, with its high-performance engine, was not really as suited to use as an everyday passenger car as the standard 356A coupe. Extended use of the car with the engine rpm below 2,500 resulted in excessive engine wear, especially the crankshaft. For racers, however, the Carrera was just what the doctor ordered.

The Carrera GT, a lightweight version of the stock Carrera, was produced in small numbers between 1955 and 1964. It differed from the standard Carrera in several ways. Rear and side windows were made of Plexiglas. The rear window was raised or lowered with a leather strap, rather than a crank operated roll-up mechanism. Door, hood, and trunk hatches were made of aluminum, rather than steel.

356 Remembered

The 356 had been the first successful sports car for Porsche as a company and allowed the company to make the successful transition from strictly a design studio to an automobile manufacturer. By September 1965, the last full production year of the 356, Porsche had manufactured a total of 76,303 356s and was clearly one of the leaders in the sports car world.

Despite its success, the 356 remained a curiosity to many Americans. The 1965 Corvette, the 1965 Jaguar XK-E, and the Chrysler powered Facel Vega, among others, were both more beautiful, more comfortable, and more powerful. And yet while many did not yet "get" the 356 for a number of reasons, many of these same people were fascinated by it nonetheless. While there has been much written on the 356, one of the most interesting observations on the car's worldwide success comes from author Laurence Meredith in his book *Original Porsche 356:* "One of the reasons why motoring enthusiasts regard cars made during the 1950s and 1960s as classics is that they often seem to have more character. With their round headlamps, metal bumpers and curving bonnets, many had 'faces' with which the car buying public could identify, and the 356 was no exception. It had a happy countenance that greeted its owner with a reassuring smile."

The 356 was superceded by the 911, a car which would further the original 356/2 concept. Unlike the 356, it debuted with a six-cylinder engine and a truly independent rear suspension. The 356C is generally considered the best of the 356 series due to its position at the top of the 356 evolutionary chain of mechanical and technical improvements. Many also consider the 356C to be the best-looking car of the series. And yet it seems now that the earlier, simpler A and B Series cars are the most desirable after all, due to their lower production numbers and spartan appearance. At the present state of modern motoring, where even Toyotas and Hondas have air-conditioning, disc brakes, power steering,

1960 Porsche-Abarth Carrera coupe
Bob Harrington

1960 RS60
Bob Harrington

power windows, and fully independent four-wheel suspension, less may actually be more.

Not many drivers today get to experience the thrill of driving a car like the 356. Modern cars of all types are fast, quiet, and handle well, but lack the personality of the less-sophisticated cars of the past. Prices have skyrocketed as more and more people have discovered them, many for the first time. While the prices continue to climb, the good news is that there are plenty still available, but not to be found again at bargain prices, as they have made the transition from the obsolete to the collectible.

Owning a 356 during the years of its manufacture permitted the owner membership in an exclusive though unofficial club of the motoring elite. The car was an "insider's" car. Those who had them knew what they were, and the opinions of the ignorant or merely uninformed who thought them nothing more than VWs with sportier bodies, did not matter. The cars were expensive for their era and generally purchased by those able to afford them. Additionally, they were reliable and dependable, unlike British cars of the era in particular, and serviced through an established and growing network of VW dealers nationwide. Parts were thus more readily available for the 356 than with many other high-end foreign cars of the same period.

Ultimately, the 356 was limited by its four-cylinder pushrod engine which had been developed as far as practical at 90 hp. The four-cam Carrera engine had proved to be expensive to maintain and unreliable for everyday use. In light of the 356's dated looks (some would now say timeless), in comparison to the Jaguar E-Type, it was time to move on. The 356 had surpassed all expectations, both in terms of its public acceptance and sales. The Porsche tradition, it was felt, could best be continued in an altogether new car—one that could hopefully expand on the successes of the 356.

Ultimately, the Porsche company used its racing successes to push sales of its passenger cars, and the revenue generated from the sales of its cars was used to further its racing victories. But the 356 had been much more than a racing car. It had evolved from the Pre-A, through the A, B, and C series, and was further refined in each of its incarnations. Porsche realized fully that, despite the allure of racing, most of its customers were not racing their cars. This led the company to continue making refinements to both handling and creature comforts throughout the lifespan of the 356.

The Porsche Crest

There are several stories about the origin of the now famous Porsche crest. Supposedly, American automotive importer Max Hoffman suggested that Porsche needed a badge or crest of some sort as a distinguishing symbol, as was the custom with premium car manufacturers in the U.S., such as Packard, Chrysler, and Cadillac. According to legend, Ferry Porsche designed a rough version of the Porsche crest on a napkin off the top of his head right then. Other stories credit Max Hoffman entirely, while others credit the origin of the crest to Ferry Porsche, and Porsche's publicity chief at the time.

Whatever its true origin, the Porsche crest is immediately recognizable worldwide. It is agreed that the six stag horns represent the Baden-Wurttemburg state, while the black horse represents Stuttgart, an area once used as a stud farm.

1965 Porsche 904/6 racing coupe
Bob Harrington

911

911 TIMELINE

1875-1951
- Professor Ferdinand Porsche

1964
- Manufacture began in September

1966
- 911S announced
- Alloy wheels introduced

1972
- E Series 911 introduced

1963
- 901 introduced in September at the Frankfurt Auto Show

1965
- First 911s sold in U.S. in February
- Targa was introduced at the Frankfurt Auto Show in September

1968
- B Series announced as 1969 model

1973
- Family removed from day-to-day company business and Porsche goes public
- 911 Turbo debuts at the Paris Auto Show

The 911 is the car upon which the Porsche company was built. While a derivative of the 356 and the earlier VW, the 911 of today has evolved into one of the most recognizable cars in the world. While other sports car manufacturers have introduced and withdrawn famous models, Porsche's 911 has continued in its basic configuration since its inception. During that entire period, now more than 40 years, the 911 has literally transformed from an unusual-looking, difficult-to-handle basic sports car into the absolute state-of-the-art machine it is today, complete with its stability management system, anti-lock brakes, electronic engine management system, and airbags. The car, while completely new, has maintained its original configuration, with an engine in the back behind the rear axle. While many automotive enthusiasts have questioned the inherent wisdom of this layout over the decades, the car has continued to develop and evolve, all the time winning the most significant motoring events in the world, leading to technical advancements that would be applied to production cars. No other marque can claim to have applied so much of what was learned the hard way to its actual production cars.

There have been several dark periods for the 911, and it was felt at one time it might be nearing its end, a victim of U.S. government regulations concerning noise and safety. A replacement for the 911 was designed and placed into production in 1977 in the form of the 928—a front-engine car that was seen as the salvation of the company when the 911 fell by the wayside. Different models of the 911 were introduced over the years and there were constant mechanical improvements, all the while with the consideration lurking in the background that the 911 might literally be outlawed in the American market with little or no notice.

There were bleak times on the horizon as Porsche moved out of the highly profitable 1980s. Porsche, always an expensive car, suffered to some degree in the early 1990s as a symbol of capitalism. The 911 at the end of the 1980s was in appearance basically the same car as it had been at the beginning of that decade, and it needed something new if it was to survive its diminishing U.S. and world sales. While cars, at least in America, had been horrible by comparison in every way to those made before 1975 and after 1990, there was a major turnaround in the U.S. in 1990, and American manufacturers began making really good cars again, further threatening Porsche sales. The 911 was revised yet again, this time evolving into the 993, and Porsche was again running at full speed, achieving success to an unprecedented degree as the 20th century ended.

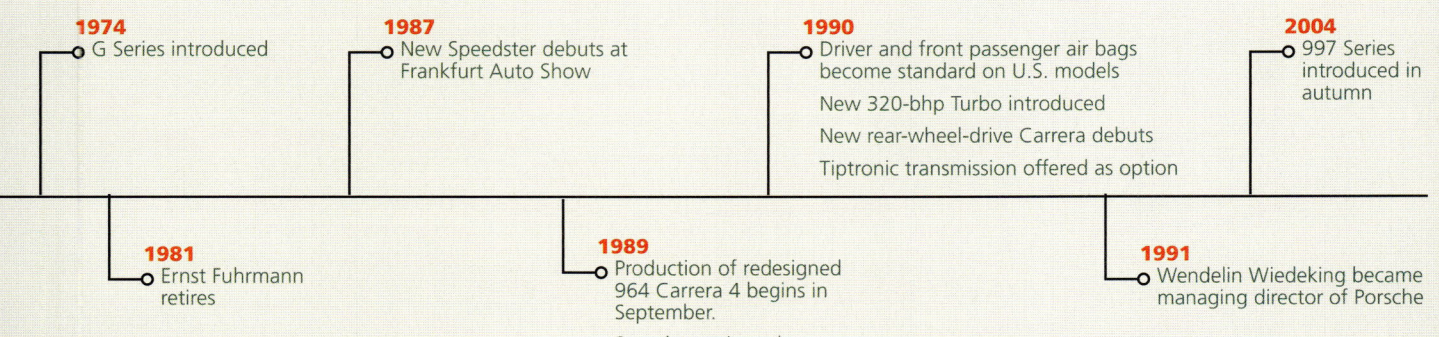

1966 911 coupe, prepared for racing
Bob Harrington

901 1964-1967

The exterior design of the car which was to replace the highly successful 356 series was eventually designated the 901 and was undertaken in 1959 by the second Ferdinand Porsche, known as "Butzi." His initial design sketches resulted in a car known within Porsche as the Type 7, of which either three or four prototypes were built under the direction of engineer Erwin Komenda. The 356 series had been more successful than anyone at Porsche had ever initially envisioned, and even as early as 1959, a mere 11 years after the first car, the Porsche name had become synonymous with a desirable lifestyle.

But Porsche, ever with an eye to the future, felt that the 356 must at some point be replaced. For its relatively high price, the 356 lacked both the room and creature comforts of other emerging marques. With this in mind attention was paid to the creation of a new car. The car under consideration was to have lower maintenance requirements and more storage space for luggage. It was also to be configured as a 2+2 (two rear seats for occasional use for short distances). It was not, however, to be a legitimate full-time four-seat car.

The new car continued the basic rear engine configuration of the 356 but, apart from its component layout, was essentially a new car. The new Porsche 901 debuted at the Frankfurt Auto Show in September, 1963. It was 6 inches longer than its predecessor, featured four-wheel disc brakes, a more modern (American type) 12-volt electrical system, rack and pinion steering, and a more powerful flat six-cylinder Porsche 1991cc engine. The new car had an 87-inch wheelbase, a width of 63.4 inches, a height of 52 inches, and a weight of 2,380 lbs.

The introduction of the opposed air-cooled single-overhead cam flat-six in a passenger sports car was one of the most significant advances in the company's history, and would largely define the Porsche engine through the end of the 20th century. The new 2-liter (1991 cc) engine replaced the four-cylinder engines of the 356 and produced 130 bhp at 6100 rpm and 128 ft.-lbs. torque at 4200 rpm. It had a forged eight-bearing crankshaft, cast-alloy pistons, and two Solex triple-choke carburetors. It featured dry sump lubrication and a cast-aluminum crankcase, a 9.0:1 compression ratio, and 80mm bore and 66mm stroke. This initial Type 901/01 engine was used through July, 1966, and is attributed to Hans Tomala and Ferdinand Piech (Dr. Porsche's nephew).

The new model had sharper lines, more glass, and less body curves, and yet the family resemblance to the 356 had been maintained, and a tradition established. The basic visual design of the 911 is attributed to "Butzi" Porsche, grandson of Ferdinand Porsche, and to Erwin Komenda, who was responsible for getting the design into production.

Structural similarities continued for Porsche with an all-steel monocoque chassis similar to that of the 356. This type of construction would become a standard for all Porsche sports cars in the future, including the front-engine cars. It was still fairly revolutionary at the time, however. In Detroit, by comparison, cars like the very large and expensive Lincoln featured similar unibody construction beginning in 1958, while Cadillac, for example, still continued with a body attached to a rigid frame. Jaguar had abandoned its body on frame construction in its sports car line with the XK-150, and created a combination unitized steel body with strut-type frame supports for the engine and front suspension in the E-Type, a direct competitor with the new 911. Rolls Royce and Bentley also switched to a unibody construction beginning with the 1966 Silver Shadow and T series, respectively.

In the 901/911, the unitized body featured a much-improved suspension, especially at the rear, with double universal joints for each of the rear axles, a decided improvement over the swing axle rear suspension of the earlier 356 cars. But then the double-jointed rear axles were still, even in 1964, a very high-tech improvement, missing until 1972 in Mercedes 350 SL, and even as late as the early 1970s Ghibli, for Maserati. The rear suspension of the new Porsche also employed transversely mounted torsion bars as with the 356 series, and a front

901/911 Technical Specifications	
Engine	Type 901/01 opposed six-cylinder
Diaplacement:	2 liter
Compression:	9.0:1
Horsepower:	130 bhp (DIN) at 6,100 rpm
Torque:	128.8 ft. lbs. at 4,200 rpm
Crankcase:	Cast aluminum
Body:	Unitized steel
Drag coefficient:	0.38
Wheelbase:	87.05 in.
Overall length:	163.90 in.
Front track:	53.27 in.
Rear track:	52 in.
Weight:	2,381 lbs.

suspension employed MacPherson struts with longitudinally mounted torsion bars and an anti-roll bar.

The new 911 was initially offered in a variety of standard colors which included Slate Gray, Ruby Red, Enamel Blue, Light Ivory, Champagne Yellow, Irish Green, and Signal Red. Optional colors of Dolphin Gray, Togo Brown, Bali Blue, and Black were offered. By 1967, the seven available standard exterior colors had been expanded to nine, and there were a host of optional colors available.

Despite the new car's exotic appearance and improved suspension, it was immediately noted that it didn't handle well, especially in the hands of an average driver. The basic problem was the result of the placement of the engine behind the rear axle. This was an inherently off-balance design, which resulted in a substantial oversteer in hard corners at speed. American motorists, in particular those used to large front engine V-8s, or sports cars like the Jaguar XK 150 or Jaguar E-Type, often found themselves sideways when driving a 911 for the first time. Subsequent experience would be gained incrementally as they learned the car's nuances, but the car's basic handling problems were obvious. The 911 was not only too heavy at the rear, it was too light at the front. It was subject to cross winds, and not particularly stable in a straight line at higher speeds.

It was especially dangerous in corners when a driver, fearing he had approached a curve too fast suddenly, removed his foot from the accelerator. At that point, the centrifugal force combined with the sudden change in camber in the rear wheels made the car even more unpredictable.

The early 911s were also noted for their understeer at lower speeds. This was again due to the majority of the weight being in the rear. What this meant in actual experience was that the car might continue to move forward a bit after the steering wheel had been turned hard, especially on a loose road surface on an uphill grade. A significant part of this problem was the positioning of the new, larger six-cylinder engine behind the rear axles. While rear traction was excellent due to the majority of the car's weight being in the proximity of the drive wheels, traction in the front was not all it could or should have been. Porsche was aware of the problem and immediately began to take corrective steps, although it was reported that some mechanics and service technicians actually placed weights in the front corners to aid the understeer problem. While this solution might sound laughable at first, if for no other reason than its pure simplicity, it was effective. Other manufacturers, including Ford, had used added weights for balance. The so-called "suicide door" Lincoln Continental convertibles of the 1960s, for example, had large round weights bolted behind the front bumper at each end, ahead of each front wheel. A similar solution was found at the Porsche factory for the 911. The remedy consisted of similarly placed 24.5-lb. weights at each end of the bumper, ahead of the front wheels. While this solution was somewhat effective, it was temporary and the 911's handling problems would be addressed and corrected through ongoing engineering advances.

Steering for the new Porsche was ZF rack and pinion, as opposed to the worm gear steering found on the earlier 356. The general consensus at that time among sports car manufacturers was that worm gear was not as desirable as a steering rack, and it was consequently phased out. By 1961, the Jaguar E Type, for example, no longer had the earlier worm gear steering of the legendary XK-120, and Porsche had most likely considered the worm gear to be dated as well. Additional safety for the driver resulted from the use of a three-piece steering column rather than a rigid tube. There had been no provision in the original design for castor and camber adjustments at the front, and there had been problems with steering and front suspension both loaded on a single ball joint at each side. Measures were taken in manufacturing to correct these oversights as well. Tires for the first 911 were 165 HR 15, mounted on 4.5 J x 15 steel wheels.

It's curious, in light of today's very high and wide wheels, why a company like Porsche would introduce its top-of-the-line new car with 4.5-inch wheels. At the time, the company simply felt that narrow tires were more suitable to the car's handling characteristics.

Brakes were single-circuit four wheel discs with cast-iron calipers, with a mechanical drum-type parking brake activated by a cable-operated handbrake lever. The initially used transmission was a Type 901 five-speed manual.

While there would be significant changes over the course of the car's long life, none would be undertaken capriciously or as a reaction to stylistic fads. Instead, the technical knowledge gained from constant racing successes would be incorporated into the basic 911, giving rise to the much used term "evolution" as it pertains not only to the 911 and its derivatives, but to the underlying philosophy of automotive development across the model range at Porsche.

It should again be mentioned that the cars for the following year are generally introduced in the previous summer or fall, thus a 1969 model was actually introduced in the Summer of 1968. For this reason it is often confusing when one reads that some new model or option was offered in a particular year. The author might mean that it was manufactured in that year while it might not have been available until the following year's model. It is especially confusing with the 911 series cars because the 911 is the only Porsche manufactured uninterrupted since its introduction. There have been many 911 models introduced and removed and reintroduced, as well as constant changes of all types. Specifications for specific markets varied as well depending on various governmental regulations.

1966 911 Targa

1966 911 coupe

1965 911

Production of the first right-hand-drive models began in May, 1965. Initial U.S. price was $6,500. Targa was introduced in 1965 (see below). A four-speed transmission replaced the five-speed as standard, with five-speed becoming optional.

1966 911

Solex triple-choke carburetors were replaced by Webers with the introduction of the 901/05 engine in February, 1966, correcting the problems associated with the earlier carburetors. Other than the change

911 Targa

The 901/911, unlike its predecessor the 356, had been initially available only as a coupe. But in 1965, the Targa, named for the legendary but now defunct Targa Florio race, debuted in September, at the Frankfurt Auto Show. It was basically a 911 with a lift-off roof panel that made it a convertible of sorts. The rigid brushed metal rear "B" pillar of the roof, affixed to the body, served as a rollbar as well as a roof support. The car originally featured a removable plastic rear window that helped its aerodynamics and did not detract from the overall appearance.

The removable rear window was soon replaced in 1969 with a fixed curved glass window (optional in 1968), which, unlike the plastic one, did diminish the car's aesthetic appearance with the roof removed. Be that as it may, the fixed glass rear window was considered by most to be a major improvement over the plastic one. Anyone who has ever attempted to unzip and then re-zip a plastic rear window into any convertible top generally abandoned the process after a few attempts. The glass rear window also provided a weather tight seal, and since it was bonded to the B pillar and surrounding body panels, it provided further structural rigidity.

The roof section over the seating area was removable and stowable under the front hatch cover. An optional softtop roof panel was available and required less room for storage, increasing available cargo space for luggage or other items.

While many people justifiably considered the earlier Targa's bulky rear roof pillar to be a detraction from the otherwise smooth roofline of the 911 coupe, there were reasons for its design. Porsche wanted to keep the new Targa's body as close to that of the coupe as possible to save machining and tooling costs by using as many interchangeable parts as possible, and this was accomplished using the same body panels, fenders and doors throughout on both the coupe and Targa. The rear pillar provided the protection of a rollbar while maintaining most of the structural rigidity lost through the absence of the rigid roof structure of the coupe body. Another problem with any convertible is increased weight resulting from chassis reinforcement to compensate for the missing roof. Porsche, in the case of the Targa, was able

Porsche

in carburetors, the engine remained the same. Production of the new Targa began in December 1966. Production for the 1967 models began in July 1966.

1967 911S, Targa

Models for 1967 were the 911 Targa and 911S. The higher-performance "S" model was introduced into the 911 series beginning in 1967 at a cost of nearly $7,000. It would immediately become the most desirable of the 911 series cars. Most of the changes were to the engine, now the Type 901/02, and included larger valves, different camshafts, forged rather than cast pistons, a 9.8:1 compression, and the addition of different Weber carbs, boosting power to 160 bhp (DIN) at 6,600 rpm, and 132 ft.-lbs. of torque at 5,200 rpm. A five-speed gearbox was standard for the S only, while the four-speed came with other models.

The S models were fitted with the new Fuchs forged alloy 4.5 J x 15 wheels as standard. These became a popular option for other Porsche models as well, and practically a 911 trademark. They were each 5 lbs. lighter than the pressed steel wheels, but also much more expensive to manufacture. Other wheel materials had been unsuccessfully tried but were abandoned due to cost or impracticability. Brakes for the new S model were ventilated single-circuit hydraulic four-wheel discs with

to keep the weight essentially the same for both the coupe and Targa models. There was also the desire to maintain the 911's basic shape as much as possible in line with that of the coupe.

Manufacture of the original Targas began in December, 1966 with the first cars for sale as 1967 models.

The introduction of the fully open 911SC Cabriolet in 1983 had a negative effect on sales of the highly popular Targa, which had up until the Cabriolet's introduction accounted for nearly 40 percent of the 911's sales overall. Even though the Targa continued to be available in the 964 series and was produced through 1994, it was eclipsed in desirability by the Cabriolet.

A radically new Targa debuted at the 1995 Frankfurt Auto Show and was offered to the public as a 1996 model at nearly $71,000. This new model from the side view, unlike the earlier Targas, was basically indistinguishable from the coupe. It had an electrically sliding glass roof panel that opened and slid beneath the rear window. The dark transparent glass panel retracted through the push of a button, rather than having to be physically removed and stored. Electric motors located behind the rear seats in combination with cables provided the mechanics. Additionally, the tempered glass panel was designed to block 100 percent of all ultra-violet rays. As with the sunroof, the glass panel of the Targa could be opened or closed while the car is in motion.

The new style Targa's lines are hardly undesirable. Gone is the large brushed metal rear roof pillar of the earlier models, replaced by the simple flowing roofline of the standard 911 coupe. While this particular body style has not received the recognition it deserves from most quarters, the Targa, especially in its most recent incarnation, is one of the most exotic of all production Porsches.

The Targa has understandably been a very successful model over what has now become a significant period of time, and served as the only Production Porsche for basically twenty years (other than the 914) which offered an open-air ride. In fact the term "Targa" is now applied to any car with a fixed rear pillar and an open roof.

wider calipers and rear pistons. The ventilated discs resulted in less brake fade, slower pad wear, and cooler operation than solid disc plates.

As with other auto manufacturers, there were continuing concerns about rust. Porsche made three 911s with stainless-steel bodies in 1967 to test the metal's rust-fighting potential. While the unpainted stainless steel used in the bodies was not subject to corrosion like normal automotive steel, it was prohibitively expensive. The lure of stainless steel as an end-all for problems of rust and corrosion has been an ongoing experiment which has never proven to be financially viable even for a company as rich as Ford. Lincoln, for example, has tried several stainless-bodied convertibles in the same dimensions as the standard production versions, but decided that the cost did not justify the effort. And even as recently as the early 1980s, the ill-fated DeLorean had been crafted of stainless steel. By 1986, Porsche would be sufficiently satisfied with its rust preventive measures to offer a full 10-year rust through warranty on the entire body.

Production of the A series cars began in July, 1967.

Reported U.S. Porsche sales for 1967 were approximately 6,700 units (10,941 total).

1968 911L racing coupe
Bob Harrington

1968 911, 911L

Models for 1968 included the 911 ($6,190) and 911L ($6,790). The Targa body was offered on the 911L for an additional $400. The 911S was not offered for sale in the U.S. in 1968 because it did not meet U.S. emissions standards for that year, but the 911L was essentially the same car without the more powerful engine of the European 911S.

There were several significant changes in the 911 for the 1968 model year, not the least of which was the belt driven "smog pump," in the U.S. market—the first in an ongoing series of increasingly restrictive steps to reduce exhaust emissions. Illuminated side markers (amber in front, red at the rear) were added to U.S.-bound cars in an effort to increase their night time visibility. Wheel rims were widened from 4.5 to 5.5 inches. Brakes for all models were upgraded from a single-circuit to a dual-circuit system.

The engine offered in the U.S. market on the 911 and 911L featured Weber carburetors and the new smog pump, and produced 130 bhp at 6,100 rpm, and 128 ft.-lbs. of torque at 4,200 rpm.

The Type 905 Sportmatic transmission was first offered on U.S. 911 models for the first time in 1968 as a $280 option. It was the 911's first automatic and consisted of a fully synchronized four-speed gearbox developed from the original 901 gearbox by Porsche and Fichtel & Sachs. A hydraulic torque converter and a single disc clutch were designed to operate through an electrically (solenoid) activated vacuum control unit set in motion by the movement of the floor-mounted shift lever. Every time the shift lever is moved, the clutch was released. The Sportmatic offered the option of shifting manually without a clutch throughout the full range of four forward fully synchronized gears, or simply selecting an automatic "drive" setting in which no shifting at all was required. The shift pattern consisted of park, and reverse to the left of a traditional "H" pattern consisting of L (low) D (drive), D3 (drive 3), and D4 (drive 4).

All 911s were fitted with dual circuit brakes as well as ventilated discs, except for the lower-priced 911T (Europe), which retained plain discs unless ordered with the Sportmatic, in which case it came with vented discs.

External dimensions remained the same as the previous year's models. August 1968 brought the introduction of the 911 B Series (as 1969 models).

Total U.S. sales for 1968 were approximately 7,458.

1969 911S, 911T, 911E

Models for 1969 were the 911S ($7,695), 911T ($5,795) and 911E ($6,995). The Targa option was available for $620. The S, which had not met U.S. emissions requirements since its U.S. introduction in 1967, was back for 1969. While the 1969 model 911 looked essentially the same as its predecessor, the 1969 model benefited considerably from the ongoing efforts at Zuffenhausen to correct the handling problems associated with the 901/911. Understeer at the front and oversteer at the rear were reduced for the 1969 year.

Significant for 1969 was the extension of the wheelbase by 2.4 inches in an effort to improve handling. The engine and transmission remained in the same location relative to the body, but the rear trailing arms were lengthened in order to move the back wheels further to the rear. This lengthening of the car was one of the only significant physical changes for the basic 911 body design for nearly the next 20 years.

The original steering rack of the type used on the 1964 901/911 was replaced with a less-expensive (to manufacture) type that had been developed for the mid-engine 914. Aluminum engine and transmission casings were replaced with lighter magnesium castings, an application of knowledge gained from racing. Front brake calipers of the 911S were replaced with lightweight alloy, and aluminum hood and trunk lids replaced the steel of the Series A cars.

1970 Porsche 911T coupe
Dan Lyons

Wheel width was increased from 5.5 to 6 inches on the 911S and 911E. All in all, the lengthening of the trailing arms (and wheelbase) rearward, while keeping the engine in its same position, in combination with the magnesium castings, altered the front-to-rear weight ratio from 41.5/58.5 to 43/57 and substantially improved handling. A larger rear caliper was introduced and total brake surface area was increased more than 20 percent per wheel.

The 1969 model year was also important because it saw the introduction of the first fuel-injected models using a Bosch mechanical system, a portent of future development. The Bosch system was standard on the S and E, but the lower-priced T still retained carburetors. A magnesium crankcase replaced the cast aluminum of the earlier 911 models. Air conditioning was optional beginning with 1969 models.

Total U.S. sales for 1969 were approximately 5,893 units.

1970 911S, 911T, 911E

The C Series was introduced in September. There were no major changes to speak of for 1970 at least in terms of overall external appearance, with models T, S, & E comprising the lineup. The big news was on the inside, where engine size was increased to 2.2 liters.

Enthusiasts of other marques continued to wonder what it was about Porsche that made it so special. So what if the engine size was increased to 2.2 liters for 1970. The Jaguar E-Type by way of comparison had a 4.2-liter engine for 5 years. And what was with those Volkswagen-type pressed steel wheels? Even the optional alloys looked cheap and poorly

Porsche

designed when compared to the exquisite chrome wire spokes of a Jaguar.

And yet, despite the outright derision from exponents of other marques, there was always the suspicion that superior "German engineering" might be the underlying reason for what on the surface looked like rather uninspired wheels.

Total U.S. sales for 1970 were 13,898, which represents inclusion of the new mid-engine 914, including the underpowered and poor-selling 912.

1970 911T
Dan Lyons

1971 911S, 911T, 911E

Models and prices remained basically the same for the 1971 year with the introduction of the 911 D Series. Total U.S. sales for 1971 were approximately 17,239, again reflecting the successful lower-priced 914. Options included the $315 Sportmatic transmission, $650 air-conditioning, and a sunroof for $360.

1970 911T coupe
Dan Lyons

1971 911 coupe

Porsche began using galvanized steel in some particularly rust-prone areas.

1972 911T, 911S, 911E

The E Series arrived. Models included: 911T ($7,250), 911E ($7,995), 911S ($9,450).

Capacity was increased for all 911 models to 2341 cc for 1972. The 911S now boasted 190 bhp, a top speed of 140 mph, and 0-to-60 acceleration in 6 seconds. A functional front spoiler was standard on the 911S to reduce the likelihood of front end lift at speed. While it was an option on the T and E, the spoiler would subsequently become offered as standard on all models beginning in 1973. The 911T was rated at 157 hp (SAE) at 5600 rpm with a 0-to-60 mph clocking of 6.9 seconds. The wheelbase of the 911 was extended to 89.4 inches. Stainless-steel exhaust was employed from 1972 on.

U.S. sales at 20,464 for 1972, were again at record numbers with the 914 leading the pack at 15,344 units.

1973 911T, 911S, 911E

The F Series arrived. Models were: 911T ($7,960), 911E ($8,960), 911S ($10,060).

The 911T received Bosch CIS fuel injection mid year. The 911S had 180 bhp, the Targa 165 bph. Both the E and S had 185/70VR-15 tires.

This was the first year for the Carrera's RS 2.7-liter engine and fiberglass engine cover with "Duck Tail" rear spoiler, a precursor of the larger "Whale Tail" spoiler that would debut in 1975. The Carrera was basically a lightweight version of the 911 S, except that the S had a 2.4-liter engine as opposed to the Carrera's larger 2.7 liter.

The Carrera was fitted with 7 x 15-inch wheels and had a stiffer competition suspension. "Cook-ie Cutter" alloys were also introduced. As with the 928's "telephone dial" wheels, these would also later find their way to the 944.

The 1973 Carrera was not sold in the U.S. as a passenger car due to its absence of a smog pump and other emission equipment. It was basically, in the U.S. at least, a racing car.

Total U.S. sales reached 23,771, of which 5,838 were 911s, and the remainder 914s.

1974 911S, Carrera

The G Series arrived in 1974. Models were: 911 ($9,950), 911S ($10,800), and Carrera ($13,575) G-Series.

It was a significant year for the 911 in many respects. The most significant physical changes for the 911 were the incorporation of the more "crashworthy" front and rear bumpers mandated by U.S. governmental regulations to survive a 5-mph collision. The aluminum bumpers were mounted on compressible shocks that would return to their original position in the event of a minor parking lot incident. Porsche easily complied with the new U.S. regulations, actually improving the appearance of the

A 1974 Porsche ad shows that year's 911 coupe.

cars. American manufacturers, however, for the most part, responded with bumpers that failed to integrate at all with overall body geometry, and in many cases actually looked like they had been added as an afterthought.

Fender flares for Porsche were also slightly exaggerated over the 1973 models and a modified front spoiler was fitted beneath the front bumper. It was a major reworking of both front and rear of the 911 series cars, something that was considered an improvement by some, while disliked by others as interfering with the 911's basic looks. For the rear, the brake lights were extended in the form of a plastic bar with Porsche lettering that connected them above the rear bumper. The new front end treatment featured a similar bumper that housed the turn signals and extended in an otherwise unbroken line across the front of the car below the hood and above the spoiler. The new front and rear changes would remain with the car for some time to come.

Equally as significant as the bumper changes were the dropping of the 911T and 911 E from the lineup. The revised 911 lineup for 1974 consisted of 911, Carrera, and the 911S. The Carrera, which had been

The 1974 911 Carrera coupe was the cover car for a Porsche brochure.
McLellan's Automotive History

introduced outside the U.S. as a street car the previous year, became available to U.S. buyers in 1974 and, apart from the U.S.-style bumpers, was virtually identical to the European model. The 1974 U.S. version, however, was equipped to meet all U.S. emissions standards. Standard transmission in the U.S. was four-speed manual with optional five-speed manual and three-speed Sportmatic. Engine size was increased from 2.4 liters to 2.7 liters (2687 cc) for all models, raising displacement to that of the previous year's non-U.S. Carrera. Bore and stroke were increased to 90mm and 70.4mm, respectively. Horsepower was raised to 143 SAE for the standard 911, and 167 for the Carrera and S.

American emission regulations had significantly begun in 1968 with the addition in U.S. cars of a belt driven smog-pump. Additional engine restrictive measurers had been taken in 1973. Despite these power drains the 911 engine, enlarged to 2687cc, managed to produce 143 bhp (SAE) at 5700 rpm. The overall length of the 911 was increased half an inch to 168.9 inches.

1974 was also the last year for pressed steel wheels as standard on the lowest priced 911 model.

The Bosch CIS fuel injection, which was similar to that introduced on the 928 in 1977, and adapted to the 2.4-liter 911T in mid-1973, was applied to all 911 models in 1974. The designation "C.I.S." stands for Continuous Injection System, and is essentially mechanical in nature, differing from the later computerized injection systems. The use of the CIS system meant the end of the carburetor. Subsequent electronic fuel injection systems would become even more efficient, but the CIS is still a marvel of simplicity.

The street version of the 911 Turbo, the new Carrera RS, had a 3-liter engine and a four-speed transmission. It was a direct by product of the racing version, which had debuted at the March 1974 Le Mans trials with a 2142 cc engine and a single, exhaust-driven KKK turbocharger. The racing version developed 516 hp at 7,600 rpm and was fitted with coil springs rather than the 911's normal torsion bar rear suspension as offered on the road-going version.

Total U.S. 911 sales for 1974 were 4,868.

1975 911

Models and prices were basically the same as the previous year for the H Series, and introduced to the U.S. market in August 1974. The 1975 year, however, saw the U.S. introduction of the catalytic converter. The theory was that the catalytic converter placed within the exhaust flow line would reduce emissions. In reality the engine has to work harder and therefore uses more gas.

The Turbo Carrera appeared for 1975 in Germany, but not yet in the U.S. It had a turbocharged CIS injection system and a top speed of 155. The non-Turbo Carreras received the "whale tail" rear spoiler as on the 935 and 930 cars. It was every bit as functional as it appeared and was unique to production sports cars. While some owners of other marques thought its appearance somewhat exaggerated, it was a feature immediately associated with the 911.

Options for the 911 remained minimal by today's standards but already distinctions were being made between performance, comfort, and appearance group options. The revised 925 Sportmatic was offered optionally as a three-speed for $425, while a five-speed was available rather than the standard four at an additional cost of $250. Warranty was extended to six years against lower body rust through and 12 months unlimited mileage.

U.S. 911 sales for 1975 were 5,024 cars.

1976 911S, Turbo

Refinements continued with the introduction of a U.S.-inspired cruise control, and a "climate control" similar to that which had been available on Cadillac for a long time. A temperature setting was selected and maintained by the system. While this system, as

1976 911S
Technical Specifications

Engine:	Opposed flat six-cylinder air-cooled
Displacement:	2687cc
Compression ratio:	8.5:1
Horsepower:	157 SAE
Torque:	168 ft.-lbs. @ 4900 rpm
Lubrication:	Dry sump with separate oil tank
Fuel supply:	Electric pump, CIS injection
Voltage:	12 volts
Battery rating:	66 amp
Alternator:	980 watt
Ignition:	Capacitive discharge
Transmission:	Five-speed, with optional three-speed Sportmatic
Body type:	Unitized steel
Suspension:	Four-wheel independent
Springing:	Torsion bars
Brakes:	Entered four-wheel disc
Wheels:	6 x 5-inch pressure cast alloy
Tires:	185/70 VR 15
0 to 62 mph:	7.8 seconds
Top speed:	134 mph

The 1976 911 Turbo and 911 Targa were an impressive tandem.

on the Cadillac, was effective after the car has been inhabited for awhile, the natural tendency for anyone entering a freezing cold car in winter, or a very hot car in the summer, is to set the controls to the maximum desired setting for immediate relief, adjusting it as needed subsequently.

The big news for 1976 was the introduction of the 930 Turbo Carrera in the American market. It had debuted at the Paris Auto Show in September 1973 with a 2.7-liter engine, but was actually manufactured with a 3-liter (2994 cc) engine. Compression was lowered to 6.5:1. Advertising at the time touted the car as the fastest production Porsche ever built, and the only factory turbocharged car available in the American market. With an advertised acceleration of 0 to 60 mph in under 6 seconds, and a top speed in excess of 155 mph, it was unlike anything ever previously available offered in the U.S. market.

The Turbo Carrera was an instant hit. Its appearance was aggressive, if not actually menacing, with its excessively flared rear fender wells, wide tires, and whale tail rear spoiler. There was the immediate sense in the beholder that the car was every bit as powerful as it looked, and it was. It was truly the ultimate sports car.

The 3-liter engine for the U.S. market produced 245 horsepower at 5500 rpm, as opposed to 260 for the European version, due largely to the presence of pollution equipment and the much-detested catalytic converter mandated for the U.S. market by the federal government. The turbocharger was provided by KKK (Kuhnle, Kopp, and Kausch).

The wheel wells had been flared to accept the larger wheels and tires necessary to handle the car's increased torque. In this case, the Fuchs alloys, a Porsche trademark for the 911 were expanded to 7 inches wide in front, and 8 inches wide at the rear x 15—a far cry from the 4.5-inch front and rear wheels of the original 911. Tires were Pirelli P7 205/50 VR 15 front, and 225/50 VR 15 rear.

The rear pressed-steel semi-trailing suspension arms of the standard 911 were replaced with cast aluminum on the Turbo. The interior appointments were essentially those of the 911 of the same year, but with leather seating surfaces as standard, a reaction to the American preference for leather over fabric seats in sports cars. Air conditioning and electric windows were expected and included at the initial price of nearly $26,000.

Total U.S. 911 sales for the 1976 model year were approximately 4,300 911S and 626 Turbo Carreras.

1977 911S, Turbo Carrera

Models for 1977 were the 911S ($14,995) and Turbo Carrera ($28,000).

For the 1977 model year Porsche was primarily concerned with the front engine experiment, consisting of the 924 and upcoming 928. Changes to the 911 were minimal, with the two-car line still consisting of the 911S, and the Turbo Carrera. Wheel diameter on the Turbo increased from 15 to 16 inches with tire size now 205/55 VR 16 front and 225/50 VR 16 rear, allowing for larger brakes and better cooling.

Total 911 sales in the U.S. for the 1977 model year consisted of 839 Turbo Carrera coupes, and 6,135 911S cars. Again figures differ. Another set states 5,709 total 911S and 517 Turbo Carreras.

1978 911SC, Turbo

Models for 1978 were the 911SC ($19,500) and Turbo ($36,700).

The 911S was replaced by the 911SC, again available either in a two-door coupe, or as a Targa. Prices continued to escalate in the U.S. due to runaway inflation and top legal speed in the U.S. was limited to 55 mph—a far cry from the Autobahn.

The engine on the new 911 was now 182.6 cubic inches, 2933cc (3 liter) with a 95 x 70.4mm bore and stroke. Horsepower was consequently increased on the standard 911 (now the SC) from 157 to 172. The new engine featured an aluminum rather than a magnesium crankcase, as well as a new crankshaft with larger bearings. In the American market large engines were going the way of the dinosaur with the last hanger on, the Lincoln 460

1976 Turbo Carrera Technical Specifications

Engine:	Opposed horizontal air-cooled six-cylinder
Displacement:	2993cc
Compression ratio:	6.5:1
Horsepower:	234 SAE
Torque:	245 ft.-lbs. @ 4000 rpm
Lubrication:	Dry sump with separate oil tank
Fuel supply:	Two electric pumps
Mixture:	CIS injection, turbocharged
Voltage:	12 volts
Battery rating:	66 amp
Alternator:	980 watt
Ignition:	Capacity discharge
Transmission:	four-speed
Body:	Unitized steel
Suspension:	Four-wheel independent
Springing:	Torsion bars
Brakes:	Four-wheel vented disc brakes
Front wheels:	Front: 7 x 15-inch forged alloy
Rear wheels:	8 x 15-in. forged alloy
Front tires:	185/70 VR 15
Rear tires:	215/60 VR 15
0 to 60 mph:	5.7 seconds
Top speed:	152 mph

1978 911SC

1978 911 Turbo
Dan Lyons

discontinued after 1978. The installation of a new, larger, clutch disc hub on 1978 models required the repositioning of the engine rearward by 1.18 inches. A "whale tail" rear spoiler became optional for the 911SC. A Sportmatic transmission was still available as an option for the 911SC, as were leather seats ($680), and a full leather interior ($1,450).

1979 911SC, Turbo

Models for 1979 were the 911SC and Turbo.

Models and prices remained the same as 1978 with the Turbo available only as a coupe and the SC still available as coupe or Targa. For 1979 the SC featured new servo-assisted brakes as standard issue. The unwieldy Sportomatic transmission was finally discontinued mid-year. The Turbo was removed from the American market at the end of the 1979 model year due to noise and exhaust concerns and would not reappear until 1986.

U.S. 911 sales included approximately 3,267 911SC, and 652 Turbos.

1978 911 Turbo

Porsche

1979 911 coupe

1980 911SC

The 911SC ($27,700) was the only model this year.

For 1980-1982, emphasis appeared to be on the front-engine cars, with the 928 having replaced the 911SC as the "top of the line." The 924 was still selling strongly and was available in a Turbo version as well as a standard model. Again, it was felt at Porsche that the 911's days were numbered. To that end, the 911SC was the only 911 model available during this period, again as a coupe or Targa. In the U.S. market, air conditioning, power windows, and leather seating surfaces were standard. A limited edition "Weissach" edition 911SC resembled the more-powerful Turbo visually, but lacked the turbocharger. The Turbo remained available in Europe, but not in the U.S. The 200,000th 911 was manufactured in 1981.

Sales of the 911SC in the U.S. reached approximately 3,459 during 1980.

1981 911SC

The 911SC ($28,364) again remained the only 911 available in the U.S., still available either as a coupe or Targa. The full body rust-through

A 911SC coupe was used to help describe torsion bars in a 1981 company ad.
Porsche NA

The 1981 911SC

warranty was extended to seven years in 1981. Of especial significance was the introduction of the 911 Cabriolet at the Frankfurt Auto show in 1981. It was the first fully open Porsche since the 356. It was presented to the press and motoring public with a 3.3-liter Turbo engine and four-wheel drive. When the car that would become the production model made its appearance two years later, it would be with two-wheel drive, rather than four.

Total Porsche sales reached approximately 11,241 in 1981. Again, the majority of these sales were at the lower end of the model range, consisting of 924 cars.

1982 911SC

The 911SC ($28,600) was again the only model for 1982. The 911SC cabriolet that would

1981 911 Special Edition cabriolet
Dan Lyons

become available for sale as a 1983 debuted at the March 1982 Geneva Auto Show. It is interesting to note the disdain which those disparagingly referred to by adherents of the front engine cars as "the rear-engine crowd" felt for the front engine cars, as Dean Batchelor related in the *Illustrated Porsche Buyers Guide*:

"In the event that a convertible was added to one or both of the front-engined water-cooled Porsche lines, it would only affect 911 sales to a minor degree in my opinion. Too many Porsche enthusiasts saw the 911SC as the last *real* Porsche, and the water-cooled models as "some other kind of car.'" He then modifies the statement by noting that "This view probably wasn't shared by those new to Porsche ranks who didn't know or care about the 'tradition.' "

The implication is clearly that anyone owning a front-engine Porsche of any type does not know or care about tradition. Such was not necessarily the case at all. The tradition was respected, it was just that there were many who could not afford a 911SC, but who could afford a 924.

This is a 1982 Porsche 911 "Slant Nose" cabriolet. Porsche purists are generally critical of such modifications, which radically change the original lines of the car.
Dan Lyons

Total U.S. sales for 1982 were 14,407, with the majority comprised of 924s.

1983 911SC, Targa, Cabriolet

Models for 1983 were the 911SC coupe ($29,950), 911SC Targa ($31,450), and 911SC Cabriolet ($34,450).

Sales of the new Carrera 3.2 began in August, 1983 (UK). Compression was increased to 10.3:1 (9.5:1 U.S.), and engine size was boosted to 3.2 liters, giving the car 231 bhp and a top speed in excess of 150 mph. Engine management was through Bosche Motronic 2 DME and LE-Jetronic fuel injection. The cars had 16-inch Fuchs alloy wheels and a new hydraulic clutch

1983 911SC
Technical Specifications

Engine:	Air-cooled, four-cycle, horizontally opposed six	Battery rating (amp/h):	66	Stabilizers:	Front: 20mm, rear: 18mm
Bore:	3.74 in. (95mm)	Generator:	980 W alternator	Brakes:	Power-assisted, with ventilated discs on all four wheels
Stroke:	2.77 in. (70.4mm)	Ignition:	Breakerless capacitive discharge system		
Displacement:	183 cu. in. (2994 cc)			Wheels:	6J x 15 front; 7J x 15 rear (alloy)
Compression ratio:	9.3:1	Clutch:	Single dry plate mechanically assisted	Tires:	Front: 185/70 VR 15
Engine output SAE net:	172 hp (128 kW) at 5500 rpm	Manual gear box:	Porsche Synchromesh		Rear: 215/60 VR 15 rear
Maximum torque SAE net:	175 ft.-lbs. at 4200 rpm	Speeds:	5 forward, 1 reverse	Steering:	Rack and pinion
		Final drive:	Spiral beveled, pinion and differential	Wheelbase:	89.5 in. (2272mm)
Fuel octane requirement:	Lead-free only			Track:	Front: 53.9 in. (1369mm)
Crankcase:	Light alloy	Final drive ratio:	31/8 = 3.875:1		
Cylinders (individual):	Light alloy	Body:	Unitized construction		Rear: 54.3 in. (1379mm)
Camshaft drive:	Double chain	Front suspension:	Independent with wishbones and shock absorber struts	Length:	168.9 in. (4291mm)
Crankshaft:	Forged steel, 8 main bearings			Width:	65.0 in. (1652 mm)
				Height (unladen):	51.6 in. (1320mm)
Lubrication:	Dry sump with separate oil tank, thermostatically controlled oil cooling	Front springs:	Torsion bars	Ground clearance (laden):	4.7 in. (120mm)
		Rear suspension:	Independent semi-trailing arms		
Fuel supply:	Electric fuel pump	Rear springs:	One traverse torsion bar per wheel	Turning circle:	34.0 (10.4 m)
Mixture supply:	Continuous Injection System			Gross weight:	3,417 lbs. (1550 kg)
		Shock absorbers:	Front and rear hydraulic double-acting	Top speed:	139 mph (225 km/hr)
Battery voltage:	12 V			Acceleration:	0 to 50 mph 5.8 seconds

1983 911SC cabriolet

The most significant addition to the 911 line was the new 911SC Cabriolet, which sold for $34,450. It was the first fully open Porsche roadster since 1964. It featured the same 183-cubic inch engine as its sister ships the 911SC coupe, and 911SC Targa, and with its top raised

911

boasted essentially the same performance figures as the coupe. Much was made at the time of the similarity of performance figures between the coupe and Cabriolet, emphasizing the roadster's low wind resistance and interior noise with the top in the raised position. In fact, Porsche boldly claimed that the 911SC Cabriolet was the fastest production convertible in the world.

The Cabriolet top was manually operated and folded rearward, and could be raised or lowered by one person. In its lowered position it could be covered with a tonneau cover. By 1987, all Cabriolet tops would be power operated. Additional bracing was required to insure structural rigidity in the absence of a fixed steel roof. An optional steel roll bar was offered from the factory, but if they ever did actually exist, they are scarce.

By 1983, the era of the so-called "yuppies" was in full swing in the U.S., and Porsche was one of this group's most desirable status symbols. The new 944 would move Porsche in a different direction for awhile, but the most desirable Porsche was still the 911—a car with continuing refinements in keeping pace with this lucrative new market. The 911 was, by the 1980s, no longer simply a basic sports car as the 356 had been. It was essentially more user-friendly and reflected the desirable lifestyle of its upwardly mobile customers.

While performance was expected and delivered in the 911, the new emphasis was on luxury. Standard 911 features included intermittent windshield wipers, tinted glass on all windows, power windows, air conditioning, reclining seats, electrically adjustable and heated outside mirrors, a quartz clock, and rear speakers with balance adjustment. These were essentially the type of creature comforts likely to be found on any new Lincoln or Cadillac of the period. These standard features were sufficient to the degree that apart from the optional roof rack, leather seats, alarm system, and digital cassette radio, most of the options were performance based, such as cruise control, limited-slip differential, fog lights, sport shock absorbers, and spoilers.

1983 was the final year for the 911SC.

1984 911 Carrera

The E series 911 Carrera ($31,950) was the only model for 1984.

The long-running SC was replaced by the Carrera. Available body styles for 1984 included the Cabriolet, coupe, and Targa. Engine displacement was increased to 3.2 liters with horsepower raised to 200 SAE at 5900 rpm. A new Bosch electronic DME (Digital Motor Electronic) Motronic injection system replaced the Bosch K-Jetronic. There was still no automatic transmission, and five-speed manual was all that was available in the U.S. Fifteen-inch 928-styled "telephone dial" wheels of cast aluminum were standard issue for the Carrera beginning in 1984. Also, beginning in 1984, the self-contained hydraulic timing chain tensioner was replaced with one that was pressurized by the engine. A Turbo look appearance group package was available which gave the Carrera a more aggressive posture, but lacked the turbocharger, which could be found on the European Turbo.

Total Porsche sales in the U.S. reached approximately 20,024.

1985 911 Carrera

As was the case the previous year, the only 911 model offered in the U.S. market was the Carrera ($31,950), still available in three body styles. Total Porsche U.S. sales for 1985 were approximately 25,306.

1986 911 Carrera, 911 Turbo

The Turbo was again offered in the U.S. with a 3.3-liter engine, but with increased power at 320 bhp due to a larger intercooler and turbocharger. It had 0-to-60 mph acceleration of 4.8 seconds and a top speed of 168 mph. Rust-through coverage for the entire body was extended to a full 10 years.

The Cabriolet and Targa were offered in an optional wide-body "Turbo Look" without the turbocharger beginning in 1986. Electric top operation for the Cabriolet became standard beginning in 1986.

Total Porsche sales worldwide for the 1986 model year were approximately 52,939, with 30,471 sold in the U.S.

1987 911 Carrera, 911 Turbo

The "Slant-Nose" option had been available in the U.S. since 1982 and would continue through 1989. It was also available for the Turbo model in 1987, and featured retractable headlights, functional side rear air vents, and a steeply slanted nose. Some felt this to be the ultimate road Porsche, but others felt that the radical shaving of the prominent fender mounted headlights, a 911 trademark, was simply too much. It was an expensive, and to some, desirable option at $23,000.

As with the "Turbo Look," efforts were made by both the experienced and amateurs to transform standard 911s into "Slant Nose" cars resembling the 935 racing cars. Some of these aftermarket transformations were done with metal, but most with fiberglass, generally with less-than-satisfactory results. Fortunately, these are not as common as they once were. The factory versions while rare in their time now look interestingly peculiar with the passage of time.

Horsepower for the Carrera was boosted to 214. The 915 trans-mission was replaced by a five-speed G50 with Borg-Warner synchromesh and hydraulic clutch.

Total U.S. sales were approximately 23,632, with 911 sales approximately as follows: coupe sales 2,916; Cabriolets 2,653, Targas, 2,232. The remaining majority consisted of front engine 944s, and a few of the expensive 928s.

1988 911 Turbo, Carrera 2, Carrera 3.2

A total of 300 limited edition 25th Anniversary models were introduced for 1988, and featured metallic blue exterior with matching color wheels and interior. The Carrera 2 was introduced, and it was the last year for the Carrera 3.2.

1989 Carrera 2, Carrera 4 (964), Speedster, 911 Turbo

Models for 1989 were the Carrera ($51,205), Turbo ($70,975), Carrera 4 ($69,500) and Speedster ($65,480).

The 911/964 was the first real reworking of the original 1963 design. The need for a new car had been based on several factors. The original 911 design had not provided for (at the time) undreamed of government regulations concerning noise and pollution, multi-speaker stereo systems, air-conditioning, or other modern technical advances. There was also a desire at Porsche to create an all-wheel-drive car based upon the commercial and racing success of the Audi Quattro. In order to accommodate the driveshaft and running gear, an all-new floorpan would be needed. At the same time the external body shape and design of the 911 would be retained visually in order to benefit from the 911's international recognition and appeal.

While the newly designated 964 resembled the previous model, in most respects, it was the first 911 to feature the new deformable (and reformable) bumpers, similar to those developed for the front engine 928 in 1977. While many considered the new bumpers (which were painted the same color as the body) to be unattractive, many more felt that the new bumpers offered a considerable visual advance over the previous generation 911 bumpers which had already been around since the mid-1970s.

1986 911 cabriolet
Dan Lyons

Engine size increased to 3.6 liters, while the classic air-cooled flat six configuration remained. There were some significant mechanical changes, however, including a twin-plug ignition. The 964 was also the first 911 to have power-assisted steering and coil springs, replacing the torsion bars which had been a 911 standard. The front suspension now consisted of MacPherson struts and lower control arms, while the rear suspension employed semi-trailing arms. The power assist was designed to operate fully at low speeds and then diminish as speed is increased. It is considered essential by most modern day motorists.

The Carrera 4 was launched in 1989 as model 964. Many owners were understandably thrilled with the all-wheel-drive, which helped the normally tail-heavy 911 negotiate corners without fear of the rear end swinging out in the hands of an inexperienced Porsche driver. The Carrera 4, with its additional mechanical weight from the front wheel drive and longitudinal drive shaft machinery, felt heavier on the road than the standard 911, and it was. But at the same time, there was the distinct feeling that the car was firmly planted, an impression which some enthusiasts used to heavier cars found reassuring.

The Carrera 4's all-wheel-drive mechanism was based on that used in the 911 which won the 1984 Paris-Dakar rally, which itself was based on that of the all-wheel-drive 959 that debuted at the 1983 Frankfurt Auto Show as the "Group B Study." A rigid torque tube of the type used on the 928 transmitted power to a secondary front differential, delivering torque at a 31/69 front to rear ratio. The system operated through ABS sensors in each wheel, which, sensing slippage, informed the electronic control unit, which then activated a clutch, transferring torque to the front wheel that had the most traction, and acting as a limited-slip differential at the rear wheels. The system was computerized and adjusted itself as necessary.

The all-wheel-drive concept in a sports or passenger car was understandably considered revolutionary at the time of its introduction in 1989, but its overall importance to the motoring world would not be fully realized for another decade.

The most interesting visual feature of the nearly $70,000 Carrera 4 was its automatic rear spoiler, which deployed at speeds between 40 and 50 mph, but retracted as soon as speeds reduced to around 5 mph. In its closed position air circulates freely into the engine compartment, while in its raised or extended position it helps reduce lift at higher speeds.

Much had been learned through racing and applied to Porsche road cars. For example, it was learned that aerodynamic lift negatively affects a car's handling at higher speeds. While no specific consideration had been given to lift in the initial 911 design, it had been addressed subsequently through a variety of front and rear spoilers, from the smaller rear spoiler of the 1973 Carrera, to the "Whale Tail" of the Turbo. Many observers felt that the rear spoilers greatly detracted from the otherwise fluid lines

1988 911 Carrera coupe
Dan Lyons

1988 911 Special Edition cabriolet
Dan Lyons

of the 911. The new 964's ingenious rear spoiler design served its intended purpose while the car was in motion, but maintained the smooth lines of the car at rest. And after all, when it was deployed, the driver couldn't see it anyway. While the spoiler's actual utility at lower speeds might be questionable, the motions of this appendage certainly gained attention in traffic.

Drag had increased over time on the 911 due to external modifications like wider fenders and the U.S.-mandated bumpers for the American market. The new Carrera 2 and 4 both had a much more acceptable drag coefficient of 0.32, ahead of the earlier front engine 924's 0.34. This was achieved in large measure to a smooth underbody and air intake modifications.

As with the original 356 Speedster (1954-57), the 1989 Speedster was to be a less-expensive model than the standard 911, and designed primarily for the U.S. market. It was a response to the desire in the lucrative U.S. market for a less-expensive open car suited primarily to warmer climates. It was to be a stripped-down version with manually operated seats, windows, and top.

The Speedster was fitted with an unlined, lower profile convertible top, one-piece side windows—that is, without the fixed vent windows of the 911—and a raked front windscreen. The windshield was intended to resemble that of the original 356 speedster and is the most similar feature of the two cars. The top, when lowered, disappeared beneath a hard cover with mock headrests, very reminiscent of the 1963 Ford Thunderbird's rear seat cover. As with the early Jaguar XK-120, the Speedster's windshield could be fairy easily removed for racing and replaced with a lower-profile driver's windshield.

The Speedster was an exotic-looking car and is highly desirable today and equally rare with a total of 2,065 built during the second run of the legendary car. Of this total, 1,894 were built with the "Turbo Look" body.

A lightweight Club Sport model was offered outside the U.S. for 1989 and was essentially a stripped-down 911, devoid of the usual luxury amenities, such as air conditioning, insulation, and power windows. The weight savings and slight engine modifications gave the car a top speed of 150 mph. But the 911 had been gaining weight since its inception. First there were the larger American government mandated bumpers, as well as the so-called "smog pumps," followed by catalytic converters. In addition to emissions equipment there were the addition of creature comforts such as air conditioning, and electric windows, mirrors, and antenna, each with its own motor, and power seats with multiple motors. Ultimately, there was the addition of a radiator and its coolant contents. While these features have added additional weight across the 911 line over the course of time, there are few who would complain, especially in the American market. Be that as it may, there are those few, who, more for aesthetic reasons than reality, would prefer a stripped-down model because it is "faster," not that they are ever likely to use even the heavier car at its full potential.

Of special significance was the reworking of the heating system for the 1989 models. Prior to this time the system had been basically unchanged from the early cars, and consisted of air heated by heat exchangers on either side of the engine and piped through the door sills to the front of the car.

Sixteen-inch wheels became standard for 1989.

Total U.S. 911 sales fell to 3,377 cars, plus 823 Speedsters. This included 1,361 Cabriolets and 860 Targas.

1990 Carrera 2, Carrera 4

The Turbo was not in the lineup for 1990. The Carrera numerical designation refers to either continuous two- or four-wheel drive. With 250 horsepower, the 1990 Carrera was one of the hottest cars around.

Porsche advertising of the period indicated that while over 85 percent of the components of both the Carrera 2 and Carrera 4 models were new, the classic profile of the 911 remained true to its heritage. Of particular significance, at least to Porsche, were the polyurethane front and rear bumpers that allowed a full color match between the bumpers and the body of the car. Things had been heading in that direction for quite some time both in America and abroad. It probably began in the U.S. with the introduction of the 1968 Pontiac GTO, which had a "rubber" front bumper that was somewhat lighter than steel and amazingly crashworthy. By 1990, even in American cars, chrome bumpers were virtually a thing of the past. Porsche had, for the most part, dispensed with even chrome trim on bumpers by the early 1970s due to the necessity of redesigning them to meet American crash standards. Beginning in 1977, a one-piece bumper would be introduced into the 928 line and eventually extend to the other cars as well. The bumpers were not merely cosmetic, they were designed to pop back to their original shape at a minimum impact, such as might occur in a parking lot mishap. The Carrera's front bumper also bore a family resemblance to that of the 928 of the same period. Additionally, bumpers contained turning lights, parking lights, and fog lights in one cluster at each end. The integrated bumpers also served to reduce drag to 0.32.

The now-famous Tiptronic transmission was first introduced with the 1990 964 Carrera 2 as a four-speed. It was a fully automatic transmission and operated as a standard automatic transmission, somewhat like the Hurst Dual Gate shifter found on some American muscle cars of the late 1960s and early 1970s. That is, that it can be operated as an automatic or, by moving the shift lever to the right, operated as a manual, but without any clutch.

1990 911 Carrera 4
Porsche NA

Unlike the Dual Gate shifter, the Tiptronic was electronic, rather than mechanical, and was a device of incredible technical sophistication. The lever transmitted signals electrically to the Tiptronic computer, which then shifted the gears as necessary. There was an automatic override in the Tiptronic that shifted the transmission upward when maximum engine speed was reached for the selected gear.

The Tiptronic was developed as a joint project by Porsche, Bosch, and ZF, with Bosch providing the electronics and ZF the case. While the option of a manual shift was desirable in theory, the precision of the Tiptronic was such that most drivers opted for the fully automatic setting for everyday driving.

1991 911 Carrera 2, 4, Turbo

Models for 1991 were the Carrera 2 ($60,700), Carrera 4 ($72,000) and Turbo ($95,000).

The Turbo returned for 1999, but unlike the two Carreras was available only in a two door coupe body. The Turbo's displacement was 201.3 cubic inches (3,229 cc). It developed 320 horsepower at 5,750 rpm, with torque rated at 331.8 ft.-lbs. at 4500 rpm. Top speed for the

Turbo was 168, with 0-60 mph in around 4.8 seconds, faster than the flagship 928's 0-60 in 6.1 seconds. The largest selling car for the year was the Carrera 2 Cabriolet at 1,031 units.

1992 911 Turbo S2 coupe
Mike Mueller

1992 Carrera 2, 4, Turbo, America Roadster

Models for 1992 were the Carrera 2 ($63,900), Carrera 4 ($75,780), Turbo ($98,875) and America Roadster ($87,900).

1992 was a pivotal year for the Porsche company. The high sales Porsche enjoyed particularly in the U.S. during the prosperous Reagan years were gone by 1992. In fact, sales in the important U.S. market had dropped to just 25 percent of what they'd been in 1988. Again, as with the so-called gas crisis of 1973, there were those who considered the internal combustion engine to be the major source of the world's problems. That in addition to a political climate which was inhospitable to capitalism in the U.S. relegated Porsche to the status of a car primarily for

RS AMERICA

1992 RS America was introduced in 1992 as a 1993 in the U.S. and Canada. A total of 701 RS Americas were built between 1992 and 1994 (297 in 1992; 328 in 1993; 76 in 1994).

The similarities between the Standard Carrera 2 and the RS America were greater than their differences. Basically, the America consisted of a standard Carrera 2 body and chassis with certain modifications to both. The engine of the RS America was the same as the standard Carrera 2's 3.6 liter engine. The body of the America had a fixed rear spoiler, unlike that of the Carrera 2. Interior options included corduroy fabric, accented with red. Differences in running gear consisted of fully manual steering as opposed to power assisted on the Carrera. Both front and rear springs and shocks on the RS were upgraded and the front suspension was fitted with a 22mm anti-roll bar as opposed to the standard 20mm. Standard wheels were 17 inch alloys.

Options were minimal and included air conditioning, a sunroof and a limited-slip differential.

---

greedy yuppies. Add to that the 911's basically dated looks, and something needed to change.

Be that as it may, an America Roadster debuted in the 1992 model year in commemoration of the very limited production 356 based America Roadsters of 1952. Unlike its earlier namesake, the 1992 version was well equipped with luxury amenities such as air conditioning and a six-speaker stereo system. As with the earlier, original version, by the time everything was said and done, the America Roadster was more expensive than the standard 911. The engine of the RS America was the same as the standard Carrera 2's 3.6-liter mill. Both front and rear springs and shocks on the RS were upgraded and the front suspension was fitted with a 22mm anti-roll bar as opposed to the standard 20mm. Standard wheels were 17-inch alloys. The body was similar to the Turbo-look Carrera 2 Cabriolet in that the rear wheel wells were widened to accommodate the wider wheels and tires. Options were minimal and included air conditioning, a limited-slip differential, and Tiptronic transmission.

Sales for the America Roadster were as follows: 297 for 1992; 328 for 1993; and 76 for 1994. Sales for the Carrera 2 Cabriolet at 654 units made it the largest selling 911 for 1992, followed by the Carrera 2 coupe at 609.

1993 Carrera 2, 4, Turbo, America Roadster, RS America

Models for 1993 were the Carrera 2 ($64,990), Carrera 4 ($78,450), Turbo ($99,000), America Roadster ($89,350), and RS America ($54,900).

1993 marked a milestone year for Porsche in that it represented the 30th anniversary of the 911. To this end a special edition wide-bodied Turbo Look commemorative 911 model was offered of which a mere 911 examples were produced.

The RS America debuted as a 1993 model and was truly a stripped-down and less-expensive version of the standard 911, somewhat similar to the various European "Club Sport" models, with emphasis on performance rather than luxury. The strictly two-seat RS lacked power steering, but employed a sport-racing suspension as standard. It was available as a two-door coupe only with an optional manually operated sunroof. The interior was as minimal as possible with plain door panels lacking map pockets, and an interior pull-down type door opening cord similar to that found on both German and British sports cars of the 1950s. Recaro seats were standard, but lacked the leather seating surfaces associated with the higher-priced cars. They were covered instead by corduroy.

1993 911 RS America coupe
Dan Lyons

A wide-body Turbo Look was available for the Carrera 4 coupe.

Sales diminished even further as prices increased, with the entry level Carrera 2 at nearly $65,000, and the Turbo priced at $99,000. Production of the 964 ended in December as preparation began for production of the all-new 993.

1994 Carrera 2, 4, Speedster, America Roadster, RS America

Models for 1994 were the Carrera 2 ($64,990), Carrera 4 ($78,450), Speedster ($66,400), America Roadster ($89,500), RS America ($54,900) and Turbo ($99,000).

The 993 Series 911s debuted at the 1993 Frankfurt Auto Show as 1994 models, and represented the most drastic revision of the 911 since its inception. Basically everything about the car was new. An entirely new rear suspension finally successfully addressed the oversteer that had plagued the 911 from the beginning, and a radically revised body style gave the car a better look while maintaining the original configuration. Weight had continually been added to the 911 over the years, and had increased from 2,315 lbs. for the 1975 coupe to 3,064 lbs. for the basic two-door coupe by the 1994 model year. A six-speed manual transmission was offered for the 993, and the optional four-speed Tiptronic S now featured steering wheel mounted push button gear selectors. Larger, four-caliper brakes were standard with 12 inch front, and 11.8 inch rear, cross-drilled disc rotors for the new series cars.

Production of the 993, the last of the air-cooled 911s, began in January 1994 and remained in place through the 1998 model year.

The Speedster was reintroduced at the Detroit show as a 1994 model and, like the RS America, featured a five-speed manual transmission, with an optional four-speed Tiptronic. Like its Speedster predecessors, it was also strictly a two-seater. It was based on the Carrera 2 structurally and was at once a mixture of both luxury and old school sports car tradition. The top was manually operated, and like the 1989 Speedster, stowed beneath a hard cover when in the down position. Seats were racing style buckets, but the car came standard with power electric windows. Unlike the America Roadster, however, this open top car was not available in a wide body Turbo-look configuration.

The Turbo again was based on the 3.6-liter engine only with a compression ratio of 7.5:1. It was again the most expensive car in the line at nearly $100,000.

1994 911 Speedster
Dan Lyons

1995 Carrera 2, 4, Turbo

Models for 1995 were the Carrera 2 ($59,900), Carrera 4 ($65,900) and Turbo ($99,000).

The Speedster and RS America were discontinued for the 1995 model year, while both the Carrera 2 and the all-wheel drive Carrera 4 were offered in coupe and Cabriolet bodies.

Many people feel that the 911 known as the 993 Carrera, which debuted in America in 1995, was the most visually appealing Porsche ever built. Since its introduction, sales have been up every year. The 993 was revolutionary particularly in terms of its appearance. Gone were the protruding bug-like headlights that had always been a hallmark of the 911. Finally, the headlights had been more fully integrated into the front fenders, providing an infinitely more attractive appearance from any angle.

The 993's air-cooled 3.6-liter engine with its new Bosch 2.10 engine management system developed an impressive 272 bhp without a turbocharger. A six-speed manual transmission was standard but an optional automatic Tiptronic was also available. The interior remained standard 911 with classic five-dial instrument cluster. Gone, hopefully forever were fabric seating surfaces, replaced by full leather. Brakes were cross-drilled ventilated four-wheel discs, behind beautiful cup style alloy wheels.

Of special significance for the 1995 was the reworking of the all-wheel drive system that had debuted with the 1989 model year 964 series Carrera 4. The new system was more than 100 lbs. lighter than the first all-wheel drive system.

The new 993 Turbo featured all-wheel drive, twin turbochargers and 18-inch wheels, and again was priced at around $100,000, depending on options.

The Carrera 2 was still the highest seller with production almost equally split between the Cabriolet (1,743) and coupe (1,767).

1996 Carrera 2, 4, 4S, Turbo

Models for 1996 were the Carrera 2 ($63,750), Carrera 4 ($69,100), Carrera 4 S ($73,350), Turbo ($105,000).

1996 marked the first time since 1977 that the 928 was not on the Porsche menu, except basically as remaining unsold stock. Its removal

---

Carrera 2 (993)
Technical Specifications (1994)

Engine:	Horizontally opposed (flat), air-cooled six-cylinder, aluminum
Displacement:	3.6 liters (3,600cc)
Horsepower:	272 @ 6100 rpm
Compression ratio:	11.3:1
Bore & stroke:	3.94 x 3.01
Torque:	243 ft.-lbs. @ 5000 rpm
Engine management:	Bosch Motronic 2.10
Transmission:	Six-speed manual
	Four-speed Tiptronic (optional)
Front suspension:	MacPherson Struts with coil springs
Rear suspension:	Independent, multi-link (LSA)
0 to 60 mph:	5.3 sec.
Top speed:	168 mph
Wheelbase:	89.4 in.
Height:	51.8 in.
Width:	68.3 in.
Weight:	3,014 lbs.

from the lineup restored the 911 to its former premier place of honor in the Porsche pantheon, and signaled the death knell for the long-running front-engine experiment that had started with the debut of the 924 in 1975. The short-lived front-engine 968, basically the last of the 944 series, also dropped off the charts as well.

The one millionth Porsche was manufactured as a 993 police car. Standard horsepower was increased to 282 with the 3601 cc (220 cc) engine that was used across the model range. The new Turbo also used the 3601 cc engine that now featured twin turbochargers, and delivered power through all four wheels. Turbo horsepower increased to 400 at 5250 rpm., with 400 ft.-lbs. of torque at 4500 rpm. The all-new Targa, now an exotic car (see Targa section), returned with its rearward-sliding glass top, a significant technical improvement over the lift-off roof panel. The Carrera 4S featured the wide rear wheel flares of the Turbo, but lacked the Turbo's rear spoiler. Prices for

1996 911 Turbo coupe
Dan Lyons

1996 911 Carrera Targa
Dan Lyons

the model year began at $63,750 for the Carrera 2, and escalated to $105,000 for the Turbo.

Although Porsche offered the Carrera 2 and 4 coupe and Cabriolet, as well as the 4S Coupe, Turbo, and Targa, the largest-selling car in the U.S. market for the year was still the Carrera 2 at 2,108 units.

1997 911

Models for 1997 were the Carrera 2 ($63,750), Carrera S ($63,750), Carrera 4 ($69,100), Carrera 4S ($73,350), Turbo ($105,000), and Turbo S ($150,000).

The new 911, dubbed the 996, appeared in autumn 1997. The Carrera S coupe, which featured the wider body of the Turbo, was introduced in March 1997 and became the entry-level 911 for the following model year.

911 71

1998 Carrera S, 2, 4, 4S, Targa

Models for 1998 were: the Carrera S coupe ($63,750), Carrera 2 Cabriolet ($73,000), Carrera 4 ($69,100), Carrera 4S ($73,000) and Targa ($70,750).

The new 911 dubbed the 996 appeared in autumn 1997. This car had been developed at the same time as the Boxster and shared a great visual similarity, especially from the front, thus giving both cars a familial similarity. Designer Harn Lagaay, once an understudy of 928's design chief Tony Lapine, had managed to retain the 911's basic appearance while basically revolutionizing the car both externally and internally. The wide-body Turbo look was available on Carrera S which had been introduced the previous year.

Total U.S. sales for Porsche in 1998 were approximately 17,243.

1999 Carrera S, 2, 4

Models available for 1999 were the Carrera S coupe ($65,030), Carrera 2 Cabriolet ($74,460) and Carrera 4 ($70,460).

1997 911 Carrera 4S coupe
Porsche NA

1997 911 Carrera coupe and cabriolet
Porsche NA4

The new 996 debuted as a 1998 model in Germany, but showed up in the U.S. for the 1999 model year. The 1999 model year represented a significant turning point for the 911, and the Porsche company. Basic models consisted of the Carrera 2 and Carrera 4, both of which were available in coupe or Cabriolet form. A heavier, 3.6-liter, 360-horsepower coupe known as the GT3 was offered, but not in the U.S.

The big news for the 1999 911 was the new water-cooled engine. For the traditionalist, this was unpardonable. Gone forever would be that unmistakable air-cooled "Porsche" exhaust, replaced by a quieter, more

911 | 73

1997 911 Turbo coupe and cabriolet
Porsche NA

subdued tone. To others, however, the birth of a water-cooled engine in the 911 finally completed the separation of the 911 from the Volkswagen. A water-cooled engine, it was felt, had been long overdue. While the lingering and long-standing doubts that the 911 would survive due to U.S. noise and safety regulations had pretty much fallen by the wayside, the fact was that these issues were still considerations at the time that development of the water-cooled engine had been undertaken. Beyond those concerns, however, was the fact that the air-cooled engine, in one form or another, had powered the 911 and its predecessors since 356/1 in 1948. But, in the current world environment the air-cooled engine was basically obsolete as a power plant for any sports car. Even beyond that, the technological limits of the air-cooled engine had been reached by the Porsche engineers. Increasing demands for accessories such as air conditioning, power steering, electric windows, and constantly restrictive emissions requirements could no longer be efficiently met with an air-cooled engine.

The new water-cooled 3.4-liter flat six (displacement reduced from the previous series' 3.6-liter) had twin plugs and four valves per cylinder, double overhead camshafts, and Variocam valve timing. Gone forever were the awkward and unattractive cooling fan and cowl housing of the air-cooled engine. For the first time, the engine of the 911 was a visual work of art in its own right. But as far as its function was concerned, the new 3.4-liter engine, with its 300 horsepower, pushed the new 996 to 60 mph in around 5.2 seconds, marginally faster than the 993's air-cooled engine. And while top speed for the 911 had been increasing constantly

This aerial view shows the 1999 Porsche Carrera 4 drivetrain and suspension.
Porsche NA

A phantom view shows the inner workings of the 1999 911 Carrera 4.
Porsche NA

1999 911 Carrera 4 coupe
Porsche NA

1999 911 Carrera cabriolet
Porsche NA

1999 911 Carrera 4 cabriolet
Porsche NA

911 (996)
Technical Specifications (1999)

Engine:	3.4-liter water-cooled flat six with double overhead cams	Horsepower:	300 @ 6,800 rpm	Weight:	2,910 lbs.
		Torque:	258 ft.-lbs. @ 4,600 rpm	Front suspension:	MacPherson struts with gas pressurized shocks surrounded by coil springs
Valvetrain:	Four valves per cylinder, double overhead camshafts, Variocam variable timing	Body construction:	Steel unibody	Rear suspension:	Independent multi-link with coil springs and gas pressurized shocks
		Transmission:	six-speed manual (standard); ZF built 5-speed Tiptronic (optional)		
Bore and stroke:	3.78 in. x 3.07 in.	Wheelbase:	92.6 in.	Wheels:	Front 7J x 17, rear: 9J x 17
Engine management:	Bosch Motronic	Height:	51.4 in.	Tires:	Front: 205/50ZR, rear 255/40ZR
Compression ratio:	11.3:1	Width:	69.5 in.		

for the standard 911 since 1965 (132 mph), the new 911 reached 174 mph, according to factory tests—the fastest production 911 yet.

The Carrera 2 and 4 were both available in the open Cabriolet for approximately $9,000 more than the standard coupe.

The new 996 was indeed a far cry from the first air-cooled 911, and offered nearly 100 comfort, performance, and appearance options, ranging in price from $5,876 for interior maple trim to $75 for a lower dash panel in a different color.

For the 1999 model year, Boxster sales soared way above those of the 911 cars, but the more-expensive Carrera 2 Cabriolet ($74,460) at 3,578 units outsold the Carrera S Coupe's 2,326, further confirming the U.S.'s love of open sports cars.

2000 Carrera 2, 4

Models for 2000 were the Carrera 2 ($65,590) and Carrera 4 ($71,020).

Again models consisted of two- and all-wheel-drive models in both coupe and Cabriolet. Engine output and displacement remained the same. Again, the more-expensive Carrera 2 Cabriolet outsold the Carrera 2 coupe, 3,802 to 2,510. But the standard Boxster outsold both of them at 7,593 units for the model year.

2001-2004 Carrera 2, 4, Turbo

Models for 2001 through 2004 were the Carrera 2 coupe ($65,000), Carrera 4 coupe ($72,000), and Turbo ($111,000).

Porsche

Both two-wheel and all-wheel-drive models continued in coupe or Cabriolet body styles with the open car costing between $5,500 and $11,000 more than the coupe. The new Turbo was available with an automatic transmission for the first time and boasted a basic price of $111,000. It incorporated twin turbochargers, delivering 415 hp and pushing the car to a top speed of 189 mph, with a 0 to 62-mph time of 4.2 seconds, despite its weight of 3,395 lbs. By comparison weight-wise, the new (2005) Jaguar XJ8 long wheelbase four-door sedan, for example, weighs only 3,777 lbs. One cannot help but wonder why Porsche kept constantly adding and withdrawing specific models such as the Turbo, the Carrera S, the Carrera 2, the Carrera 4S, etc. One possible explanation might be that a model was withdrawn from the market for redevelopment on occasion. Still, it seems unnecessary, as did the frequent alteration of engine displacement.

Carreras received a larger 3.6 320 bhp engine for the 2002 model year, while a Performance Kit option introduced for Turbo boosted power by 30 bhp to 450 bhp, and torque from 413 to 457 ft.-lbs. VarioCam timing and full-time all-wheel drive, as well as Porsche Stability Management (PSM), were standard but with an overide button. Turbo standard wheels were 18 inches, while the Carrera 4 had stock 17s. The excessively large tail wing of earlier Turbos has been replaced by a modest fixed-wing spoiler.

911 Turbo Specifications (2003)

Body:	Galvanized steel two-door coupe with 2 + 2 seating
Engine:	Flat opposed six-cylinder water-cooled
Displacement:	3600cc
Horsepower:	420 bhp at 6000 rpm
Transmission:	Six-speed manual, optional five-speed Tiptronic.
Drive train:	Fulltime four-wheel drive with PSM
Front suspension:	MacPherson struts, pressurized gas dampers
Rear suspension:	Multi link, coil springs

2001 911 Turbo coupe
Porsche NA

2001 911 Turbo coupe
Porsche NA

911 | 77

2004 911 Turbo coupe
Porsche NA

2004 911 Carrera 4S cabriolet
Porsche NA

2004 911 Targa
Porsche NA

Porsche

40th Anniversary 911

A limited edition 40th Anniversary model was introduced for the 2004 model year in commemoration of the 911. Other models consisted of the standard 911 coupe, Targa, and Cabriolet, the 911 Carrera 4S in coupe or Cabriolet, the Turbo in coupe or Cabriolet, and the GT2 and GT3. Production of the 996 Series continued until the introduction of the new, second generation water-cooled 997 (as a 2005 model) in Summer 2004.

40th Anniversary 911 Technical Specifications

Engine:	Water-cooled, horizontally opposed six-cylinder
Displacement:	3.6 liters
Horsepower:	345 bhp
Length:	174.5 in.
Height:	51.4 in.
0 to 62 mph:	5 seconds
Top speed:	177 mph

2001 911 Carrera coupe (left)
Porsche NA

2001 911 Carrera cabriolet (middle)
Porsche NA

2001 911 Carrera 4 cabriolet (bottom)
Porsche NA

911 | 79

2003 911 Turbo coupe
Porsche NA

2003 911 Carrera coupe
Porsche NA

2003 911 Targa
Porsche NA

GT2

The GT2 is the fastest production 911 to ever be offered for public consumption, although, admittedly in limited numbers. With its twin turbochargers and 477 horsepower (at 5,700 rpm) flat-six it achieves a top speed of 198 mph and could go from 0 to 62 mph in a searing 3.9 seconds. Torque is, as would be expected, equally impressive at 472 ft. lbs. (between 3,500 and 4,500 rpm). The car is lighter (3,131 lbs.)

Porsche

than either the 911 Carrera 2 (with Tiptronic), or Turbo models due to the absence of all-wheel drive, Porsche Stability Management, and any other electronic control systems. In other words, there are no additional protective systems to overide a driver's potential carelessness.

Visually the GT2 resembles the Turbo coupe with its high-placed side air intakes behind each door handle. The main visually distinguishing feature, however, is the unusual and exaggerated surface rear spoiler.

GT3

The GT3 is another supercar version of the regular 911. Like the GT2, it is available in a two-wheel rear drive configuration only. It is equipped with an adjustable rear spoiler, 18-inch wheels, and wider tires, as well as a redesigned front air dam to help handle the extra 60 horsepower (above that of the standard 911 Carrera). Top speed performance at 150 mph is not as stunning as that of the GT2's 198, or the Turbo's 189.5

2003 911 GT2 coupe
Porsche NA

2004 911 Carrera 4S coupe
Porsche NA

2004 911 GT2 coupe
Porsche NA

(manual). Like the GT2, it has fixed six-piston monobloc front calipers and fixed four-piston rear brake calipers.

2005

Models for 2005 were the Carrera ($69,300), Carrera S ($79,000) and Turbo S ($131,400).

The latest edition of the 911 appeared as the 997 in summer of 2004 as a 2005 model. This is especially significant because the 996 has been the most successful of all the 911s so far. Again, the 997 is obviously a 911, but even more futuristic in appearance than its predecessor. It resembles the 1995-1998 993 series (the last of the air-cooled cars) more than anything else, especially at the front where the lighting pods which previously, in the 996, housed multiple function lights including headlights, fog lights, washers, and turn signals have been replaced by individual units, as on the more traditional 911s. The 997 now has separate headlights with washer nozzles beneath the headlights as in earlier models. The headlights, however, are oval rather than round as on the 993s, although this is a minor point and likely not immediately noted. Turn signals are again housed in separate lenses beneath the headlights at each end of the polyurethane bumper. Air intakes are still housed in the lower section of the front bumper with a larger center section flanked at each end by horizontally split intakes.

While the new car can hardly be called retro, the more traditional headlights hearken back to earlier days as do the turn signals. The front air intakes, however, are in keeping with the more modern appearance of not only the Boxster, but, stretching the comparison somewhat, even to the Cayenne. The sleek body features an aluminum front hood and engine hatch cover. Despite ongoing rumors of an eight–cylinder 911, Porsche has continued with the traditional flat six. Models offered in the 997 line initially include the 355-hp Carrera S and the 325 hp Carrera. The Carrera retains its 3.6-liter engine for 2005 while the Carrera S features a 3.8-liter flat six. Both cars are equipped with a new six-speed transmission.

A Turbo S version based on the 996 continues for 2005 and is available in either coupe or cabriolet versions.

Conclusion

The 911, replacement for the 356 series is still standing after more than 40 years, having been threatened with extinction numerous times under various pretexts. The car of today, a marvel of technical sophistication unimaginable in 1964, still retains its ancestral influences, both in terms of its now timeless shape, its adherence to its original rear engine design, and its original purpose. While Porsche successfully experimented with front-engine cars, and even the new Cayenne SUV, it is still the 911 which best defines Porsche as an automobile company. No other sports car manufacturer has kept any model in continuous production as long as Porsche has the 911.

2004 911 GT3 coupe
Porsche NA

2004 911 Turbo interior

2004 911 Turbo Cabriolet

2004 911 Turbo Cabriolet

84 *Porsche*

2005 911 cabriolet
Porsche NA

2005 911 S
Porsche NA

911

912

912 TIMELINE

1965: Targa body introduced in September

1966: Track width was increased

1967: 912 gained a five dial instrument cluster from the 911

While the six-cylinder 911 had successfully replaced the 356 series, there was still a vacancy within the company lineup for a less-expensive entry-level car. It was hoped that a Porsche with a smaller engine and smaller price would fill the bill by attracting buyers who otherwise wouldn't be able to afford a Porsche. To this end the 912 was conceived and introduced to the U.S. market in September, 1965.

The 912 offered an entry level Porsche at a substantially smaller price ($4,700) than the top-of-the line 911 ($6,500). It was virtually identical in exterior appearance to its more-expensive sister. The interior was more basic than that of the 911, and plastic was substituted for the 911's wood trim. Instrumentation was also minimal, with three gauges instead of the five found in the more expensive 911. The 912 engine was the same air-cooled, opposed four-cylinder 1600cc pushrod version found in the late 356C, using two twin-choke carburetors. The engine, while achieving greater torque, however, suffered a loss of 5 horsepower because it was, by all accounts, "detuned" in an effort to make it smoother running. The standard gearbox was a fully synchronized four-speed, with an optional fully synchronized five-speed available at higher cost, and a Fichtel & Sachs single dry plate clutch standard for both. The electrical system was now a standard 12-volt system, replacing the earlier 6-volt system common on many non-U.S. cars. The body was identical to that of the 911 and, to the untrained eye, they were indistinguishable.

Perhaps the greatest problem for 912 owners was that they expected the same performance from the four-cylinder 912 as offered by the six-cylinder 911. While such an expectation might seem illogical, given that every buyer knew that the 912 had a four-cylinder engine, the illusion persisted. After all, the 912 looked just like a 911. How much difference could two cylinders make anyway? A top speed of 116 was acceptable for the time, but acceleration to the standard 60 mph at between 11 and 12 seconds was not particularly breathtaking. In the American market, the 1965 Pontiac GTO was available with a 389-cubic inch engine with three two-barrel carburetors. 1965 also marked the introduction of Oldsmobile's spectacular 442 muscle car. The American buyer expected more than adequate power in any car he purchased. The very concept of a sports car implied performance. The 1965 Jaguar E-type, for example, debuted its larger 4.2-liter engine in 1965, and while it was certainly much slower than a 1965 427 Corvette off the line, it was capable of frightening performance from 60 mph upward. The idea of a four-cylinder

1969:
Wheelbase increased by 2.25 inches. Production discontinued

1968:
U.S. models were fitted with front and rear running lights mandated by the U.S. government

1975:
912 reintroduced as 912E to fill gap between 914 and 924, using 914 engine with 5-speed manual gearbox standard
Production discontinued

912 Technical Specifications (1965-1969)

Engine:	Opposed flat four-cylinder pushrod, air-cooled (taken from the 356C)
Displacement:	1582cc
Bore & Stroke:	3.25 x 2.91 in.
Horsepower:	102 @ 5800 rpm
Torque:	91 ft.-lbs. @ 3500 rpm
Transmission:	Four-speed manual standard. (5-speed optional 1966-1969)
Body:	Unitized steel-Rear engine-Rear wheel drive
Front suspension:	MacPherson strut
Rear suspension:	Semi-trailing with swing axles and torsion bars
Weight:	2,190 lbs. (950 kg.)
Weight distribution:	46/54 front/rear
0 to 60 mph:	11.5 sec.
Top speed:	116 mph

engine in an E-Type body, or in a Corvette body would have been inconceivable even in theory to an American performance car buyer. Be that as it may, had such a thing been offered, the American buyer would still have expected outstanding performance. The Porsche reputation promised performance and it was expected.

Ultimately, the 912 suffered as a result both of over expectations and a price that was not equaled by the car's performance. The problem with performance may be attributed to the 1600cc SC engine, a vestigial remnant from the 356. The optional $75 five-speed transmission was available to boost performance, but it employed a racing shift pattern that many owners found inconvenient.

The first 912 series sold 30,300 cars total, not an unimpressive figure for its era. It is generally considered that the 911 replaced the 356, but since the 912 continued with the same engine as had been offered on

1966 912 coupe
Dan Lyons

the last 356 models, it could be argued that the 912 was the actual replacement for the 356, not the 911.

It should be mentioned that the 912 was originally named the 902, following the 901, which was renamed 911 due to legal claims from French automaker Peugeot. Peugeot claimed legal right to all three-digit car numbers with a zero in the middle place. So the 901 became the 911 and the 902 became the 912. Porsche conceded the numerical designations to Peugeot, but refused to relinquish the 900 series designation for competition models. It seems petty in retrospect that Peugeot would be so trivial, but Porsche conceded and the 911 proceeded to become possibly the most recognized sports car in history.

1976 912E

With the 914 no longer in production and the controversial 924 and 928 not yet available, Porsche was left with a decided void at the lower end of its product line. The upper end was more than adequately covered in 1976 with the 911S and Turbo Carrera. In order to fill this vacancy, the four-cylinder 912 was reintroduced—this time designated as the 912E. The "E" (Einspritzung) referring to the new car's new Bosch D-Jetronic fuel injection system, the same found on the last European 914s.

Conclusion

While some Porsche enthusiasts today still consider the 912s to have been underpowered, the 912s were not without merit for their respective times. Every evolutionary step taken to improve safety and handling with the 911, except for the engine, was equally applied across the board to the 912. The 912s were full-fledged Porsches and were nearly identical in appearance to their more expensive sisters.

Today the original 912 and later 912E are as desirable as they were during their respective times. If the original 912 was a mistake, as some detractors feel, then the 912E was a compound mistake, one Porsche should not have made again, given its experiences with first series. That the 912E was discontinued after only one year with sales of approximately 2,000 units indicates that Porsche must have felt it made a mistake, one that should, and was quickly corrected.

On the other hand, for those who particularly like the body style and overall looks of the 911, the original 912, and later 912E look as good today as when first introduced.

1976 912E
Technical Specifications

Engine:	Opposed flat four-cylinder-air cooled (same as in 914)
Displacement:	2.0 liters (1971 cc)
Compression ratio:	7.6:1
Horsepower:	86 at 4900 rpm
Torque:	98 ft.-lbs. at 4000 rpm
Lubrication:	Forced circulation
Fuel system:	Electric pump/electronic fuel injection
Electrical system:	12 volts
Battery rating:	44 amp/hr.
Alternator:	980 watt
Ignition:	Coil ignition
Transmission:	Five-speed
Body:	Unitized steel
Curb weight	2,395 lbs
Suspension:	four-wheel independent
Springing:	Torsion bars
Brakes:	Four-wheel disc brakes
Wheels:	5.5 x 15-inch steel
Tires:	165 HR 15
0 to 60 mph:	11-12 sec.
Top speed:	115 mph

914 & 914/6

914 TIMELINE

1970
914/4 and 914/6 were introduced
16,231 produced in 1970

1971
21,440 produced in 1971

1972
Last year for the 914/6
A new energy-efficient 1.7-liter fuel-injected engine allowed the use of 91-octane gas

The car known in America as the Porsche 914 first appeared at the Frankfurt Auto Show in September, 1969, the same place the 901 had first appeared in 1963, and began being sold in Europe in February 1970 as a "VW-Porsche." In America, the VW designation was dropped altogether and the car known simply as the Porsche 914 began selling in March of the same year, just in time for spring and summer. The car was actually a joint venture involving Volkswagen, Porsche, and coachbuilder Karmann, of VW's Karmann Ghia fame.

While the 914 represented Porsche's first large-volume production car without a rear engine behind the back axle, it was not the first or last mid-engine Porsche. Porsche's first experimental cars were actually tube-framed, mid-engine models, while the first manufactured Porsches, including all 356 (other than 356-1), 911, and 912 models were rear-engine cars exclusively. The 914 became the first in a continuing series of Porsche cars to break with that longstanding tradition.

The 914 came into being as a result of several factors taking place at approximately the same time. As many of the features found in modern passenger automobiles, such as four-wheel independent suspension, functional air ducts and scoops, four wheel disc brakes, and various types of spoilers grew out of knowledge gained from racing, so did the idea of mid-engine placement. Cars like the mid-1960s Ford GT 40, MK II, and MK IV, as well as offerings from both Ferrari and Lotus in Formula I cars, had clearly established that, in racing at least, mid-engine placement was the optimum positioning for balance, weight distribution, and handling.

By 1965 at Indianapolis, and 1966, with Ford's first, second, and third placement at Daytona, Sebring, and LeMans, both front- and rear-engine locations seemed obsolete, at least as far as racing was concerned. More significantly, it was possible that mid-engine configuration would soon be widely used not only in racing cars and existing exotics like the Lamborghini Miura, but also in higher number production sports cars. In fact, the mid-engine De Tomasso Pantera, successor to the mid-engine Mangusta, debuted in 1972, while the Maserati Bora and Merak began production in 1971 and 1973 respectively. Other, more common, lower-priced mid-engine cars also entered showrooms throughout the world in ensuing years, such as the Fiat X-19, the Toyota MR

1974
1.7-liter engine was bored to 1.8 liters with carburetors in Europe and fuel injection in America

Cars sold in U.S. were fitted with awkward new government-mandated bumper guards

1973
914 Optional 2.0-liter engine was offered for 1973

Cars with the larger engine also came with eight-spoke alloy wheels

1975
The last year for the 914

Total production 118,947 (including 914/6)

1970 914

2, and the Pontiac Fiero, proving not only the soundness of the mid-engine concept, but that other manufacturers considered the idea a good one.

Porsche's successful racing cars had employed a mid-engine configuration mostly for balance. A mid-mounted engine with a driver in front and a gearbox to the rear provide in many cases a near 50/50 front-to-rear weight ratio giving a car excellent balance. While the mid-engine makes sense in a racing car it poses specific problems for a passenger car, even a sports car. The engine and its associated heat and noise are very close to the driver and passenger. The engine is also difficult to access for servicing. And in the case of an air-cooled engine, the noise level is worse. A water-cooled engine is generally quieter since the mechanical aspects are insulated to some degree by the water jacket surrounding some of the internal components.

That Porsche sought to apply racing technology to the production of an inexpensive sports car was highly commendable. It was also self-serving in the best possible way. Porsche was known exclusively as a manufacturer of sports cars and was well respected in the highly competitive racing world, a well known proving ground for innovations ultimately applied to passenger car production. By 1970, Porsche had scored significantly with impressive wins in its class in nearly every important road race worldwide. That its racing successes should be passed on to its production cars was a worthwhile objective and a Porsche tradition. The late Steve McQueen's portrayal of Porsche racing in the early 1970s movie *Le Mans* further glamorized not only racing, but Porsche in general. James Dean was a folk legend known for nearly as much for his love for the 550 Spyder as his acting.

Porsche had already decided to discontinue the 912 due to poor sales and as early as the mid-1960s had started planning a replacement. With

Porsche

that decision having been made it was considered that another, lower-priced sports car should be offered to the public—hopefully one which would generate greater sales volume than the 912 (30,300). The prices of the 911s and 912s had steadily increased to the point where they were considered expensive cars by the American buyer. The cost of undertaking an entirely new car from scratch was a significant consideration for the Porsche company, which was then still small by modern standards. Ferry Porsche turned to VW's head, close friend Heinz Nordhoff, with the idea of manufacturing a car that would serve both companies by carrying both names. Nordhoff and VW were interested in introducing another car to the VW line. Porsche wanted a lower-priced sports car to replace the 912, and Volkswagen wanted to offer something a bit sportier than its then current line of fairly basic transportation. The Volkswagen Beetle was a top-selling car at the time, so Porsche could benefit from the proven marketing skills of VW in Europe and the U.S., while VW and Audi could both benefit from the prestige associated with the Porsche name. Audi was basically an unknown brand in America in 1969, despite its long-term success in the European market.

It was agreed between Ferry Porsche and Heinz Nordhoff that Porsche would design the car and Volkswagen would manufacture it at the Karmann factory in Osnabruck, using Volkswagen's 411 four-cylinder engine. Porsche would be then able to purchase the car bodies at a reduced rate, and install Porsche engines as desired. The original agreement between Ferry Porsche and Heinz Nordhoff was derailed when Kurt Lotz took over VW after Nordhoff left the picture due to illness (he died in 1968). To many Americans, the question arises as to how Lotz was able to change, if not actually disregard most of the terms of the original agreement between Nordhoff and Ferry Porsche? Why,

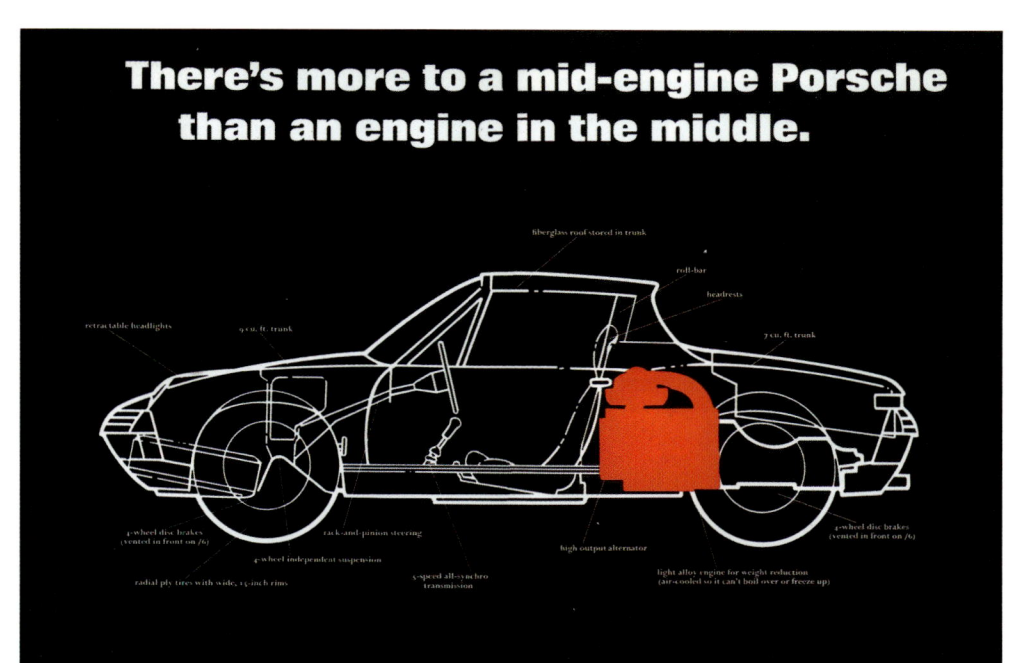

In 1970 literature, Porsche showed the mid-body placement of the 914 series engines.

one wonders, didn't Ferry Porsche simply tell Lotz that the deal he made with Nordhoff would stand as originally agreed or simply not come to pass at all? It is logical to assume that Volkswagen was owned by Porsche and that Lotz held his job at the pleasure of Ferry Porsche. But such was not the case. Lotz was free to enter into any agreements that he found acceptable and avoid those which he felt were not in Volkswagen's best interests.

To resolve problems associated with Nordhoff's departure, a new company was established called Vertriebsgesellchaft (VG), which was owned by both VW and Porsche. The 914 would be imported in America through the new Porsche-Audi distributor network, and sold only as a Porsche, while in the rest of the world it would be known as a Volks-Porsche, or VW-Porsche. Sales of the 914 in the U.S. would be, as with other Porsche models, through the new Porsche-Audi dealer network. Porsche and Volkswagen would each provide a sales director for the new company. By selling Audi in Porsche dealerships, the Audi brand would gain credibility by association with Porsche in the U.S. market.

The basic exterior design of the car was handled by German company Gugelot Design GmbH located about 50 miles from Stuttgart in Neu Elm. Apparently, Porsche didn't want the car to resemble the traditional 911, but it was also to be sportier than the VW Beetle or Karmann Ghia, another car with declining sales, which it was intended to replace. The original design from Gugleot was to have been front engine, but with the decision having been made to make it a mid-engine car, Butzi Porsche redesigned it to accept mid-engine placement.

The body was to be a steel monocoque construction with thick port and starboard side rail sills similar to those found on the highly desirable Jaguar E Type. The car was styled as a "Targa," with a structurally rigid rear top brace behind the back seat, joined to the front windscreen by a removable fiberglass top. (The Targa design had debuted at Porsche in

Note the massive bumper on the 1975 914.

914 Technical Specifications

Engine:	NOTE: The 914/4 came with three different four-cylinder engines during its lifespan; a 1.7 liter (1970-1973), 1.8 liter (1974-1975), and 2.0 liter (optional 1973-1975)
Engine type:	Volkswagen, mid-engine, air-cooled, opposed four-cylinder
Cylinders:	4
Bore:	3.54 in. (90mm)
Stroke:	2.60 in. (66mm)
Displacement:	102.3 cu. in. (1.679cc)
Compression ratio:	8.2:1
Horsepower:	SAE 85 (80 hp/DIN) at 4900 rpm
Maximum torque:	SAE: 109 ft.-lbs. (13.4 mkp) at 2800 rpm
Horsepower per liter:	51 SAE (48 DIN)
Valve arrangement:	Overhead
Valve drive:	Pushrods
Camshaft drive:	Gear type
Crankshaft:	Forged steel, four main bearings
Wheelbase:	96.5in. (2450mm)
Track, front:	52.8 in. (1337mm)
Track, rear:	54.3 in. (1374mm)
Overall length:	157.0 in. (3985mm)
Overall width:	65.0 in. (1650mm)
Overall height (unloaded):	48.0 in. (1220mm)
Ground clearance (loaded):	4.7 in. (120mm)
Turning circle:	approx. 33.5 ft. (11 m)
Dry weight (DIN):	1,982 lbs. (900 kp)
Max. permissible weight:	2,687 lbs. (1220 kp)
Max axle load, front:	1,430 lbs. (650 kp)
Max axle load, rear:	1,430 lbs. (650 kp)
Top speed:	approx. 110 mph (177 km/h)
Power/weight ratio:	25.2 lbs/hp/SAE
Fuel consumption:	Approx. 26.2 mpg
Lubrication:	Pressure lubrication
Carburetion:	Bosch electronic fuel injection Solex carburetors on European four-cylinder cars
Rated voltage:	12
Battery:	45 Ah
Ignition:	Battery, coil and distributor
Clutch:	Single dry plate
Number of speeds:	five forward, one reverse, fully synchronized
Axle ratio:	4.429:1 (7/31)
Frame:	Welded, pressed steel sections unitized with body
Brake disc diameter:	Front: 11.0 in. (281mm)
	Rear: 11.1 in. (282mm)
Rims:	4 J x 15 (steel)
Tires:	155 SR 15 tubeless
Steering:	ZF rack and pinion
Steering ratio:	1:17.78
Price:	$3,500 U.S.

1965 with the 911 and 912 models). The spare tire (stored horizontally), luggage compartment and fuel tank were placed in the front of the car, while the engine was placed directly behind the vertical seat back, but ahead of the rear axle. A rear area would also serve for additional storage as well, including a place for the removable fiberglass top. The gearbox was placed horizontally behind the engine and midway between the rear wheels, with shift linkage housed in a tunnel between the two seats.

From the standpoint of economics it made sense to use as many components from existing sources as possible. The front suspension was taken entirely from the more expensive 911 and included the traditional torsion bars located lengthwise front to rear at each side of the car just inside each front wheel. The steering rack and front suspension struts were also from the 911. For the rear suspension, coil springs surrounding shock absorbers were affixed to semi-trailing arms, with double-jointed drive shafts, giving the car a truly independent rear suspension minus the "swing arms" found on both earlier Volkswagens and Porsches.

The standard engine was initially an air-cooled, fuel-injected 102.4-cubic mill with a cast-iron block—a VW 80-bhp four-cylinder taken from the VW 411E, although engine size would increase later. It was manufactured completely at the Karmann facility at Osnabruk.

The original 914 offered mid-engine configuration, a low center of gravity, four-wheel disc brakes, independent suspension, a removable fiberglass top, rack-and-pinion steering, and the Porsche name, were packaged together at an affordable price. Initial pricing was approximately $3,500 for the standard 914. Available options were minimal, but included grained vinyl for the side top supports and chrome bumpers as part of a $200 appearance group option. It was an all-new design for the American market that had never been offered anything comparable previously. For Porsche, the cost of developing an entirely new car had been diminished as a result of the association with Volkswagen, but there was no guarantee the new car would be successful.

The 914 was offered for sale in some interesting colors during its day, including orange, yellow, red and light blue. Possibly the most unusual of all was the insect-like pale green. The interior was well designed if spartan, and included a fixed passenger seat and an optional center console. What was irritating to American owners was that in some cases the radios were affixed with volume and tuning knobs stamped with the VW logo. Standard wheels for the 914 were 4.5 x 15, four-lug, slotted, pressed steel with small chrome hubcaps nearly identical to those found on the VW Beetle. Optional 5.5 x 15 Mahle alloy wheels were available at increased cost. The steering wheel for the European VW-Porsche had the familiar Volkswagen Wolfsburg crest in the center, while the U.S. Porsche version had the stamped Porsche shield instead. While no reference was intentionally made to the 914's VW heritage in the U.S., the car did not look anything like the 911 or 912 familiar to American Porsche owners.

Be that as it may, the 914 was never considered by most of its American buyers to be anything other than a full-fledged Porsche. That the 914 was considered an affront to some members of the rear engine crowd at the time, or even now, for that matter was understandable, especially in light of the 911's substantially greater cost. That sentiment, while not without some justification at the time, was irrelevant to most 914 owners. They had bought a Porsche, and that's what they got.

The car was not particularly well received initially by most automotive reviewers for either its performance or appearance. It was not really a full-fledged Porsche, and yet not quite a VW, either. The criticism was more detrimental to Porsche than to VW, because more was expected from Porsche.

I remember my first ride in a 914. A friend of mine traded in his 1968 Oldsmobile 4-4-2 and ended up with a brand-new four-cylinder Porsche 914. The Porsche did not have anything near the blinding acceleration of his 4-4-2, to put it mildly. It was also considerably closer to the ground, a frightening thought in what I imagined to be an underpowered car. At that time (1970), not that many Americans had that much experience with anything from Porsche, especially college students in their late teens or early twenties. Compared to a contemporary Camaro, a Pontiac G.T.O., or an Olds 4-4-2, the 914 was more of a curiosity than a serious contender. The 914 at first seemed unusual in appearance to the American eye. While it was somewhat rounded at either end, it was basically a flat, rectangular box and lacked the fluid lines of its contemporaries. This is not to say the car was ugly, it was more "European," for lack of a better word, and to that degree, unconventional by general American standards.

It should be remembered that when the 914 hit the American marketplace in 1970, the U.S. was at the zenith of the "muscle car" era. The larger the engine the better. It was much more important to the average motoring enthusiast to have a car that exceeded 130 miles per hour than to have a car that handled well at a lower top speed.

Most of the possessors of muscle cars I knew were high school students. They frequently raced their cars on one particular straightaway outside of town. Speed was the overriding consideration.

1974 914
Dan Lyons

Adolescent racing never involved a curvy road racing course. It was all about speed.

So the 914 entered the world at a time of abundant and inexpensive gas to compete with what? Its competition included the British MG-B, the Triumph TR-4, and the all-new Datsun 240Z—the car which would basically introduce the U.S. buyer to Japanese imports and revolutionize the market. Be that as it may, the 914 was heavily advertised in America and referred to affectionately as "The Sun Porsche." It was invariably portrayed as a fun car, something exciting to drive, affordable, and always ready to have its top removed at a moment's notice for a day at the beach or an afternoon of around town shopping.

In retrospect, the 914 was a wonderful car for its time, and sold more than 120,000 units between 1970 and 1975. It opened the door to a much wider American audience for Porsche than that which had previously existed. The 914 basically made the Porsche name a household word, at least in the U.S. The car was everything it was advertised to be. It was fun to own and drive, and it provided the thrill of an open car without the hassles previously associated with an open sports car. It had roll-up windows and a lightweight one-piece detachable and stowable (on board) roof, rather than the problematic curtains and tops of earlier, more traditional sports cars such as the Austin Healey Sprites, MG Midgets, and earlier Triumphs. With its nearly 50/50 weight ratio, handling was impressive, and performance, while not phenomenal, was adequate. When seen for its many qualities, the 914 may be one of the most important sports cars of the modern era. Today, as cars continue to appear more generic in design with less individually distinct features, the 914 is even more appealing visually than it was initially.

1974 914

In terms of its value, the 914 is generally affordable to buy, and parts are readily available and fairly inexpensive. But this is changing as more and more people look beneath the surface at the 914. It really was a wonderful car. Its price is steadily increasing though not rapidly, and there are a great many Porsche owners and enthusiasts who consider it not only an excellent investment in the long run, but an affordable and fun car to use and enjoy now. While the 914 may be a good buy, meaning that you will not likely lose much money by buying a nice example at a reasonable price, it is unlikely that it will ever be very valuable from a purely monetary standpoint, though it is likely to appreciate.

While somewhat difficult to work on due to the location of its engine, it is a simple car mechanically when compared to the 944, 968, or 928, for example. For someone wanting to have an open sports car, a 914 in good condition is just as enjoyable today as it was when first offered to the public in 1970.

In retrospect, the 914 probably should have been fitted only with the six-cylinder engine. But then again, this would have defeated its purpose of being an inexpensive entry level Porsche. As it was, many at the time felt it was overpriced already, especially when compared to other similarly priced sports cars mentioned above. The car's appearance was considered to be unattractive to some, and downright ugly to others during its manufacturing run. Still, these cars have passed the test of time. How many open sports cars of the early 1970s, especially in the 914's price range, had a removable top, rack and pinion steering, four wheel disc brakes, and a fully independent suspension front and rear? And certainly the success of the very popular mid-engine Boxter of today is clearly traceable to the 914.

The purpose of the 914 was to replace the 912 with a less-expensive model and to open the door to a wider range of Porsche buyers. In that sense, the 914 fulfilled its purpose admirably.

Porsche

914/6

The 914 was a controversial car from the outset. Rejected by many purists as debasing the Porsche name, it drew flack for a number of reasons. The most obviously disappointing aspect of the car for some detractors was its looks. It was equally disrespected for its lackluster performance. There was little to be done as far as looks were concerned once the car was in production. It was what it was visually, and either you liked it or you didn't.

The 914/6, a six-cylinder version of the 914 featuring the 2.0-liter engine from a 1969 model 911T, was introduced in late 1970 in an attempt to bring the car's performance on par with the Porsche name. The 914/6's overhead-cam flat six-cylinder engine, with its twin triple-choke Weber carburetors had 110 bhp and was considerably more powerful than the standard 914's VW four. According to Porsche sales literature of the time, the car accelerated from 0 to 60 mph in 9.9 seconds and reached a top speed of 125 mph—a substantial improvement over the stock 914's 0 to 60 in 12.5 seconds and 110-mph top speed.

Again, as with the standard 914, the emphasis was placed upon the car's race inspired layout as described in this 1970 catalog:

1970 914/6 GT
Bob Harrington

1970 914/6
Dan Lyons

Underneath the louvers and Porsche name was the mid-body mounted engine.
Dan Lyons

The 914/6 was clearly identified by its chrome script.

"To begin with, it has everything the 914 has. On top of a 2-liter engine which gives the 914/6 a top and cruising speed of 125 mph. And high power engine that it is, the high rpms, small displacement, large bore and short stroke make it efficient enough to deliver about 26 mpg. Like the 914, the /6 has a unitized, welded body, which makes it virtually one piece and rattleproof. Like the 914, it has a 4-wheel independent suspension to smooth out the roads. Along with wide wheels and radial tires that help do the same thing. Like the 914, it has a removable

Porsche

fiber-glass roof that stores under the rear trunk lid. (There's a window underneath the built in roll-bar, so you don't get as much of a draft as you think). Like the Porsche 914, a five-speed stick shift is standard and you can get Sportmatic as an option. And an electric rear window defogger, and a center armrest and console, and tinted front and side windows.

"The 914 and the 914/6: The first mid-engine Porsches not designed exclusively for the racetrack."

The more expensive 914/6 came with 5.5 x 15-inch five-lug Porsche steel wheels. Optional alloy wheels, chrome bumpers, and vinyl sides for the top pillars did not radically alter the car's basic appearance, but did improve its visual appeal. While nothing could be done for the car's looks for those who objected, the six-cylinder removed all complaints about the car's performance, and brought the 914 up to the level of the 911. Additionally, with its lower center of gravity and more forgiving drive train configuration, it actually handled better.

The 914 bodies that were fitted with the Porsche six-cylinder 911 engines were also produced at Osnabruk, but had the engines fitted on the 911 assembly line at Stuttgart along with the 911s. It has been said that by the time the 914/6 body had been assembled and sent to Stuttgart for completion, that it was as expensive for Porsche to manufacture as the 911—a direct result of the departure from the original agreement which had been structured by Ferry Porsche and Heinz Nordhoff.

The 914/6 was also more "luxurious" in that it had minor improvements over the four-cylinder model, including 911-style instrumentation,

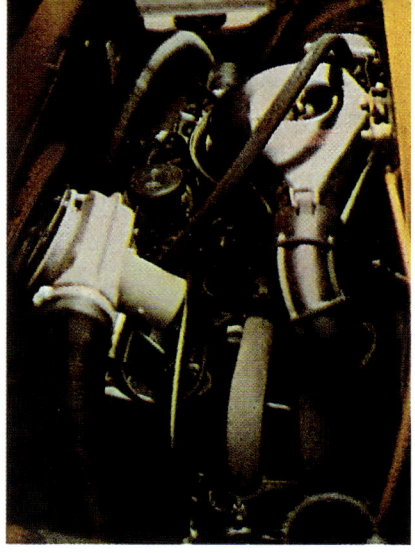

There wasn't much room for the four-cylinder engine in the 914. The six-cylinder engine was an even tighter squeeze.

1970 914/6
Dan Lyons

914/6 Technical Specifications

Engine type:	Horizontally opposed six, four-stroke cycle, air-cooled
Bore:	3.15 inches (80mm)
Stroke:	2.60 inches (66mm)
Displacement:	121.5 cubic inches (1.991 ccm)
Compression ratio:	8.6:1
Horsepower SAE:	125 (110 HP/DIN) at 5800 rpm
Maximum torque SAE:	131 ft.-lbs. (16 mkb) at 4200 rpm
Horsepower per liter:	62.5 SAE (55 DIN)
Valve arrangement:	Overhead in-V
Valve drive:	One overhead cam per bank of cylinders
Camshaft drive:	Chain
Crankshaft:	Forged steel, eight main bearings
Wheelbase:	96.5 inches (2450mm)
Track, front:	53.6 inches (1361mm)
Track, rear:	54.5 inches (1382mm)
Overall length:	157.0 inches (3985mm)
Overall width:	65.0 inches (1650mm)
Overall height (unloaded):	48.4 inches (1230mm)
Ground clearance (loaded):	5.4 inches (128mm)
Turning circle approx.	33 ft.
Dry weight (DIN):	2,070 lbs.
Max. permissible weight:	2,780 lbs.
Max. axle load, front:	1,430 lbs.
Max. axle load, rear:	1,540 lbs.
Top speed:	approx. 125.5 mph (201 km/h)
Power/weight ratio:	19.8 lbs/HP/SAE
Fuel consumption:	Approx. 26.2 mpg
Lubrication:	Dry sump
Carburetion:	Triple-throat Webers, one per bank of cylinders
Rated voltage:	12 volt (alternator 770 w)
Battery:	45 Ah
Ignition:	High-capacity discharge ignition with battery, coil and distributor
Clutch:	Single dry plate
Number of speeds:	five forward, one reverse, fully synchronized
Axle ratio:	4.429:1 (7/31)
Frame:	Welded, pressed steel sections unitized with body
Front springing:	Longitudinally mounted round section torsion bar, one per wheel.
Rear springing:	Coil springs with hydraulic, double-acting telescopic shock absorbers, one per wheel-and rubber buffers
Service brake:	Dual brake system, hydraulic disc brakes on all four wheels, internally vented discs in front
Hand brake:	Mechanical disc brake on rear wheels with control light
Brake disc diameter:	Front: 11.12 inches (282.5mm)
	Rear: 11.26 inches (286mm)
Rims:	5 J x 15 (steel)
Tires:	165 HR 15 with tube
Steering:	ZF rack and pinion
Steering ratio:	1:17.78
Original price:	$6,000 U.S.

ventilated front disc brakes, and three-speed windshield wipers. The 914/6 was not a great commercial success and was discontinued after 1972 with total sales of 3,351.

In hindsight, the 914/6 was a wonderful car, despite its poor sales, and is every bit as much of a true Porsche as any 356 or early 911. Due to its low sales, however, and early cessation of production, it is substantially more expensive now than the standard 914, which outnumbers it by basically 30/1. The 914/6 is one of the more desirable production Porsche models ever made, and as such was way ahead of its time. Again, the 914, especially the 914/6, paved the way for everything other than the 911 series hat followed, especially the Boxter. There is no doubt that prices will continue to rise for the fairly rare 914/6 model, and it is generally considered to be a much better investment than the standard 914.

1970 914/6

916

The 916 was what the 914 should have been, but wasn't. There were a total of either 11 or 20 916 prototypes built in 1972, depending on which figures you're reading. The 916 was very similar in appearance to the 914, using essentially the same body. The main visual differences included the 916's flared fender wells front and rear, and bumpers the same color as the body. The bumpers on the prototypes were actually fiberglass and probably would have been replaced by deformable polyurethane to meet U.S. standards had the car ever made it into full production. The roof on the 916 was metal and fixed, in contrast to the removable fiberglass panel roof of the 914. The car was definitely more aggressive in appearance than either the 914/4 or the 914/6, with wider 7-inch, five-lug alloy wheels. The car was fitted with an air-cooled 2.4-liter 911S, six-cylinder engine, with a five-speed manual transmission. The interior seating consisted of leather bolsters with fabric inserts.

There were other more or less experimental 914s, including two 1969 914/8s. The first was a red one featuring the 908's 3-liter flat eight-cylinder engine that produced 300 horsepower. It was used by Ferdinand Piech. The other, a silver street-registered model with four carburetors and a 250-horsepower engine was presented to Ferry Porsche on his 60th birthday. Like the limited production 916 cars, each of the eight-cylinder models had a fixed roof.

While hindsight is 20/20, it's probably accurate to say that had the initial 914 lineup been a standard 914/6 with an optional 914/8, instead of a 914/4 with an optional 914/6, the successful car might have been extraordinarily successful. But the 914 project might have been doomed at the outset after the departure and subsequent death of Heinz Nordhoff. The original deal between Norhoff and Ferry Porsche would have resulted in a considerably less expensive body manufacturing cost for Porsche and enabled a higher performance car to be offered to the public for less money. Be that as it may, a total production run of 120,000 for a sports car was respectable by anybody's standards at the time, and the idea of offering a six-cylinder 914 as the base model would have defeated the purpose of introducing a lower-cost Porsche to the U.S. market.

Ultimately, in the case of the 916, the decision was made not to put it into production. The projected cost to the customer would have been between $14,000 and $15,000, a significant, if not actually prohibitive, amount of money at the time.

916 Technical Specifications

Engine type:	Flat six-cylinder, air-cooled
Bore/stroke:	3.31 x 2.77 in. (84 x 70.4mm)
Displacement:	143 cu. in. (2341cc)
Compression ratio:	8.5:1
Horsepower:	190 bhp @ 6500 rpm
Torque:	159 ft.-lbs @ 5900 rpm
Valve placement:	Single overhead cam
Fuel supply:	Bosch mechanical fuel injection
Fuel rating:	Minimum 91 octane
Tank capacity:	16.4 U.S. gallons
Transmission:	Five forward speeds, one reverse
Final drive ratio:	4.43:1
Clutch:	Single dry plate
Body type:	Steel unitized
Steering:	Rack & pinion
Front suspension:	Independent torsion bar with MacPherson struts
Rear suspension:	Independent with semi-trailing arms and coil springs, anti-roll bars front and rear
Brakes:	Vacuum assisted, four wheel vented discs (11.1 in. front, 11.4 in. rear)
Wheels:	7-inch alloys
Tires:	Michelin XVR 185/70 x 15 in.
Wheelbase:	2450mm
Overall length:	156.9 in.
Width:	68.3 in.
Height:	48 in.
Front track:	1391mm
Rear track:	1445mm
Ground clearance:	5.1 in.
Curb weight:	2,000 lbs.
Top speed:	145 mph
Acceleration:	0 to 60 mph: 5.8 seconds

924

924 TIMELINE

1975
Production begins on the higher-powered European 924 in November, 1975

1976
First U.S. deliveries as 1977 models in April, 1976

1977
Optional five-speed transmission introduced

1979
Five-speed became standard with three-speed automatic still optional

Turbo model introduced

While the 911 descended from the 356 and the 356 from the Volkswagen, the four-cylinder 968 developed from the 944, which itself evolved from the 924, the first of the real non-traditional Porsches. The 924 was Porsche's first step into full production of a front-engine configuration automobile and would replace the 914 as the entry-level car from Porsche. Actually, the Porsche 924 began its life as a Volkswagen, and contrary to popular myth, was started after the 928 project was already underway.

The car that would ultimately become the Porsche 924 was never intended to be a replacement for the Volkswagen Beetle. The car that became the 924 had been planned to be a VW sports car, designed for VW by Porsche using existing VW and Audi parts. The same safety concerns that threatened the 911 series in terms of possible U.S. safety regulations, yet to be written, likewise endangered the very existence of the VW Beetle as well. Since Chrysler, General Motors, and Ford all manufactured front engine, water-cooled, rear-wheel drive (except for GM's Eldorado and Toronado) cars, it was no doubt felt that any impending American safety regulations would not involve attacks on that traditional, time-tested drive train. It would, therefore, be both desirable and necessary to add another car to the Volkswagen company's line with a car featuring that same configuration. Hopefully the new car could be put into service while meeting all existing and even potential American safety regulations. In the meantime, the VW Beetle continued to be manufactured and sold as long as possible.

Ultimately, Porsche knew that sales of the as-yet-unfinished 928, as well as continued sales of the 911 needed to be augmented in the interim with some other lower priced, entry level car. Despite controversy over its lineage, the 914 had been extremely successful during its 6-year run. With the desire to create an entry-level Porsche, Porsche bought the car which it had developed for VW, and then lacking facilities for production of the car, made a deal with VW-Audi in which it would manufacture the car under Porsche supervision. It was ultimately a win-win arrangement for all concerned, and the new car subsequently became the Porsche 924, and not a Volkswagen sports car as originally intended.

But interaction between VW, Porsche, and Audi was nothing new. In fact, many detractors referred to the Porsche 356 and some subsequent Porsche

1981
100,000th 924 produced
Disc brakes became standard for all models

1985
Production of the 924 ceases in July 1985. Production of 924S begins

1982
924 replaced in the U.S. market with the 944

1988
Last year of production for 924S

THE 924. THE FIRST PORSCHE AVAILABLE WITH FULLY AUTOMATIC TRANSMISSION.

The Porsche 924 gives you everything you've always wanted in a Porsche.

Styling. That special Porsche kind that stops people in their tracks as you drive by. Clean, classic lines that appeal to the eye and, at the same time, register an incredibly low 0.36 drag coefficient in wind tunnel testing.

Handling. With the excitement that only Porsche can deliver. The 924's unique trans-axle system gives this car an almost perfect 50-50 weight distribution. And the most breathtaking cornering you've ever experienced.

Convenience. Beneath that incredible, wraparound glass hatchback lies more carrying space than you ever expected in a sportscar. Wherever you go in your 924, you can take the things you need with you.

And now automatic transmission. The 924 is the first Porsche available with an optional fully automatic transmission. Now you can have the thrill of driving a Porsche with the ease of automatic.

But the best thing about the Porsche 924 is the fact that you can get one with standard transmission for less than $10,000.* That's not inexpensive. But it is less than you'd expect to pay for a Porsche.

*Suggested retail 1977—924 Std. Trans. From $9395 P.O.E. Transportation, local taxes, and dealer charges, additional.

Porsche emphasized an automatic transmission in its 1977 924 series ads.

models as "glorified Wolkswagens," a term not without some merit. The 356 had employed much of its running gear from Volkswagen, as had the 914. The car that became the 924 shared brake, steering, and engine components with VW as well. While many 911 owners disliked the 924 from the outset, any contempt for the 924 cannot logically be the result of its sharing parts with Volkswagen, since that practice was a long-standing tradition at Porsche prior to the introduction of the 924.

In terms of manufacturing efficiency, Porsche was already building two completely separate cars: the 911, and the soon-to-be-introduced luxury 928 touring coupe. These two cars shared little, so manufacturing costs were increased. In America, General motors, Chrysler, and Ford had a long-standing tradition of selling a wide variety of products using as many interchangeable components as possible between brands. This more efficient and economical manufacturing technique had not yet been as successfully applied with European manufacturers. On the other hand, American manufacturers generally suffered the expense of creating new bodies for their major brands every year or two, which was inconceivable to European manufacturers. Porsche, for example, intended for every car it created to keep the same body for its entire production run. What changes took place were generally improvements beneath the surface such as improved brakes, increases in engine displacement, or larger wheels. Purely cosmetic changes were generally minimal.

The same concerns about engine type and placement that had resulted in the decision to place the upcoming 928's engine in the front also applied to the 924. And the decision to abandon the air-cooled engine in the 928 also applied to the 924. It was felt at both Porsche and Volkswagen that the air-cooled engine had pretty much reached the limit of its utility. It would remain in both the 911 and the Beetle, but the other models would use water-cooled engines. The air-cooled engine was threatened

1981 924 Porsche
Porsche NA

1978 924

with extinction many times, but managed to survive in Porsche 911s until the 1990s.

The question naturally arises, if a water-cooled engine had been decided upon, why wasn't the water-cooled engine placed in the rear, in keeping with Porsche tradition? One of the requirements originally outlined for the new car was that it was to be a 2+2 coupe. A water-cooled engine in the rear, along with the transmission, would have substantially reduced interior space and basically eliminated a back seat. Radiator placement in the front would have reduced trunk space. So the decision was made to place the engine and the radiator in one location at the front of the car. The 924 engine was to be a water-cooled front-mounted 1984cc single overhead-cam Audi slant four-cylinder—a total departure from anything previously bearing the Porsche crest. The 40-degree slant configuration allowed a lower front profile than an upright inline four. Like the Jaguar E-Type, the engine consisted of a cast-iron block with an aluminum head. This technology was actually on the verge of obsolescence, as all-aluminum engines were about to become the standard. In the case of the

924, the initial engine was 121.1 cubic inches, and was fueled by a Bosch K-Jetronic CIS system.

The 1984cc engine remained the standard engine on the 924 (1976-1985), the 924 Turbo (1979-1984), and the 1981 924 Carrera GT and the 1982 924 Carrera GTS. The engine size was increased to 2479 cc in 1986 with the introduction of the S model and remained constant through the end of the model's production run in 1988. Actually, the 2479cc engine was taken from the 944, which had replaced the 924 in the U.S.

It was decided that, like the 928, the 924's gearbox would be located at the rear of the car, and power from the engine transmitted through a rigid enclosed torque tube via a 20mm driveshaft. The torque tube was fixed, literally bolted to the engine and clutch housing at the front, and the transmission (or torque converter) at the rear. This eliminated the need for a double-jointed driveshaft. The single-plate diaphragm-type clutch was located at the rear of the engine. Unlike the 928, however, whose transmission was located ahead of the rear axle, the 924's would be placed behind the rear axle. In either example, the engine and transmission, the heaviest individual components of the car, being situated at opposite ends of the car created a much better weight ratio, nearly 50/50, and consequently more neutral handling. The transaxle itself was also, like the engine, taken from an existing Audi.

The four-cylinder 924 and its descendents were discontinued after the 1995 model year. Since the four-cylinder period in Porsche history is over, at least for now, it is possible to examine them objectively and without prejudice, and the 924, which at the time was unduly criticized, largely for its break with tradition, can now be judged on its own considerable merits.

Porsche had determined that the 911 was likely on the way out altogether. The American market had traditionally exceeded half of Porsche's sales worldwide so something entirely new had to be produced to replace the 911, and that was to be the eight-cylinder 928, which was already under development. With restrictive U.S. safety regulations already in place, and more likely on the horizon, any new car, regardless of price, should follow the same format as had been established for the 928. That is, it should have a front engine, rear-wheel drive, and probably be a four-seater as well, employing the basic 2 + 2 layout used on most GT coupes, full-sized front seating for driver and passenger, with cramped rear seating for two additional passengers. Its four cylinders would come from an existing engine. Optimal handling could be established by balancing the front engine with a rear transmission, either manual or automatic. The American market had become more sophisticated since the 914 debuted in 1970, and now, air conditioning and other features, at least in America, were more of a necessity than a luxury. A new car was needed to fill these requirements.

Just such a car had been under development by Volkswagen and Porsche since 1972 at Porsche's Weissach testing and development center. Kurt Lotz, the head of VW during the 914 period, left his post and was replaced by Rudolph Leiding, who had been running the Brazilian division of Volkswagen. Leiding immediately cancelled all existing projects. He then hired Porsche to develop a sports car using existing Volkswagen and Audi parts. While the car that would eventually become the 924 was under development by Porsche for Volkswagen, the 928 project was already underway at full speed at Porsche.

It was a natural outgrowth of the work that had already been done in the development of the 928 that the same layout should be used on the car being developed for Volkswagen, that is front engine, rear transmission, torque tube, and rear-wheel drive. Unlike the 928, which was all Porsche from bumper to bumper, the new VW would be composed entirely of existing mechanical components from VW and Audi, making the car cheaper to build and subsequently less expensive for the customer.

The car, designed and developed by Porsche had been financed by Volkswagen, but at the conclusion of development, Volkswagen suddenly abandoned the car after having invested more than $50 million, suddenly deciding that a sports car wasn't a project it wanted to pursue. This was the direct result of Leiding's departure from VW and his replacement by Toni Schmucker. The car which had been developed by Porsche for VW under Leiding's direction had been completed as agreed by Porsche, and was in fact, ready for production. Despite the fact that the car was ready and that VW had already paid Porsche, the car was not of interest to Schmucker. He felt that the last thing VW needed at the time was a sports car. VW made it clear that it had no intention of producing the car. When that information became public, that the car was not going to be built at the VW plant as expected, a large number of workers were likely to be without jobs.

At this point, Porsche, having designed and engineered the car, felt that it had developed an excellent product. Porsche still needed an entry-level car so it bought the project back from VW in its entirety. This was accomplished with the financial aid of the government of the Baden-Wurtenburg state, which did not want to see idle workers at the VW plant, where the car had originally been intended to be built. Porsche now had the car but lacked the facilities to build it. The Porsche facilities were already operating at full throttle in production of the 911 and upcoming 928. Another agreement was structured between VW and Porsche, one in which construction of the new car would be handled by Volkswagen

1981 924

1981 924 Turbo

under Porsche supervision, at the NSU factory at Neckarsulm, north of Stuttgart. (Audi-NSU had been bought by Volkswagen from Daimler-Benz in 1969). The new Porsche, which had been originally dubbed the EA 425, was given the project designation 924 by Porsche.

The question arises that if VW had kept the car designed by Porsche, what was Porsche intending to use as its entry-level car, since the 914 was on the way out. The fact was that Porsche intended to keep the 911 in production along with the higher-priced 928. While the 911 was expensive for any entry-level car, it can be accurately cited that Porsches have always been expensive.

While there is a distinct visual similarity between the flagship 928 and the 924, especially at first glance, the 928 was all Porsche from drawing board to the showroom. Such was not the case with the 924, however, despite its similar appearance. The degree to which the 924 was actually a Volkswagen/Audi rather than a Porsche becomes obvious when looking at the components from VW that were used in its construction. The rear suspension, for example, was taken entirely from the VW Super Beetle, while some front suspension parts came from the Volkswagen Rabbit and some from the Beetle. Steering came from the Rabbit, while brakes were taken from the Beetle.

The 924 was a wonderful car and fulfilled its intended purpose as an entry-level Porsche. It sold well, and there are still many of them on the road today. It was a credit to the Porsche design team that a car which it had designed for another company was good enough on its own merits to bear the Porsche name with no modifications.

The standard model had four-lug, pressed-steel wheels. One wonders now, and at the time of the car's introduction, why four-lug wheels were used. In the U.S., a four-lug wheel was generally viewed as unimpressive, to put it mildly. Even inexpensive cars in the U.S. had five-lug wheels. And yet, even the 924's expensive contemporary, the Maserati Merak

1980 924
Dan Lyons

924
Technical Specifications

Engine type:	Water-cooled, front mounted 40-degree slant (starboard) four-cylinder
Block:	Cast iron
Head:	Aluminum
Valves:	Two per cylinder, single overhead camshaft
Displacement:	1984cc
Weight:.	300 lbs.
Compression:	9.3:1 (Europe) 8.0:1 (U.S.) 8.5:1 (U.S. model with automatic transmission)
Horsepower:	119 SAE @ 5800 rpm (Europe) 95.4 SAE @ 5500 rpm (U.S.) 110 SAE @ 5750 (U.S. model with automatic transmission)
Bore:	86.5mm
Stroke:	84.4mm
Torque:	122 ft.-lbs.
Fuel supply:	Bosch CIS K-Jetronic
Ignition:	Breakerless transistor (U.S.)
Electrical:	12 volt
Transmission:	Standard four-speed synchromesh manual Optional automatic three-speed
Clutch:	Fichtel and Sachs single dry plate diaphragm type
Body:	Unitized steel (hot dipped galvanized beginning in 1978 as a rust preventative)
Front suspension:	MacPherson struts with equal length A arms both sides, 20mm anti-roll bar
Rear suspension:	Independent, semi-trailing links, 18mm anti-roll bar
Steering:	Rack and pinion
Wheels:	5 J x 14 (6 J x 14 alloy optional)
Track:	Front: 55.8 in.
Rear:	54. in.
Wheelbase:	94.5 in.
Brakes:	Vacuum-assisted dual-diagonal
Front:	Solid disc
Rear:	Drum type (four-wheel discs standard beginning in 1981)

had a four-lug wheel, so perhaps it was more a European tradition than a manufacturing shortcut.

The 924 came with a fully independent suspension, front and rear. It should be remembered that in the U.S., even as recently as the late 1970s, a fully independent suspension was almost unheard of in cars produced by the "Big Three." The Chevrolet Corvette is the only readily available high-performance car that comes to mind. Even today, America's most successful sports cars, the Pontiac Trans Am, the Chevrolet Camaro, and the Ford Mustang, still lack this most basic element of high-performance handling. As far as handling is concerned, based upon its suspension, front to rear weight ratio, and steering, the 924 was far ahead of its competition in the U.S.

The lines were smooth and fluid with a long forward sloping hood and credited to Dutch born Harm Lagaay, an understudy of 928 chief Tony Lapine. Lagaay would ultimately be the design force behind the highly successful Boxster. Further, the 924's low drag coefficient of 0.36 made it one of the most aerodynamically efficient cars in the world. Actually, its drag coefficient was less than that of the most expensive Porsche, the 928. There were some problems associated with the large one-piece glass lift-up rear hatch, itself a manufacturing innovation at the time. Although it provided good rear visibility, it gave the car a greenhouse effect, which on a hot day was nearly impossible for the air conditioning system to cool. The car was at once very attractive, affordable, and to many looked like a Porsche, though not a 911. While there was obviously no similarity visually or otherwise to the 911, the car was accepted as a Porsche by U.S. buyers, as had been its 914 predecessor.

The car was not immediately popular, and first-year sales were a mere 5,145 copies. Sales reached 23,889 the following year, however, and the car was well on its way to breaking the 100,000 mark 1981. It should be remembered that the 924 was not an inexpensive car, at least not in the U.S. With an initial base price of nearly $9,500, the car was cost about the same as an entry level Cadillac, and that was without the 924's optional air conditioning.

The 924's interior was spartan but adequate, and featured an offset steering wheel with more space at the top than the bottom, supposedly to provide the driver with more legroom and increase instrument visibility. The seats were available in standard fabric, vinyl, or optional leather.

924 Turbo

The 924 Turbo brought the 924 into the serious performance category when it was introduced in 1979. Torque was increased from 122 ft.-lbs. to 181 ft.-lbs. and top speed was boosted from 125 to 140 mph. The engine short block was assembled at the Neckarsulm plant and sent to Porsche's Zuffenhausen where a different head was installed and the Kuhnle, Kopp, & Kausch Turbocharger was fitted.

Advertising at the time talked of refinements tested in the 911SC and the 928 being adapted to the 924 turbo, including five-lug wheels, and ventilated disc brakes configured in a dual-diagonal hydraulic system, although U.S. Turbo models had front disc-rear drum brakes, as opposed to the European front and rear discs. The dual-diagonal system means the left front wheel is on the same circuit as the right rear wheel, and vice versa. The theory behind this is that should one system fail for any reason, diagonal front and rear wheels on the same channel would still be able to stop the car because there would be active braking both front and rear, on each side of the car. This was the same brake system pattern employed on the early 928s. The 924 Turbo had larger, 15-inch wheels as well and floating brake calipers that could stop the car in 148 feet from 60 mph on a dry road. Tire size was 185/70VR-15.

Visually the Turbo is distinguished by the four longitudinal intake slots above the front bumper and an aviation-inspired intake on the starboard side of the hood. A front or chin spoiler further reduced drag from 0.36 to 0.34 and a rear spoiler was affixed at the base of the rear window, similar to that which would appear on the 1980 European 928 S. Other visual differences included alloy wheels and gravel guards behind the rear wheels.

Interior modifications on the 924 Turbo included a 911 type three-spoke steering wheel and a leather shift boot. Amazingly, the first 924 Turbos to reach U.S. shores had the bizarre and dizzying "Op-Art" interiors that were originally standard on the 928. (See 928 chapter).

Other mechanical modifications to the Turbo included a beefed-up front suspension to accommodate the heavier engine, stiffer shocks, and a larger driveshaft to handle the extra torque provided by the turbocharger. The Turbo model was available only with five-speed transmission.

924S

Although the 924 was discontinued for the U.S. market after 1982 and replaced by the 944, it resurfaced in the U.S. in June 1986 as the 924S, and was everything the 924 should have been all along. It had 147 horsepower, a top speed of 134, and made if from 0 to 60 mph in under 8.5 seconds. While it resembled the 924 in every detail physically, except for its 928-style telephone dial wheels and rear window spoiler, it was essentially a 944 beneath the surface with its 2.5-liter engine and similar brakes, drive train, and suspension. What differentiated the 924S from the 924, apart from its improved running gear, was its list of standard

The 1987 924S—note the 928 style wheels.

features, which included: electrically adjusted mirrors, air conditioning, and power steering, antenna, and windows. It again became the entry-level Porsche at a price of approximately $20,000, but by this time the 924 was not particularly interesting to U.S. buyers any longer, despite its considerable improvements over early 924 models. The 924S, while the best of the bunch, was still a 924, and the 944 was more attractive than any 924 to most American buyers.

There were several limited-production 924 models including the 1977 Championship edition (2,000 units) produced to commemorate Porsche's victory in the 1976 World Championship of Makes. This car had an all-white body with white wheels and red, white, and blue body stripes.

Another was the 210-horsepower 1981 924 Carrera GT (400 units) and the 245-horsepower 1982 Carrera GTS (59 units).

928

928 TIMELINE

1971
- Official start of 928 project in October

1973
- Full-scale model presented to the Porsche Board of Directors in October

1980
- 300-horsepower 4.7-liter S debuts in Europe with slotted wheels, larger brakes, and front and rear spoilers

1983
- Automatic transmission in U.S. and Japan raised from three to four speeds

1972
- Basic design finalized

1977
- 928 is presented to the world in March at the Geneva Auto Salon
- 928 becomes the official pace car for the 24 Hours of Le Mans in June

1981
- S appearance group offered in U.S., but without the larger engine

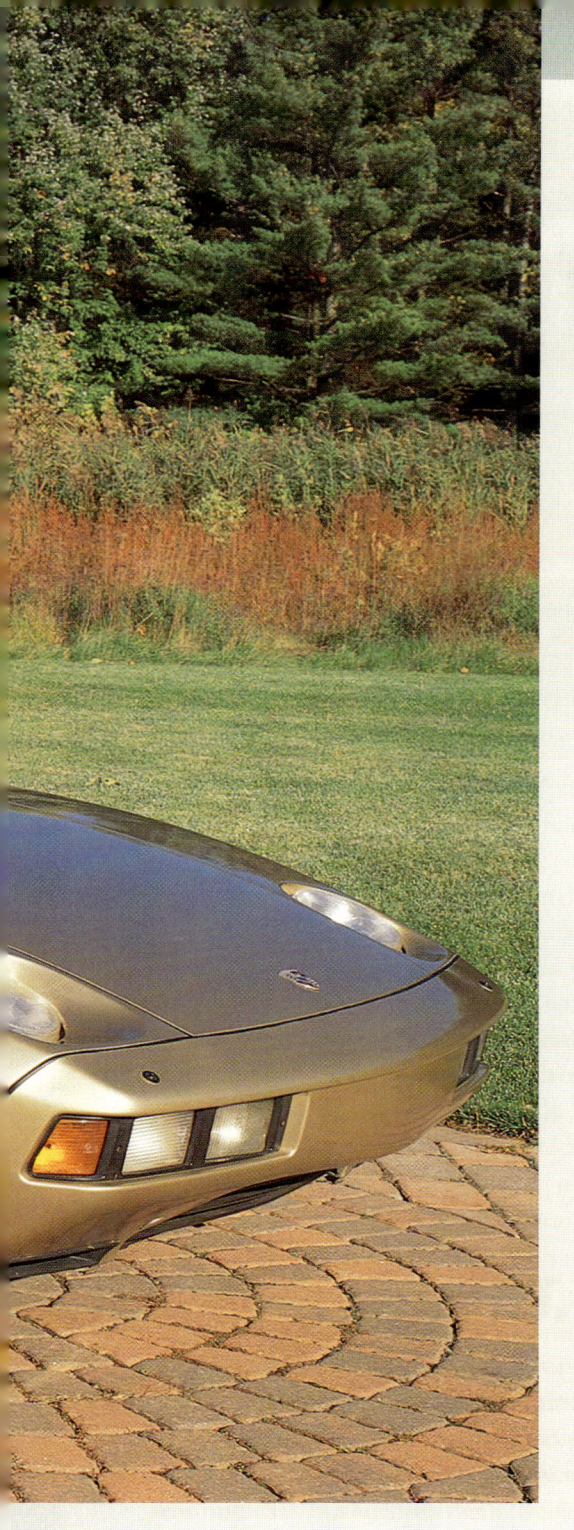

Many will remember the government-mandated "safety regulations" that began effecting the American automotive marketplace in the late 1960s. Many of these requirements were worthwhile, while some of them were merely annoying. The first major government intervention began with the 1968 model year and included among other things, engine belt-driven 'smog pumps.' Continuing improvements included the 1969 "side door guard beams." While the term "side door beam" calls to mind some heavy piece of galvanized metal like that of a highway guard rail, most of them turned out to be fairly minimal, and in many cases today actually have become little more than a hollow metal tube with about the same diameter as a broomstick.

Beginning in 1968 and continuing into the present, there were constantly changing regulations for automobile manufacture. The most significant of these were the 1973 front bumper requirements. The front bumper must be able to withstand a crash at 5 mph. This is why, beginning in 1973, so many American cars looked unwieldy until designers learned to incorporate the bumper more smoothly into the basic lines of each particular car. While this was certainly a good idea, it was often unworkable for sports cars, as in the last of the Porsche 914 and the later MGB, where the otherwise essentially good lines of the cars were ruined by massive hunks of rubber affixed to both ends of the cars.

Perhaps the most significant of all of these requirements resulted from the U.S. establishment of the Enviormental Protection Agency in July, 1970. The EPA became seriously concerned with reducing harmful exhaust gases and their effects on the atmosphere, as well as improving gas mileage. The most observable effects of these regulations began in the U.S. with the 1975 model year introduction of the greatly maligned catalytic converter, an item which many enthusiasts replaced immediately with a length of hollow steel pipe. Whether the increased gas required to force exhaust through the restricted airflow of the catalytic converter justifies its existence is debatable. What was not debatable is that not only would the American government be actively regulating future automobiles, there was no way to guess which area some do-gooder with unlimited taxpayer funds would focus on next. The unpredictability of future regulations became a serious consideration for all automobile manufacturers, not only the U.S. "Big Three," but those companies outside the U.S. which depended on U.S. sales to a large extent for their very existence. Bumper regulations effectively killed the Jaguar E-Type, removing the wings from the knock-off wheel hubs, getting rid of the glass over the

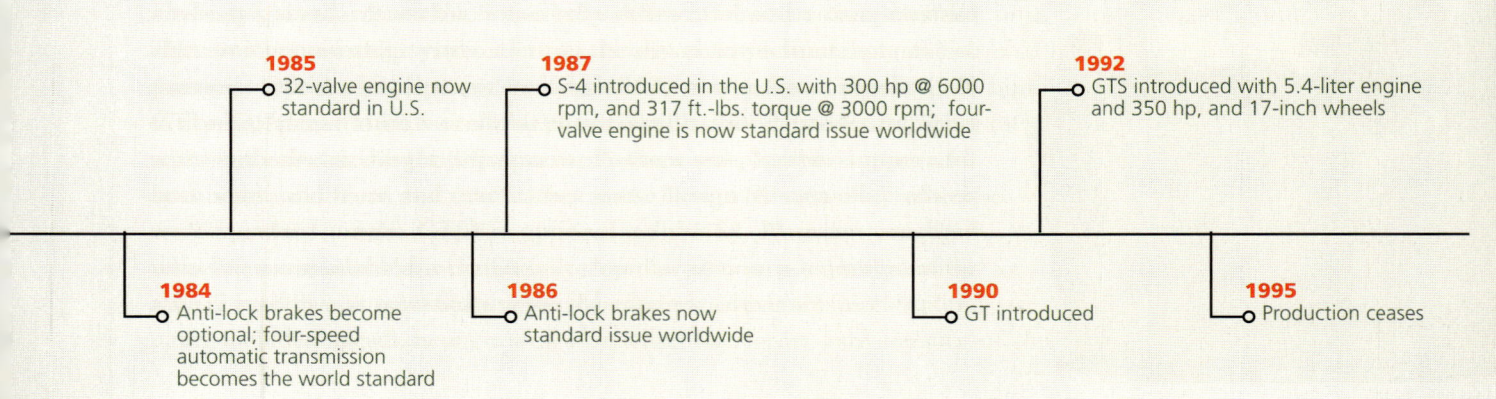

1985
32-valve engine now standard in U.S.

1987
S-4 introduced in the U.S. with 300 hp @ 6000 rpm, and 317 ft.-lbs. torque @ 3000 rpm; four-valve engine is now standard issue worldwide

1992
GTS introduced with 5.4-liter engine and 350 hp, and 17-inch wheels

1984
Anti-lock brakes become optional; four-speed automatic transmission becomes the world standard

1986
Anti-lock brakes now standard issue worldwide

1990
GT introduced

1995
Production ceases

1979 928
Dan Lyons

headlights, and replacing the instrument panel toggle switches with less-intrusive rocker switches.

For Porsche, which had only air-cooled, behind-the-rear-axle engines (with the exception of the 914), the implications were especially ominous. With America as its largest market, and anything possible, something had to be done. Not only would Porsche have to meet existing regulations, but might even have to anticipate and prepare for future ones. It was not out of the question, given the emerging political climate at the time, that the rear-engine Porsche could become illegal in the face of so many regulations.

And then, there was also an underlying question at Porsche: How long would people continue to buy the 911, anyway? It had had a long

Porsche

1983 928
Porsche NA

and successful run, but maybe its time was up. Porsche officials decided it was time for a new car—not merely another car, but a totally new vehicle that would meet and exceed all current and any likely U.S government regulations, and probably replace the 911 altogether. In the meantime, as long as people wanted the 911, and as long as it wasn't outlawed by emerging noise, pollution, and safety regulations, it would remain in production. With this in mind, the idea for what would eventually become the 928 began taking shape in 1971.

The development of an entirely new car from the ground up, with no preexisting components, was a major undertaking for any auto manufacturer, especially for a smaller company like Porsche. It could afford no mistakes. The 914 had been a successful project for Porsche, but it had been undertaken with VW and Audi, and the car which ultimately became the 924 had been paid for initially by VW. For Porsche to design and build a new car from the ground up was a major undertaking. That the car would be the most expensive production car the company had ever offered to the public was even more challenging. Lastly, and even more significantly, the break from Porsche tradition by offering a front-engine car, not merely as a second option to the 911, but as the top-of-the-line flagship was a daunting proposition.

While many car buyers, especially outside the U.S., considered the 914 to have been a VW, and not really a Porsche at all, considering its VW engine, it had at least been true to Porsche's original concept: a mid-engine, air-cooled car as had been the case with the 356-1. But to manufacture a front-engine car as a planned replacement for the clearly established 911 flew in the face of 30 years of tradition. An expensive V-8 powered front-engine GT car might be little more than an overpriced Chevrolet Corvette.

As rumors of the car's development made the rounds reactions were varied. In the U.S., as elsewhere, Porsche purists were shocked. Many other Americans, however, were intrigued. Porsche's reputation as a racing giant was legendary, as was the mysterious concept of "German

928

Perhaps the Porsche 928 should have no hood.

Putting its handsome V-8 engine on public display, might be the easiest way to show the world the quality of creative thought that Porsche has devoted to this, its newest car.

For the 928 does not otherwise brag of its brilliance. Among cars that wear their status symbols like brassy badges, the 928 is unassuming. It does not need the pretentious ornaments of other autos, for under its hood, under its skin, is the clarity of engineering expression for which Porsche is famous, polished to unprecedented perfection. Its voice is heard by the knowing driver.

The 928 is not a symbol, but the reality. It is the reality of a high-performance car that is also quiet, a car that corners superbly and also rides well, a small and sleek car that is also roomy, and a luxury car that is also built for long life.

In these ways and more, the 928 is Porsche's redefinition of the sports car.

engineering." The American car buyer had been raised on a V-8, and four or six-cylinder engines were not particularly exciting to most American performance car enthusiasts. In fact, many of the potential U.S. buyers for the 928 had personally owned or had friends who had owned American muscle cars, all of which had big V-8 engines—the larger the better. Even cars like the Cadillac Fleetwood Brougham reached 120 mph at the test track. Performance was expected in the U.S., and that was achieved in the American psyche with a large V-8 power plant.

By 1972, the muscle car era was on the way out. The upcoming fuel crisis slowed down the muscle cars and forever

1977 928

Porsche

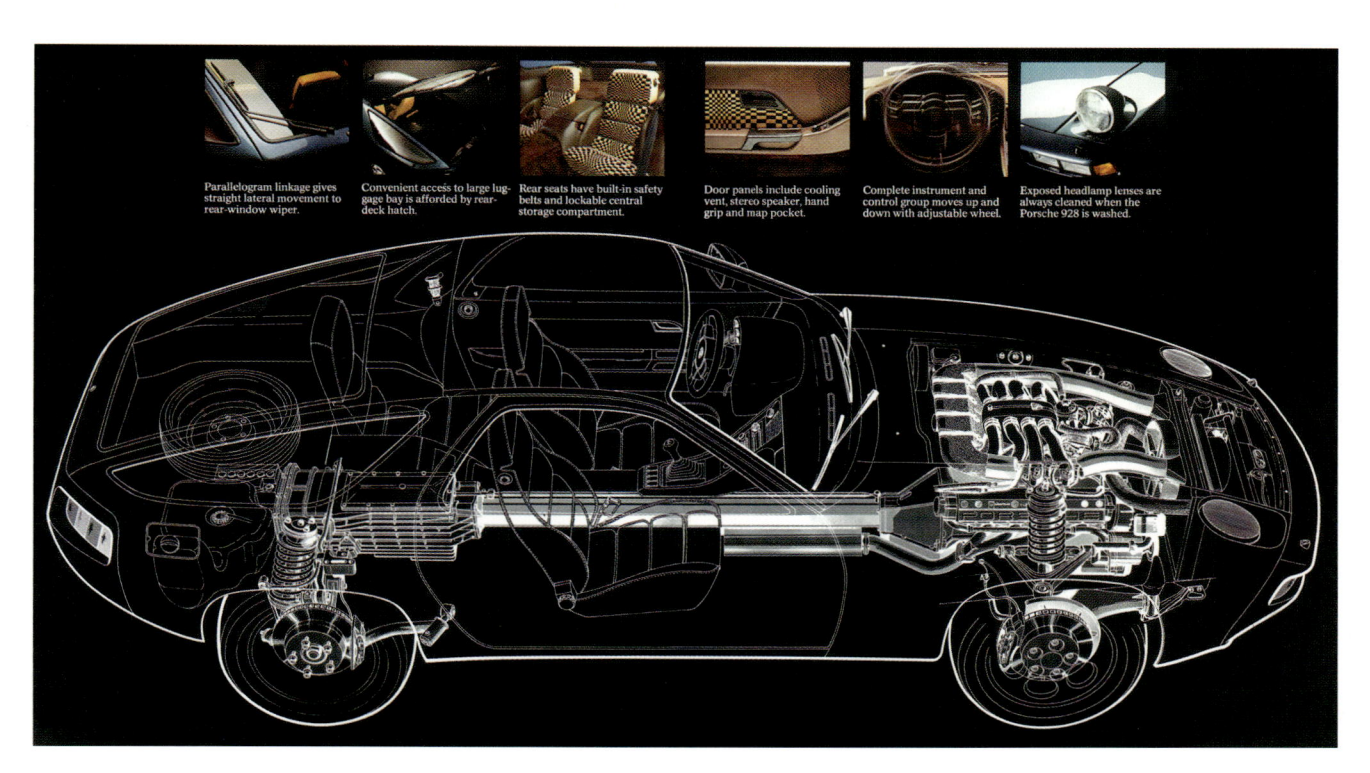

Parallelogram linkage gives straight lateral movement to rear-window wiper. | Convenient access to large luggage bay is afforded by rear-deck hatch. | Rear seats have built-in safety belts and lockable central storage compartment. | Door panels include cooling vent, stereo speaker, hand grip and map pocket. | Complete instrument and control group moves up and down with adjustable wheel. | Exposed headlamp lenses are always cleaned when the Porsche 928 is washed.

A phantom view shows the internal components of the Porsche 928.
Scott Faragher

changed the inherent concepts of cars in general from that point (1973) forward. And yet, for many of us who had known and loved these muscle cars, as well as those who had wanted them as teenagers but were unable to afford them, the lure of speed and power were ever present in the background, just waiting for the day when it would be possible to express them in a modern car.

The 928, nearly 30 years after its debut, is frequently referred to as "the answer to a question," rather than something that should have existed anyway, on its own. And yet, it was the answer to several significant questions, most importantly, "What is the greatest closed GT coupe Porsche could build?"

But that's what the 928 was, the best GT coupe that the best engineers and designers in the automotive world were capable of creating. When the decision had been made to create the replacement for the 911, literally everything was on the table—front-engine, mid-engine, or rear-engine. That Porsche elected to go with a front-engine design was the result of several significant considerations, not the least of which was that the front-engine, rear-wheel-drive layout was the most common in the U.S. market. This configuration, with a few notable exceptions such as the front-wheel-drive Cord of the 1920s and 1930s, the 1960s Corvair, and the 1960s and 1970s GM Toronado and Eldorado, had been the U.S. standard. A rear engine had been planned for the failed Tucker in the late 1940s, and had shown up in the revolutionary Corvair, the car which was the primary subject of Ralph Nader's famous book *Unsafe at Any Speed*. In light of the negative publicity generated from that book, rear-engine cars were suspect in general.

928 | 121

928 Technical Specifications (1978)

Engine type:	Front-mounted, water-cooled, V-8 (90 degree)
Bore/stroke:	3.74 ins. (95.0mm)/3.11 ins. (78.9mm)
Displacement:	273.0 cu. in. (4474cc)
Compression ratio:	8.5:1
Horsepower SAE net:	219 bhp @ 5250 rpm
Maximum torque:	254 ft.-lbs. @ 3600 rpm
Valve placement:	Overhead valves, hydraulic lifters
Valve train:	Overhead cam, one per bank
Camshaft:	Single spur belt driven
Crankshaft:	Forged, five main bearings
Lubrication:	Pressure lubrication, sickle pump
Fuel supply:	Two electric fuel pumps in series
Fuel/air mixture:	Continuous injection system
Fuel requirement:	Lead-free only
Battery:	12 volt, 88 amp hr.
Alternator:	1260-watt maximum
Ignition system:	Breakerless transistor
Clutch:	Twin disc, dry diaphragm type
Transmission:	Rear transaxle, fully synchronized
Number of gears:	Five forward, one reverse
Final drive:	Direct beveled drive
Drive axles:	Double constant velocity joints
Shift lever location:	Floor shift in tunnel console
Final drive ratio:	2.7500:1
Automatic transmission (no charge option):	Three-speed with torque converter
Body type:	Unitized construction
Front suspension:	Independent
Rear suspension:	Independent

Porsche introduced the new 928S version of the car in a 1982 ad.
Porsche NA

The car that would replace the 911 had to be able to adapt and conform to safety regulations, both current and future. To that extent, the front-engine, rear-wheel-drive layout was considered the safest since U.S. auto manufacturers would not be likely to be attacked en masse by regulators. They were too powerful and had too many lobbyists. Additionally, if the truth could be spoken, it is most likely that the engineers at Porsche itself felt that the front-engine, rear-wheel-drive configuration was probably the best for a closed GT car. In fact, one of Porsche's top designers of the time said repeatedly that "...an arrow fired backward will, at some point revert to its natural trajectory." This statement, if followed to its logical conclusion, essentially means that the placement of an engine-behind-the-rear-axle is inherently a bad design, no matter how much it is tampered with in the attempt to make it workable. That Porsche has been able to make it work to the extent that it is a testament to its engineering skill.

928 Technical Specifications (1979)

Type:	Front-mounted, water-cooled, 90 degree V-8	Engine lubrication:	Pressure lubrication, sickle pump	Wheel rims:	Pressure-cast light alloy 7 J x 16 (automatic-7 J x 15)
Number of cylinders:	8	Fuel supply:	Electric fuel pump	Tire size:	225/50 VR 16 (automatic-215/60 VR 15)
Bore:	3.74 in. (95.0 mm)	Fuel/air mixture:	Continuous injection system (CIS)		
Stroke:	3.11 in. (78.9 mm)	Transmission:	Five-speed manual or optional three-speed with torque converter	Steering:	Power assisted rack and pinion
Displacement:	273.0 cu. in. (4474 cc)			Engine:	6.9 qt. (6.5 liter)
Compression ratio:	8.5:1	Clutch:	Twin disc, dry, diaphragm type	Transmission:	4.0 qt. (3.8 liter)
				Fuel tank:	22.7 gal. (86 liter)
H.P. SAE net (kW):	219 (164) at 5250 rpm	Transmission:	Rear transaxle, fully synchronized	Wheelbase:	98.4 in. (2500mm)
Max. torque:	245 ft.-lbs. at 3600 rpm	Gears:	Five forward, one reverse	Track, front:	61.1 in. (1551mm)
				Track, rear:	60.2 in. (1530mm)
Fuel requirement:	Lead-free only	Final drive:	Direct beveled drive	Overall length:	175.7 in. (4462mm)
		Drive axles:	Double constant velocity joints	Width:	72.3 in. (1836mm)
Engine design:	Water-cooled, V-8 (90 degree) front-mounted	Shift lever location:	Floor shift in tunnel console	Height (unladen):	51.6 in. (1311mm)
Crankcase:	Light alloy crankcase/cylinders	Final drive ratio:	2.7500:1	Ground clearance at maximum load:	4.9 in. (125 mm)
Cylinder heads:	Light alloy	Type: automatic:	Optional three-speed with torque converter		
Valve placement:	Overhead valves, hydraulic lines			Turning circle curb -to-curb:	29.3 ft. (9.6 m)
		Top speed:	130+ mph.	Battery voltage:	12V
Valve train:	Overhead cam, one per bank	Acceleration:	0 to 60 mph 7.7 sec.	Battery capacity:	66 amp/hr
Camshaft drive:	Single spur belt drive	Body:	Unitized construction	Alternator output:	Max. 1260 watt
Crankshaft:	Forged, five main bearings			Ignition system:	Breakerless transistor ignition

Porsche traditionalists understandably bristle at this statement, while at the same time almost bragging that "you have to learn how to drive a 911, especially some of the earlier ones, or you can lose control easily." The new car, the replacement for the 911, would not have any of those lovable but dangerous idiosyncracies of the rear-engine cars. It would be engineered for perfect balance and absolutely neutral handling, so that it would not falter in a turn with full power applied.

The engine placement having been decided, the positioning of the other components was also addressed simultaneously. The best placement for balance would be a transmission at the rear, beneath the rear seats and ahead of the rear axle. These components would be joined by a rigid steel tube (containing a driveshaft) connecting to the back of the engine and to the front of the transmission, ahead of the rear axle. This was an extremely advanced design, and holds up as well technically now as it did at the time. The fuel tank and battery were also housed at the rear, along with an inflatable spare tire, itself part of a growing space conservation trend that had been adopted by cars as diverse as the Cadillac Eldorado convertible and the Maserati Merak.

The wheels on this 1983 928S indicate that this car is equipped with an automatic transmission.
Dan Lyons

The 928 project was started before the 924, although the 924 was completed and offered for sale before the 928. Much of what had been learned in the development of the 928 was applied to the 924, thus enabling the 924 to be brought to the public much faster than the 928. Additionally, the 928 had its own engine, developed from scratch, while the 924 had an Audi engine. In fact, every part of the 928 was new.

As logical and advanced as this configuration was, it was still not sufficiently satisfactory for the Porsche engineers. They were determined to build the best closed GT coupe in the world. To this end, the rear suspension had to be better than the 911's. Despite the fact that the independent rear suspension had been around as early as 1936 (Mercedes), it was still basically unknown in U.S. passenger cars other than the 1963 and subsequent Corvettes. Both the American-made Corvair (prior to 1965), and even earlier Pontiac Tempest had originally used a swing axle rear suspension, but not with great success. Porsche had employed an independent rear suspension beginning with its 356. Its problem was also a swing axle, which caused the car to misbehave in a sharp curve taken at high speed.

The swing axle consisted basically of a hinged differential attached to a rigid axle housing. If one of the rear wheels hit a bump, it would not transmit that energy through the axle to the other rear wheel, it would simply absorb the bump and move on. This arrangement was admittedly superior to a rigid live axle in most everyday driving situations. When a car with this suspension was pushed, as on a curvy road at high speed, handling could become unpredictable and dangerous as the rear suspension reacted to the centrifugal forces of the curve. This problem was corrected to a large degree at Porsche, as elsewhere, by the addition of a second universal joint in each axle, beginning with the 901/911. But the rear suspension had not yet been perfected, and problems of oversteer needed to be addressed and overcome once and for all. The engineers

Porsche

at Porsche's Weissach facility decided that the development of the 928 provided the best opportunity to design the perfect rear suspension, one that would not only be predictable in a curve, but one which would compensate for a driver's error in approaching a curve too fast and then letting off the accelerator, or worse, hitting the brakes, after the curve had already been entered too fast. The multi-link suspension of the 928 was a marvel of engineering technology and helped make the 928 the best-handling car of its time.

The body ends consisted of polyurethane collapsible front and rear bumper shells placed over longitudinal aluminum bars mounted to port and starboard collapsible shock absorbers. While non-steel bumpers had been successfully used on other cars, most notably the 1968 Pontiac GTO, and later Chevrolet Corvettes, it was determined that a rigid, densely constructed bumper would not work in the required application. The GTO's bumper was flexible, but it was hard and heavy, and would transmit collision impact to the surrounding hood and fenders, thus failing to protect the rest of the body in a 5-mph collision. Now, nearly every manufacturer worldwide uses the type of bumper arrangement used on the 928, but it was revolutionary for the time. The bumper had to survive a 5-mph crash. It also had to return to its original shape, thus it had to be deformable and reformable, basically on its own. Additionally, it had to be the same color as the body since there would be none of the traditional chrome. This presented problems since paint had to be matched and applied evenly to three different surfaces while still remaining the same color. The polyurethane bumpers, aluminum hood, front fenders and doors, and the steel body surfaces each reacted differently to paint. Equally as significant was the requirement that the finish should age at the same rate on all surfaces.

Tony Lapine, former GM designer, and head of the Porsche Design Studios, had worked as a designer at GM for over a decade before moving to Porsche. Given his experience with American cars, as well as

The wheels on this 1984 928 are forged, rather than cast alloy.
Dan Lyons

The 1988 928 S4 had a rounded front end.
Dan Lyons

with GM's legendary designer Bill Mitchell, he was the perfect choice for the 928 assignment. The shape of the 928 was revolutionary for the time. It was low, wide, and rakish, and its appearance has understandably been likened to that of a shark. The long, sloping hood and wide front fenders were punctuated only by the pop-up headlights, whose lenses remained exposed, even in the lowered position—an obvious influence from the earlier Lamborghini Miura. The stern was blunt and appears chopped, despite its rounded edges.

The 928 truly looks different from any angle. Some reviewers were shocked by the car's unusual appearance, but Lapine said at the time, "A car which is liked immediately will not hold up over time." The body shell consisted of aluminum alloy doors, hood, and front fenders. The rest of the body was constructed of galvanized steel, so given the components, the incidences of rust in these cars, even now, is rare. The lightweight alloy only saved around 80 lbs. over steel. This begs the question of whether the slight weight savings of aluminum was worth the extra rigidity and occupant protection an all-steel body would have afforded, especially in a side-impact collision.

Engine

The engine was every bit as advanced as the rest of the car. It contained a Reynolds alloy block with linerless cylinders cast in two sections. The heads were also aluminum with hydraulic valves, and initially one overhead camshaft per cylinder bank. The engine as first offered was a 4.5-liter V-8 fixed at a 90-degree angle to fit within the car's sloping hood. It was fueled by a Bosch mechanical Continuous Injection System (CIS), which consisted of a fuel distributor with eight emanating fuel

126 Porsche

lines to individual injectors in each cylinder. The fuel distributor was fed by two electric fuel pumps to maintain adequate pressure. Of particular interest was the use of a plastic fuel tank rather than the traditional steel tank. A plastic tank was used primarily because the tank had to fit in the minimal rear space available. The expense involved with fabricating a metal fuel tank of the shape required was prohibitive. Ultimately the decision to use a plastic fuel tank was the most efficient and best use of the available space. It was also interesting from a technical standpoint, and not subject to rust or leaks at seams.

Displacement and horsepower increased over the 928's lengthy production run, first in Europe to 4.7 liters in 1980 with the European S (1983 in the U.S.), and to 5.4 liters (1992), with four valves per cylinder (1985-1995 in the U.S.). Another interesting feature of the 928's engine was its timing belt, which took the place of a chain. It was, at nearly 7 feet in length, the longest belt of its type in the automotive world. I asked one of the 928's designers why there was not a 928 Turbo. He answered matter of factly that the engine as it was configured could be expanded upon as needed without the necessity of a turbo.

1990 928 GT-2
McLellan's Automotive History

1990 928 GT-2
McLellan's Automotive History

Transmission

The 928 was offered initially with both a five-speed manual transmission and a three-speed automatic. The automatic was consistent with the presentation of the 928 as a luxury GT, especially for the U.S. market, where it was generally preferred over the manual. By the time the 928 was introduced into the American market, the highly successful Mercedes Benz 450 SL had been out for several years. It came standard in the American market with an automatic and had sold well. It was felt that the type of customer who bought the 450 SL or the V-12 Jaguar XJ-S (also automatic in the U.S.), would prefer an automatic transmission over a manual. But the five-speed was available for the serious sports car driver, or anyone else who wanted one. For 1983, the three-speed automatic transmission was replaced with four-speeds in the U.S. and Japan, and became standard worldwide the following year.

Interior

The original interior of the 928 consisted of front and rear seats with leather bolsters and fabric surfaces. The fabric consisted of strange geometrical patterns and soon became known as the "op art" interior, with some derision. Actually, the strange pattern was available in several colors and suited the advanced design and physical appearance of the car at the time of its introduction in 1977. It was not considered desirable in the U.S., where motorists had preferred interiors of a single color since the early 1960s. Today these "op art" interiors are rarely seen in the U.S. at all, and are usually in poor condition, since fabric did not hold up as well as leather.

Wheels

One of the most distinguishing visual features of the 928 were its wheels. The car debuted with two different sets of wheels, but the 16-inch cast alloy "telephone dial" wheels were arguably the most exotic wheels ever placed on a sports car up to that time. The wheels were 16-inch bright cast alloy with an emphasis on the space between the spokes, rather than the spokes themselves. That space consisted of five raised oval holes projecting upward from the surface of the wheel. The visual intent of the designers was certainly achieved. The 16-inch wheels came stock on manual transmission models.

For some reason, 15-inch versions were standard on models with automatic transmissions. The 15-inch wheels are, however, completely

The power came from the 32-valve engine in the 1991 Porsche 928 GTS.
Porsche NA

1991 928 GTS
Porsche NA

1997 928 GTS
Porsche NA

different from the 16-inch versions, though both versions are referred to as "telephone dial" wheels. The 15-inch versions have five large ovals, but the ovals are situated on a more or less flat surface and do not project like those of the 16-inch wheels. While similar in appearance, the 15-inch versions are far less appealing visually. The success of this design can be measured by the fact that similar wheels appeared on the Lamborghini Countach and on the subsequent Diablo. The Lamborghini wheels were obviously heavily influenced by those of the Porsche 928.

Offered at the same time in different countries, and later in the U.S. were 16-inch forged wheels with slotted perimeters. These wheels would become standard issue on the later U.S. S models, but were available elsewhere earlier. The 16-inch forged wheels are generally considered to be of a higher quality than the cast wheels simply due to the method of manufacturing. As a side note, the forged wheels are, however, almost identical to those found on the later 1986 Ford Mustang. Wheels would continue to evolve, and aftermarket wheels are common today on the 928, but it is still the earlier wheels that truly defined the car as it first appeared.

The 928 was touted as a grand touring, luxury, and performance car. Among the luxury features offered were: air conditioning, power steering, cassette player and stereo radio, pop-up headlights, a fold-down vanity mirror, power windows, electric rear window wiper and defogger, tinted glass, front and rear sun visors, deep pile carpeting, a power antenna, four-speaker stereo radio, adjustable pedals, shift lever, steering column and instrument cluster, automatic transmission, and a self-defrosting outside mirror.

But the Porsche name was synonymous with performance, so there had to be equal attention to performance considerations. A full grouping of gauges were conveniently positioned in front of the driver and included an electronic tachometer, oil pressure gauge, and voltmeter. The car offered a fuel-injected V-8, rack and pinion steering, and fully independent suspension with the revolutionary Weissach axle.

Optional equipment for the 928 was fairly minimal and included a limited-slip differential, electrically adjustable and heated mirror on the passenger side, anti-theft system, electric sunroof, and power seats.

Ultimately, the emphasis on the 928 was placed on its exclusivity as well as its performance and luxury. A Porsche brochure from 1978 suggested that few people would own a 928 and that not every Porsche dealer would even have one. So what did Porsche think when the car was finally released? One anonymous Porsche insider felt upon his first drive that the car was underpowered. The car had originally been intended to house a 5-liter engine, but in a concession to the alleged fuel shortage it was felt that a 4.5 liter power plant would be sufficient. In reality, the 4.5-liter engine was more than adequate, especially in Europe, where it was not restricted by the U.S. required catalytic converter. While the engine was adequate, and performance of 0 to 60 mph in 7.7 seconds and a top speed of 130 mph impressive, it was not blinding.

This was not the general consensus among members of the press however, who dubbed the car a "supercar" from the outset. It was nearly impossible to lose in a curve and was indeed luxurious by the standards of the time. Be that as it may, Porsche immediately began taking corrective measures to increase the 928's horsepower. The 928S debuted in Europe

The phantom view definitely shows what made the 1991 928 GTS special.
Porsche NA

as a 1980 model with a larger 4.7-liter engine and 300 horsepower. Additional body modifications included a front chin spoiler and a rear tray type spoiler positioned around the rear window, as well as slotted, forged 16-inch wheels. There was no point in making a faster car for the U.S., where the top legal speed was 55 mph. Nevertheless, Americans wanted the available power, whether or not it could be legally used. For this reason many of the so-called "gray market" S models made their way to U.S. shores prior to 1983, when the U.S. received a 4.7-liter engine. In the meantime, a concession was made to the U.S. market beginning in 1981 with the 928S appearance group, which featured the wheels and spoilers of the S, but not increased engine size or horsepower.

928S4

1987 was a pivotal year for the 928. The car continued the four-valve-per-cylinder 5-liter engine that appeared in 1985. It produced 320 bhp and a top speed of 165 mph. The most significant changes were in the car's overall appearance. The front bumper was reworked with more rounded edges. The chin spoiler was replaced with an air dam integrated into the front bumper. The rear bumper was rounded as well, giving the car a longer appearance. Taillight lenses were stripped of their vertical dividers and repositioned flush with the bumper surfaces rather than indented. A new wing-type free-standing spoiler replaced the lower, curved spoiler that had hugged the rear hatch and rear window. Sills were added to the lower portion of the car, carrying the theme from the front bumper, along the lower edge and into the rear bumper. The S4 designation referred to the fourth series in the car's manufacture, rather than to the four-valve-per-cylinder configuration, as many have thought.

The 928 GTS in action
Porsche NA

1993 and 1995 928 GTS
Porsche NA

Continual technical innovations brought the S4 to the status of one of the great GT cars of all time. It had been reported that 70 percent of all 928s sold in the U.S. had been sold with automatic transmissions. Perhaps as a response to this, a four-speed automatic became the standard with a five-speed manual transmission as a no-cost option.

The S4 was the car that elevated the 928 to true "super car" status worldwide.

928 S4, 928 GT, and 928 GTS

The GT featured a 330-bhp (at 6200 rpm) engine and was available only with a five-speed manual transmission. Top speed was claimed at 171 mph with 0 to 60 mph at 5.6 seconds. For the 1990 model year there was no difference in external appearance from 1989. Optional equipment was minimal, but by then the 928 S4 and 928 GT came well equipped by anybody's standards with a limited-slip differential and a computerized electronic monitoring system alerting the driver to such nuances as tire pressure. Optional equipment included a CD player, Sport shocks (928 GT only), "preparation for cellular phone installation," heated seats, Sport seats with electric height adjustment, Positrol seat, lumbar support for both seats, and front and rear leather seats. Design 90 cast-alloy wheels were standard on the GT, but optional on the S4. Platinum anodized wheels were available for the S4 only. Another option, a requirement for the US market was modification for the catalytic converter.

928 S4 & GT Technical Specifications (1990)

Number of cylinders:	8
Displacement:	302 cubic inch (5.0 liters)
Bore & stroke:	3.94 x 3.11
Horsepower:	S4: 316 @ 6,000 rpm
	GT: 326 @ 6,000 rpm
Torque at rpm (SAE net):	S4: 317 @ 3,000 rpm
	GT: 317 @ 4100 rpm
Compression ratio:	10.0:1
Engine design:	Water-cooled V-8, front-mounted
Fuel supply:	EZK-LH fuel/ignition system
Fuel type:	Premium unleaded
Crankcase, cylinder head:	Light alloy
Crankshaft:	Forged, five main bearings
Valve train:	Dual overhead-cam per bank, hydraulic lifters, spur belt & chain drive
Battery:	12V/72 amp/hr
Alternator:	115 amp
Ignition system:	Electronic, EZK controlled
Transmission:	Rear transaxle
Number of gears:	5 for S4; 5 for GT
Final drive ratio:	2.54:1
	2.23:1
Body:	Unitized
Front suspension:	Independent double A-arms, coil springs
Rear suspension:	Independent Weissach design
Stabilizers:	Front 28mm, rear 22.5mm
Shock absorbers standard:	Double acting, hydraulic
Brakes:	Power-assisted, fixed-caliper. ABS
Brake disc size:	Front: 11.97 in.
	Rear: 11.77 in.
Steering:	Rack & pinion, hydraulically assisted
Ratio:	17.75:1
Turns (lock-to-lock):	3.00
Turning circle:	37.7 ft.
Wheels (standard):	928 S4
	928 GT
Front:	S4: 7J x 16 forged alloy, 225/50 ZR 16
	GT: 7.5J x 16 (60mm offset) cast alloy, 225/50 ZR 16
Rear:	S4: 8J x 16 forged alloy, 245/45ZR 16
	GT: 9J x 16 (60mm offset) cast alloy, 245/45ZR 16
Wheels (optional S4):	Front: 7J platinum forged alloy or 7.5 J x 16 (60mm offset) cast alloy
	Rear: 8J x 16 platinum forged alloy
Top track speed:	165 mph
	171 mph
0 to 60 acceleration	6.0 sec.
	5.6 sec.
1/4-mile	14.5 sec.
	14.1 sec.
Coefficient of drag	0.34
Fuel consumption (city/hwy):	S4: 15/19
	GT: 13/19
Wheelbase	98.4
Overall length:	178.1 in.
Width:	72.3 in.
Height:	50.5 in.
Track, front:	61.1 in.
Track, rear:	60.9 in.
Ground clearance:	4.7 in.
Curb weight:	S4 3,549 lbs., GT 3,505 lbs.
Front headroom:	36.5 in.
Front legroom:	43.5 in.
Trunk capacity (seat up):	6.3 cu. ft.
Trunk capacity (seat folded):	20.5 cu. ft.
Fuel tank:	22.7 gal.
Engine oil:	8.0 qts.
Windshield washer:	8.0 qts.
Transmission:	9.8 qts.
Coolant:	16.9 qts.

Help for restorers

The first 928s are nearly 30 years old now, and certain parts have become difficult to find. Many of the mechanics who worked on them have now retired as well. While there are many companies selling new, used, or rebuilt parts for Porsche cars in general, 928 International specializes in 928s exclusively. The company was founded in Anaheim, California, in 1986 by Mark Anderson, an avid 928 racer familiar with every aspect of the 928, from the early 4.5-liter cars through the four-valve GTS, and everything in between. Over the last nearly 20 years, the company Mark started has grown into the absolute best worldwide source for parts of all 928 models. If you are restoring a 928 or just keeping one on the road, contact 928 International.

928 International
2900 East Miraloma Avenue D
Anaheim, CA 92806
Phone: 714-632-9288
FAX: 714-632-9328
Email: mr928@928intl.com
http:/www.928intl.com

Porsche

Both active and passive safety features were advertised at the time, including the "safety cell," which consisted of rigid roof and pillar structure and side impact bars, as well as the rigid torque tube which transmitted impact forces to the front or rear as required. Crumple zones were highlighted by the deformable bumpers. Anti-lock vented four-wheel disc brakes, great maneuverability and acceleration, and the car's optimum weight distribution made handling almost neutral. Thanks to a hotter camshaft, the GT had slightly better performance numbers than the S4.

The GTS was introduced in 1992 as a 1993 model and was a blazing-fast, low-production model that still stands as one of Porsche's most impressive cars. With about 350 hp, it was basically a revved-up version of the 928, and was the last 928 produced, exiting in 1995.

The wheel sizes were slightly larger and the fenders slightly more flared. The brakes were huge 12.68-inch models, and were accompanied by Brembo four-piston calipers.

The $81,000 GTS was simply one of the hottest cars in the world for its time and marked the high-water mark for the 928 series.

Conclusion

The 928 became increasingly more expensive as time passed, and sales diminished accordingly until it and the 968 were withdrawn from the market, victims of poor sales. The 911, the car the 928 had been designed to replace, never fell victim to the dreaded U.S. regulations after all, and has now been in production more than 40 years, while the front-engine cars passed into history. Given the fact that each of the front-engine cars had been an improvement over its predecessor, one wonders why they didn't sell better. It is true that the 968 and the 928 were incredible cars by anyone's standards, but they no longer generated either the excitement or the controversy that they had at the outset. Additionally, prices had continued escalating and the last of the 928's cost around $90,000—a huge amount of money for a car that was past its peak. The four-valve 928 had been out for a decade by 1995, and the car had nothing radically new to say.

The front-engine cars had been extremely successful, and had pushed the small Porsche company into position as the major contender in the sports car world, but by 1995 they were, for lack of a better word, "old." Still, the 928 GT and GTS, especially the 5.4-liter GTS with 350 horsepower, is probably the best production Porsche ever made, and possibly even now, the best GT coupe ever produced.

Today, the prices of all of the 928s vary widely, depending on model and condition. The later cars are still the most valuable, generally speaking, but again it's a matter of individual choice. While the earlier models with the CIS injection are generally the least valuable, they often represent the best value for the money.

Was the 928 the last of the V-8 front-engine Porsches? Not really. The Cayenne has emerged as the newest Porsche to carry a V-8, and who knows, a newer V-8 front-engine car may on the horizon. Still, one cannot help but wonder if the 928 would have survived if it had received the same attention bestowed upon the 911, specifically a Turbo version, all-wheel drive, or a convertible body.

944

944 TIMELINE

1981
The 944 is presented at the Frankfurt Auto Show in September

1985
Turbo model introduced raising horsepower to 217 bhp

Interior and instruments reworked from the 924 style, replaced by more modern oval-style cluster

1987
Antilock Braking System (ABS) offered as optional on 944S and Turbo.

Airbags offered as option for standard 944

1982
The 944 becomes available for sale in the U.S. in May, as a 1983 model

1986
Double overhead-cam four-valve-per-cylinder engine offered with 944S in mid-year

944S introduced

The 924 had had a successful run since its 1975 debut, but was old news by 1981. It had also been haunted by its VW-Audi ancestry, a circumstance that was less of a problem for the U.S. buyer than elsewhere because the 914 had also been sold as a Porsche in the U.S., but as a VW-Porsche in the rest of the world. It was felt at Porsche that the 924 needed to be upgraded in terms of appearance, performance, and lineage. The 924 had basically evolved as far as it could with its Audi engine, despite the fact that there had and would be more models than just the basic 924. There was also the realization at Porsche that there should perhaps be some middle ground in the front-engine lineup between the two extremes of the 924 on the lower end and the 928 at the top.

The next logical step on the evolutionary ladder would be a new car to fill that void. It would have the same configuration as the 924, be clearly traceable to its predecessor visually and technically, yet still be essentially a new car. Moreover, it would have a Porsche engine. The new car had been rumored for several years before it debuted at the Frankfurt Auto Show in September 1981 as a 2 + 2 coupe called the 944.

While there were immediate and obvious visual similarities between the Porsche 924 and the later 944, the 944 was a much more serious contender for the American buyer on the way up. For the buyer of the 944, any considerations about the relative merits of the front engine versus rear engine debate were of no consequence. After all, the 924 had been around since 1975, and whatever controversy there may have been initially had died down. The 924 had been a successful car for Porsche in terms of its sales (110,500), and it had also scored many significant racing victories under the Porsche name despite its VW-Audi credentials.

There were still those who hated all of the front-engine Porsches, regardless of their merits, or their wide acceptance by the public, and didn't like the 924, the 928, or the 944. For that group, it was a tough decision as to which of the three cars was most despicable. The 924, as the first front-engine Porsche drew a lot of fire from purists for its break with tradition. The 928 was even more odious because it stepped in as the top of the line Porsche with absolutely no prior credentials, supplanting the time-tested and race-proven 911. And the 944 would be hated for its stunning looks, excellent performance, and wide acceptance by the public.

1989
S2 is introduced in January
Cabriolet also available as an S2
3-liter engine introduced in 944 S2 model
944 SE introduced in UK only
Porsche celebrated the 300,000th water-cooled four-cylinder car

1991
Announcement was made in January that production of four-cylinder cars was to be moved from Neckarsulum to Zuffenhausen
Turbo cabriolet available
Production of the 944 S2 ended in July

1988
944 S given the Turbo's rear underbody spoiler

1990
944 S2 coupe and S2 cabriolet only models offered for 1990
ABS brakes and driver and passenger airbags become standard for all models

1992
944 replaced by 968

1982 944
Dan Lyons

But for many more Porsche enthusiasts, the front-engine, rear-wheel-drive layout was perfect. That Porsche as a company was actively pursuing this line of development was considered to be a great step forward, particularly among American buyers, many of whom still regarded the 911 as a "souped-up" Volkswagen, despite its high price. The incredible eight-cylinder 928 had also made its appearance by 1977, so it was perceived by the public that Porsche was on the way up and was a company that offered the most advanced sports cars of the era, regardless of price. The new 944 represented the best sports car available in its price range, and to some owners, was one of the best sports cars at any price.

It should also be remembered that Porsche still felt that the 911 would at some time be discontinued, a victim of U.S. noise, safety, or emissions regulations, or simply declining public interest. Should this eventuality occur, Porsche would be left with only front-engine cars. The 944 would be a welcome addition to the Porsche lineup on its own merits, with or without the 911.

The 924, while successful as Porsche's first front-engine car and as the entry-level Porsche, was basic like the 914. The 944, on the other hand, despite its obvious visual similarity to the 924, was actually a sports luxury car, with features such as electric power windows and outside mirrors, air conditioning, fog lights, electric sunroof, and tinted windows. These features were very advanced for the time, especially for a sports car. In 1981 when the 944 debuted (as a 1982 model), there were still plenty of people around who remembered the MG A, TC, TD, B, and Midget, Austin Healey Sprite, the Jaguar XK 120, 140, and 150, and other sports cars which were little more than an engine, frame, and body. These cars were often unreliable, had frequent electrical problems, and were cold in the winter and wet in the rain, with heaters and defrosters which were in many cases, almost useless.

Porsche

Prior to the 1980s, Porsche sales in the U.S. market were also minimal when compared to those of General Motors, Chrysler, or Ford (and still are), but then it must be remembered that Porsche sold sports cars exclusively. The 911 and 912 were, prior to the 1980s, sold mainly to knowledgeable enthusiasts in limited numbers. The 914 had been successful in the American market. It had, during its 1970-1975 run, been more than an entry-level Porsche, it had been an introduction to Porsche for many U.S. buyers, many of whom were college students and would move to the 924 and 944 later as their age and income increased.

But for Porsche to really establish itself as a big seller, especially in the U.S. market, it needed an affordable car that maintained the performance, reputation, and status associated with the Porsche name. Moreover, it had to be a car that had high performance and was highly reliable since, for many of its owners, it would be a fulltime car as opposed to something just used solely on weekends. This dual purpose was fully realized for Porsche with the 944. That the 914 had been an important car in the American market is without doubt. It, in a sense, paved the way for the acceptance of the revolutionary 924. But it was ultimately the 944, with its exotic looks, handling, and performance, that made the Porsche name truly significant as a major contender in the U.S. market for the first time.

1985 944
Dan Lyons

1985 944
Dan Lyons

Body

The 944's wider body and more aggressive stance were immediately noticeable and different from the 924. While the 924 was not particularly attractive to some observers, and downright ugly to others, it was generally conceded among nearly every sports car enthusiast that the 944 in contrast, was a beautiful and very desirable car. The body shell of the 944 evolved from that of both the 924 Turbo and the 924 Carrera as can be clearly noted by the similarities between the 944's flared front and rear fenders, which in the case of the 944 were part of the actual steel body structure rather than add-on fiberglass panels as with the 924 Carrera GT. But the similarity of the 924 Carrera's fenders, as well as those of the 944, can be clearly traced even further back to the 928, a car whose significant influence extended to the 924, 944 and later 968. Be that as it may, the visual similarities between the 924 and the 944 are unmistakable, and it's obvious that the 924 is the earlier car. The 944 headlights are of the covered pop-up type found on the 924, further distinguishing it from the visible lenses of more expensive 928's headlights.

Much attention was given to the development of the 944's body, and its appearance, however appealing, is in typical Porsche fashion, the result of extensive wind tunnel testing for a variety of reasons. Reducing wind noise, dissipation of water, airflow around and through the car into the passenger compartment, engine cooling, lift and turbulence are all considerations addressed in the 944's development. The 944's basic body shell was subject to literally hundreds of hours in the wind tunnel, enabling the engineers to determine the optimal size and location of a variety of components extending all the way from air intakes to door handles, mirrors, and front and rear spoilers. While the standard 924 did not have a rear spoiler, the 944 came standard with a large rear spoiler surrounding the base of the rear window and extending backward, essentially the same as on the 924 Carrera GT. Since speed and undesirable lift are related, and lift decreases a car's handling, traction, and directional stability, the 944's new rear spoiler served the car well. The 944's front, or "chin" spoiler was minimal but effective, providing the car with a .35 drag coefficient. In shape, the chin spoiler was similar to that of the 924 or early 928, and was incorporated into the basic under-the-bumper body panel rather than as an additional bolt-on as on the 928S. The aerodynamic considerations incorporated in the 944's design were more than just visually appealing. The low drag coefficient and small 20-sq. ft. (1.85 m2) frontal area decreased overall wind resistance and gave the 944 approximately 20 mpg on city roads and 27 mpg on the highway—not bad for a high-performance car.

The earliest anti-rust measures employed by Porsche consisted of galvanizing the lower body shell, primarily the floor pan and fender wells, as on the early 928. The entire 944 body, however, received rust protection in the form of galvanized sheet metal and offered an initial seven year guarantee against rust through, which was later extended to a full 10 years. This was a significant consideration in the U.S.-market, especially in the northern states where salt was widely used to melt road ice, with highly corrosive effects on all cars. Nearly every non U.S. car, from Rolls Royce all the way down to the Austin Healey Sprite, had been subject to the likelihood of severe rust damage. Many early Porsches,

In 1982, Porsche introduced the 944 series with a personal invitation from Dr. Ferry Porsche to test-drive the car.
Porsche NA

Jaguars, and other sports cars literally disintegrated due to rust prior to the use of galvanized metal in rust-prone areas, such as the bottom of the car, suspension components, and wheel wells.

The 944 was not a heavy car at 2,778 lbs. by U.S. standards, but then it lacked the lighter alloy hood, doors, and front fenders of the more-expensive 928, which would have reduced weight even further. But even in the 928, the total reduction in weight of aluminum over steel was just at 80 lbs., a significant consideration in a racing car, but not in a luxury sports car. Given the choice, it's likely that some in the American market would have opted for an all-steel construction anyway, even in the 928 for increased structural rigidity and crashworthiness, especially in side-impact incidents. In any case, while Porsche clearly felt that aluminum was the more desirable metal for hood, doors, and fenders, it was not used on the 944 due to its added expense.

Maximum performance was promoted in this 1983 Porsche 944 ad.
Porsche NA

The 944 received subtle visual changes during its manufacturing run. Among them were the S2's underbody rear spoiler and Turbo style nose. The most significant body change was the introduction of the Cabriolet, or convertible, in 1989, making the 944 the first front-engine Porsche available from the factory in a convertible model. In the U.S., convertibles are generally considered more desirable than in Europe, where the closed GT is preferred. Consequently, the cabriolet model will usually be more expensive than a coupe of the same model year. It should be kept in mind that the steel top of the 944 coupe is an integral part of the car's basic structure and contributes greatly to its rigidity. The convertible body lacks the strength and structural rigidity afforded by the top, despite the fact that it has received extra bracing in compensation. As a result, there is noticeably more flex in the ride and handling of the cabriolet than in the coupe.

Porsche

Standard exterior colors included Black, Copenhagen Blue, Alpine White, Pastel Biege, and the popular Guards Red. Metallic colors were available at extra cost in Sapphire Metallic, Stone Grey Metallic, Kalahari Metallic, Garnet Red Metallic, Graphite Metallic, Mahogany Metallic, Zermatt Silver Metallic, and Crystal Green Metallic.

Engine

The most significant improvement of the 944 over the 924 was its Porsche engine. The 944 engine as initially offered was a highly advanced 2.5-liter (2479cc), (151.27 cu. in) water-cooled four-cylinder, single overhead-camshaft engine with two inline valves per cylinder (one intake, one exhaust), which produced 143 hp at 5800 rpm. Like the engine of the flagship 928, the 944 block was constructed of linerless Reynolds 390 alloy, a decided improvement over the cast iron block used in the 924's Audi engine, bringing the engine's total weight to approximately 340 lbs. The cylinder head was also made of lightweight alloy, as was the case with the 924, and hydraulic tappets were used as on the 928. The crankshaft had five bearings and powered the single camshaft with a toothed-belt of the type found on the 928. Bore and stroke were 3.94 in. (100mm) x 3.11 in (78.9 mm).

As was the custom at Porsche, engine displacement would increase with the passage of time, rising from 2.5 to 2.7 (not available in the U.S.), and finally to 3 liters. The problem with any large-capacity four-cylinder engine, and this applies equally to all three 944 engines, is that a large-displacement four-cylinder engine, generally speaking, anything over two liters, is difficult to balance and vibrates excessively. Since Porsche did not want to reduce the engine displacement to diminish vibration, and intended to use a four-cylinder engine in the 944, a remedy was employed in the creation of the engine that consisted of two counter-balanced shafts which rotated in opposite directions. This feature would be used on all single overhead cam and the later double overhead cam engines. Each shaft is powered by a jointly shared double-sided single belt from the crankshaft, and rotates in opposite directions (from each other) at twice engine speed. The shafts are weighted at the firewall end and are dynamically and statically balanced with all other crankshaft driven components to keep vibrations minimal at all speeds. This design is attributed to Frederick Lanchester (1911). The patent was held by Mitsubishi, and Porsche ended up paying that company a fee of approximately $8 per car, concluding that the design could not be sufficiently improved upon to justify additional time and expense for research and development. There was a reported power loss of 5 hp required to operate the machinery involved.

It has been frequently stated that the 944's 30-degree slant configuration engine was literally half of a 928 engine, but this is inaccurate, despite the visual similarity between the 944 and 928 valve covers and air intake pipes. That the development of the 944's engine had been influenced by the knowledge gained from the 928 was, however, indisputable, especially in terms of the use of aluminum alloy components, including block and pistons. It's probably safe to say that the knowledge gained in developing the 928 engine allowed the introduction of the 944 engine faster than would have occurred otherwise.

The slant configuration was also nothing new. It had been used on the 924's Audi four-cylinder at a 40-degree slant, but even as early is the late 1950s had been offered in the U.S. by Chrysler in some of its models as the "Slant Six." The slant configuration placed the engine diagonally within the engine compartment, thus allowing a lower side profile and a reduced frontal area than would be achieved if the engine were a standard upright inline.

The initial 944 engine offered two valves per cylinder, as had been the case with the 924, and early 928, but a four-valve-per-cylinder engine was offered beginning in 1986 with the S model. The engine consists of double overhead camshafts that were operated by a toothed belt powered by the crankshaft, which spins the exhaust cam. The intake camshaft is in turn connected to the exhaust camshaft midway by a chain. Engine displacement was increased to 3.0 liters (2990cc), (182.5 cu. in.)

in 1989 with the S2 model, and horsepower grew to 208 at 5800 rpm. The 944 also received gas-filled strut engine cover supports as with the 928, replacing the primitive stick support standard on the 924.

The L-Jetronic injection system was used with the Bosch Digital Motor Electronic system (DME). Basically the system functions as follows: An electric fuel pump transfers fuel from the tank, through a fuel filter, and into a fuel rail, which transports the fuel at constant pressure to the individual injectors located between the fuel rail and the intake ports. The control unit activates the injectors at the optimal moment based upon information from the airflow sensor, temperature and oxygen sensors, and throttle position sensor. The duration the individual injectors are opened determines the air to fuel mixture within the combustion chamber. Fuel passing through the fuel rail that is not used is rerouted back to the fuel tank.

Performance

While most front-engine enthusiasts understandably wanted the V-8-powered 928, just because it was the top-of-the-line car, there were few complaints about the 944 from its owners regarding its power or performance. An inline four-cylinder engine was not something anyone in the U.S. market was likely to brag about, especially for buyers who'd previously owned large displacement eight-cylinder cars, and yet the 944's acceleration (0 to 60 in 8.3 sec), as well as top speed (130 mph),

The 1986 944 looks like it belongs in the passing lane.
Porsche NA

The 1986 944 was ideal for a curving mountain road.
Porsche NA

were impressive by anyone's standards. And the 944 was low slung and closer to the road than most American cars, which gave the driver an even greater sense of speed and power. Additionally, the car was extremely well balanced and handled nimbly in corners.

The introduction of the Turbocharged model in 1985 increased horsepower to 217 bhp and boosted top speed to more than 150 mph. Zero to 60 mph was reached in 6 seconds. This was true performance by anyone's standards in America and elsewhere.

Transmission

The 944 had the same basic engine, torque tube, transaxle-gearbox layout as the 924. Like the 924, but unlike the 928, the 944 had the transmission behind the rear axles rather than in front (as on the 928), providing additional rear seat room, as well as improved balance and handling over that of the 911's behind-the-rear-axle engine. While the 944's component layout was similar to that of the 928, the presence of the gearbox behind the rear axles in the 944, as opposed to its location in front of the rear axles in the 928, required that the collapsible spare tire be stowed vertically, rather than horizontally as in the 928.

The 944's three-speed automatic was a little slower off the line from a dead stop than the five-speed manual transmission, but top speeds were identical. The 944, while actually more similar to the 924 than to the

1986 944 interior
Porsche NA

Among the key components of the 1986 944 was its rear-mounted transmission.
Porsche NA

928, was perceived by most of its customers to be closer to the 928 than to the 924. As such, it was more of a "luxury" sports car than the 924, and for many customers, more suited to an automatic than the 924 was.

Brakes

The 944 had four-wheel discs with a hydraulic booster, which by 1983 were pretty much the world standard on any upper-end car. The 944's brakes, taken from the 924 Turbo, were ventilated to reduce fade at high speeds, and calipers were initially of the floating type. Unlike the earlier 928s, the 944 did not have the dual diagonal braking system, but instead offered a dual-circuit system with front brakes on one circuit and rear brakes on a second. Braking was excellent, with the car stopping in 46 meters from a speed of 100 km/h (62 mph). The parking brakes were fixed to the rear wheels only and were of the mechanical drum type, similar to those on the more expensive 911 and 928. Like both the 911 and the 928, the 944's parking brakes were engaged or released with a floor-mounted hand lever. The braking system also was fitted with fluid level indicator lights and a hand brake warning light. Brakes were equipped with four-piston calipers in 1985 to keep up with the Turbo's increased performance. By 1987, four-channel anti-lock brakes were optional for the 944, but standard issue in 1989.

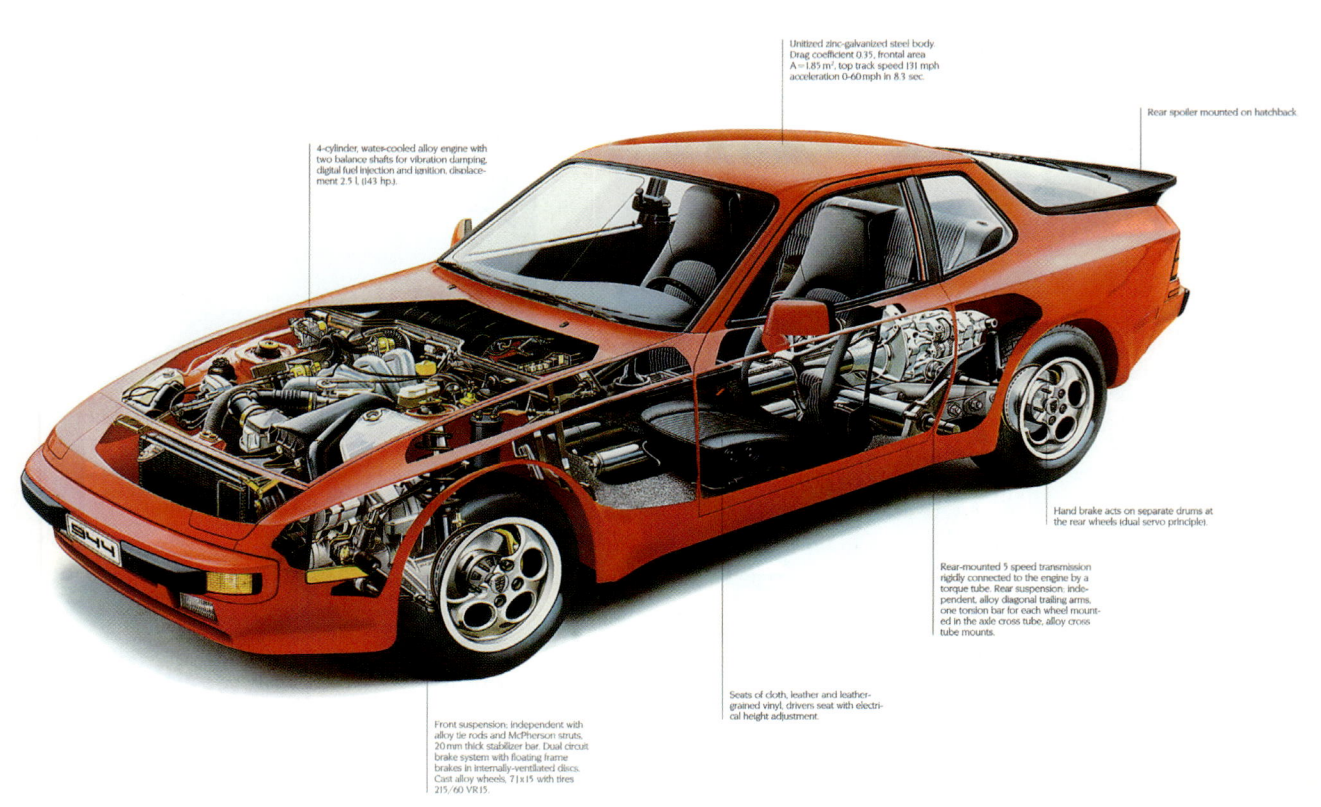

Porsche

Chassis and suspension

As one member of the 924's design team said, "the entire drive train, engine, torque tube, and transaxle are suspended from the rest of the car." This, of course, is obvious, but not something generally dwelled upon. Most people are more impressed with the single unit produced by the combination of these three elements. But the drivetrain unit is indeed separate from the body, and joined to it at various places, though not rigidly.

One of the problems associated with this rigid torque tube layout in the 924 was an excessive level of vibration, some of which was transmitted to the passenger compartment. It was determined at Porsche that the 944 would not have the same problems. One source of the vibration, the engine, had been successfully addressed with the twin balance shafts, and yet due to the combination of the engine, torque tube, and transmission into a single unit, any vibration from any of the separate components was likely to extend to the others to some degree. The engine mounts (one on each side) designed for the 944, unlike those of the 924, were freeze-proof, liquid filled rubber which allowed the liquid to move from one chamber to the other as the engine shifted.

Today, many of the original engine mounts have ruptured, so this is an area which should be checked specifically by any potential buyer. Rear mounts, as well as those for the steering rack, were traditional rubber.

The power plant in the 944 was the 2.5-liter, 143-hp four-cylinder engine.
Porsche NA

Wheels and tires

The 944 debuted with five-lug wheels, replacing the standard four-lug stamped steel wheels of the original 924. Fuchs alloy wheels similar to those of the 911 were available from the outset on the 944. The exotic and highly popular cast-alloy "telephone dial" (7Jx15) wheels similar to those originally offered on the manual 928 models were available on the 944 beginning in 1985, as also found on the 924 S models. The later, forged slotted disc wheels of the 928 S (7J x 16 front and 8J x 16 rear) were also offered on the 944S. The wheels were of a much higher quality than those of the standard 924 as well, being constructed of either forged or cast alloy, rather than pressed steel. Beginning in 1990, seven-spoke alloy wheels with 225/55ZR 16 tires were available.

Many 944 owners, as part of a growing trend in nearly all cars, have elected to replace original wheels with later, larger-diameter wheels. These replacements, in the case of Porsche, will usually be found to be the later 911 Turbo or Carrera Cup type. Generally speaking, replacing original equipment wheels with something from a later car, or even aftermarket wheels not even from the same manufacturer, has a negative impact on any car's value.

Interior

The initial interior offered on the 944 was nearly identical to that of the earlier 924 model, prompting some minor complaints at the time. Gone, however, was the strange off-center steering wheel of the 924, replaced by a simple, smaller round wheel of the same type offered on the European 928 and 911 models. U.S. models were offered with the four-prong steering wheel found on U.S. 928s. These would subsequently be replaced with steering wheels containing airbags. In 1985 the dashboard and instruments were reworked into a much better arrangement more in line with the car that the 944 had become.

The interior was luxurious. The car had power windows, leather seats, air conditioning, and well-placed instruments and controls. The emphasis again was on luxury. Gone was the presentation of the 944 as an entry-level car. And interior and seating options reflected the new direction Porsche had taken with the 944. Optional leather was offered in all U.S. 944 models from the very first. In 1986 it was available in black, brown, burgundy, and light grey, with matching carpet selections. A "Special

1987 944S
Porsche NA

Leather" option was available in Pearl White, Buff Skin Brown, Cancan Red, and Champagne but was more expensive than the standard optional leather. While the choice of leather color options might seem more than sufficient, a special leather interior could be custom ordered at extra cost, matched to a customer's sample. Three different upholstery fabrics were offered in the same four colors as the optional leather. These included a wide Pinstripe Velour, a narrower striped Pinstripe Flannel, and Porsche Lettered Cloth. Interior and fabric selections varied over the duration of the 944's production run, but the abundance of selections indicated the degree to which Porsche as a company had expanded the concept of its least-expensive car.

The interior and seating surface choices available in the 944 were in an altogether higher category than those of the 914 or 924. The presence of a back seat in the 944 enabled it to be accurately described as a 2 + 2 coupe, but it was not a place any passenger of average or larger size would care to remain for any extended period. It conveniently folds down for increased storage in the rear cargo area.

While not as obvious, a great deal of attention had been paid to occupant safety. The 944 was padded heavily on the floor and inside roof with energy absorbent materials, as were the dashboard and sun visors. All interior materials were also flame retardant. Switches, door handles, glovebox latch, and all instruments were either energy absorbing or recessed. Other safety features were engineered into the design of the 944 in case of an accident. Crumple zones front and rear were incorporated in the basic design. The rigid torque tube layout greatly diminished the possibility of the engine entering the passenger compartment in a front impact crash. The strong roof pillars were designed to protect passengers in the unlikely event of a rollover, and steel side door beams were designed to lessen passenger exposure in a side impact collision.

White letters and numbering were applied to black instrument backgrounds for greater visibility with red needle indicators. Instruments on the central panel included speedometer, odometer, tachometer, temperature gauge, fuel gauge, battery charge indicator, trip odometer, and oil pressure gauge. Other features included brake pad wear indicator, digital clock, halogen lights, heated washer nozzles, and heated outside mirrors activated via the rear window defogger switch. All controls were logically positioned.

944 Turbo

The 944 Turbo was introduced in 1985 and available only with a manual gearbox. Assembly was performed at the Audi plant in Neckarsulm, rather than at the Porsche facility in Zuffenhausen as was the case with all 944s. The turbocharged engine provided 217 horsepower at 5800 rpm. Torque was boosted from 144 ft.-lbs. at 3000 rpm to 243 ft.-lbs. at 3500 rpm. Engine improvements for the Turbo included a larger oil pump, thicker cylinder walls, forged pistons, a compression ratio reduced to 8.0:1. It also had sodium-filled exhaust valves, and ceramic exhaust port liners. Driving impressions indicated that there was a minimum time lag before the turbo kicked in and that the boost provided was smooth, predictable, and highly efficient. Suspension upgrades for the Turbo included increasing the front stabilizer bar diameter to 22mm and the rear to 18mm. Pressed-steel front suspension arms were replaced by cast alloy. A larger-capacity plastic fuel tank (as on the 928) replaced the steel tank

Again, as with the 924, the Turbo model had a more aggressive visual appearance, especially from the front with its bumper incorporated into the front section as with the 928. Like the 924 Turbo, the 944 Turbo had longitudinal slots absent in the standard models, this time below the car's centerline, and elongated. It also had a lower rear spoiler located beneath the bumper for enhanced cooling of the gearbox and fuel tank, and enhanced airflow.

The Turbo was important for a number of reasons. It was priced slightly above the base priced 911, a first for the highly popular four-cylinder models, and as such, a direct challenge to the sovereignty of the 911. Secondly, the 944 Turbo's

944 Technical Specifications (1986)

Engine type:	Front mounted, water-cooled, four-cylinder inline
Crankcase, cylinders:	Light alloy, two part
Cylinder head:	Light alloy
Valve placement:	Overhead
Valve train:	Overhead camshaft, hydraulic lifters
Camshaft drive:	Spur belt drive
Crankshaft:	Forged, five main bearings
Engine lubrication:	Crankshaft driven, crescent gear pump
Fuel supply:	Electronic fuel injection, DME controlled
Emission system:	Three-way catalyst. Oxygen sensor
Bore:	3.94 in. (100mm)
Stroke:	3.11 in. (78.9mm)
Displacement:	151 cu. in. (2479cc)
Compression ratio:	9.7:1
Maximum horsepower SAE net:	143 at 5800 rpm
Maximum torque SAE net:	137 ft.-lbs. at 3000 rpm
Fuel requirement:	Regular unleaded
Battery voltage:	12 V
Battery capacity:	63 amp/hr
Alternator output:	Max. 1610 watts
Ignition system:	Fully electronic, DME controlled
Clutch:	Single disc, dry
Transmission:	Transaxle, rear
Number of gears:	5 forward, 1 reverse (manual)
	3 forward, 1 reverse (auto)
Final drive:	Hypoid drive
Final drive ratio:	3.889 (manual)
Body design:	Welded, unitized construction; double-sided zinc galvanized steel
Front suspension:	Independent coil/shock absorber struts
Rear suspension:	Independent trailing diagonal arm, one torsion bar each
Shock absorbers:	Double acting, hydraulic shock absorbers, front and rear
Stabilizer:	Front 20mm
Service brake:	Dual circuit, power-assisted ventilated discs, front and rear
Wheels:	7Jx15 cast alloy
Tire size:	215/60 VR 15
Steering:	Power-assisted rack and pinion
Engine coolant:	9.0 U.S. qt. (8.5 ltr)
Engine oil:	6.3 U.S. qt. (6.0 ltr.)
Transmission:	2.7 U.S. qt. (2.6 ltr.) (manual)
	6.9 U.S. qt. (6.5 ltr.) (auto)
Fuel tank:	21.12 U.S. gal. (80 ltr.)
Windshield washer tank:	6.3 U.S. qt. (6 ltr.)
Wheelbase:	94.5 in. (2400mm)
Track, front:	58.2 in. (1477mm)
Track, rear:	57.1 in. (1451mm)
Length:	168.9 in. (4290mm)
Width:	68.3 in. (1735mm)
Height (unladen):	50.2 in. (1275mm)
Turning circle-curb to curb	33.8 ft. (10.3 m)
Top track speed mph:	131 mph (210 km/h)
Acceleration 0-60 mph:	8.3 sec. (manual)
	9.8 sec. (auto)
Fuel economy (city/hwy):	20/27 mpg (manual)
	19/24 mpg (auto)

handling and performance exceeded that of the standard 911. And while the styling and quality of the 924 might not have equaled that of the standard 911 for some, nobody could dismiss the overall appearance, quality of construction, interior appointments, or luxury features of the 944 Turbo. As they say rustically, "It was a hoss." There was some disrespect, if not downright hatred, of any Porsche that wasn't rear-engine. One high-ranking Porsche official noted that "there were people at Porsche who actually refused to even sit in a front-engine Porsche." The 928 was entirely in a league and class of it own, but the 944 Turbo truly added insult to injury.

The Turbo was the first truly international car built by Porsche for all markets. Prior to its introduction there were varying considerations of fuel octane, crashworthiness, and emissions regulations requiring that cars be altered for sale in different ways for different countries. The 944 Turbo was designed to meet the most stringent world manufacturing standards.

1987 944S
Porsche NA

944S

The 944S was the next logical step in the development of the standard 944 and was introduced in 1986. As with the 911S, the 928S, and the 924S, the S designation represented an evolutionary step up the ladder from the original version, and since it had occurred in the previously mentioned models, an S model was expected by the public at some point in the development of the 944. This expectation materialized in mid-1986 in the new 944S, and in the Porsche tradition meant an increase in power and performance over the previous standard model. The S featured slotted, or "telephone dial," wheels visually similar to those found on the 928, furthering the visual relationship between the two cars. But otherwise, the visual similarity between the 944 and the 944S is so minimal that, except for the S script at the rear, the two cars were basically indistinguishable. The 944S debuted with air-conditioning, power windows, fog lights, outside rear view mirrors, and sunroof as standard.

The big news was the new four-valve per cylinder engine, with its new double-overhead camshaft head affixed to the existing 2.5-liter aluminum alloy block. Both intake and exhaust shafts are connected by a steel chain midway down the engine (between the second and third cylinders), while the exhaust cam is driven by the crankshaft via a toothed belt similar to that found on the 928. Horsepower increased to 188 hp at 6000 rpm, due both to the compression increase from 9.7:1 to 10.9:1 an extra camshaft, and larger intake and exhaust ports. Torque was also increased to 170 ft.-lbs. at 4300 rpm. (The two-valve 944 engine reached its maximum torque output in the 3000 rpm range). A top speed of 142 mph was claimed by Porsche along with a 0 to 60-mph time of 7.8 seconds. But the question arises: why a four-valve engine? Ultimately the four-valve engine, while more efficient in racing, was applied to passenger cars as an answer to dealing with increasing emissions regulations.

1987 944 Turbo
Porsche NA

Continuing developments in technology resulted in the offering of both driver and passenger airbags on the 944S in the U.S. market only. Other options included cruise control, heated seats with lumbar adjustment, and rear seat backs that folded forward individually as on the 928. Instrument and dashboard arrangements were the same as the standard 944.

The gearbox used on the 944S was a five-speed manual with a final drive ratio of 3.89:1, while the suspension and chassis were basically the same as found on the previous year's 944 Turbo.

Turbo S

The Turbo S was produced only in 1988 in a limited edition of 700. It used a turbocharger on the standard 2.5-liter engine to boost horsepower to 247 and bring top speed to 162 mph. Other features included a more rigid suspension consisting of stiffer springs and shocks and larger stabilizer bars. Wider wheels and tires were fitted on the Turbo S with 7 x 16 rubber on the front and 9 x 16 tires at the rear. It is interesting that in 1988 there were four different 944 versions offered for sale, a large number for one model. They were as follows: the standard 944, the 944 Turbo, the very rare 944 Turbo S, and the 944S. All but the 944S used the 2.5-liter single overhead cam engine with two valves per cylinder.

944S2 Cabriolet

1990 994S2 coupe
Porsche NA

The cabriolet first offered in 1989 as an S2, boosted the prestige of both the 944 and the Porsche name, furthering the reputation of the 944 as a desirable and luxurious sports car. It was the first of the Porsche front-engine cars to be offered in an open top version from the manufacturer, an option not offered in either the earlier, entry-level 924, or the top-of-the-line 928. The convertible top was electrically operated after the windshield was manually unlatched. The top was covered with a tonneau cover in the down position. There was no optional or aftermarket removable hardtop available with some convertible models.

The 944 cabriolet was equally stunning visually, with the top in either the raised or lowered position, although visibility was poor with the top raised as in most smaller convertibles. The windshield was slanted rearward to a greater degree than in the coupe, giving the appearance of a lower profile, and the coupe's rear side windows were deleted, replaced instead by the side panels of the convertible top. Otherwise, the bodywork and running gear were the same as the S2 coupe. From a purely structural perspective, additional bracing was required to replace the body's rigidity sacrificed by the loss of the top. The resulting increase in weight was approximately 150 lbs.

944S2

The S2, introduced in 1989, was available in either coupe or cabriolet body, and is preferred by many as the best of the 944s, even above the 944 Turbo. It also generally considered to be the best looking of the series with its front end treatment similar to that of the 944 Turbo, but without the possible additional maintenance expense associated with the turbocharger. The nose treatment of the S2 was reminiscent of that found on the higher priced 928, not from a particular visual similarity, but from the fact that the separate bumper that had characterized the 944 since its inception (except for the Turbo) had been replaced with a more rounded unit that seemed to modernize the car's appearance.

944SE

The 944SE, like certain Club Sport versions of the later 968 and 928, was introduced in the UK market only (1991) and featured a 225-horsepower engine and a heftier suspension. More importantly, it lacked many of the comfort and luxury features, such as air conditioning as part of the intention to reduce its weight as much as possible.

944 Options

As the 944 progressed and developed, the list of standard equipment increased as well. Among the standard features on the 944 were air conditioning, tinted glass, electric rear window defroster, fully carpeted rear luggage area with fold-down seats, storage pockets in doors, three-point inertia reel front seatbelts and rear lap belts, four-spoke leather covered steering wheel, leather-covered shift lever, vanity mirrors, transistorized tachometer, full instrumentation, digital quartz clock, power windows, heavy-duty 63-amp battery, electrically adjustable and heated outside mirrors, all-glass lift-up hatchback, pop-up halogen headlights, windshield with graduated tint, front center armrest with storage, anti-theft device for wheels, upshift indicator light for manual transmission, brake pad wear indicator light, electric rear hatch release, flush-mounted fog lights, rear spoiler, power-assisted rack and pinion steering, power-assisted four-wheel vented disc brakes, steel belted radial tires, double-sided zinc-galvanized steel body, front stabilizer bar, four-wheel independent suspension, synchronized electronic ignition and fuel injection, reclining bucket seats, intermittent electric wipers, and windshield mounted antenna. It would seem that with as many standard features as available on the 944, there would be little room for options.

But optional features were available at extra cost in addition to the 944's extensive list of standard offerings. These included automatic transmission, full leather seats, digital cassette radio, heated front seats, limited-slip differential, protective side molding strips, electric rear wiper, removable sun roof with electric tilt, alarm system, electric door locks, cruise control, metallic paint, headlight washers, larger 7J x 16 front and 8J x 16 rear forged alloy wheels, and wheel centers in Grand Prix White, or White Gold Metallic.

1990 944S2 cabriolet
Porsche NA

Conclusion

By 1986 the Porsche lineup was extensive, consisting of the 928S, the 911 Targa, the 911 cabriolet, the 911 coupe, the Turbo, the 944S, and the 944 Turbo. The 944 lineup had by 1989 become extensive itself with the 944, 944S2 coupe, 944S2 cabriolet, and 944 Turbo. By 1990, however, the 944's availibility had diminished to just two models: the S2 coupe and S2 Cabriolet. Each had the 3-liter, four-valve-per-cylinder 208-hp engine—the earlier 2.5- and 2.7-liter engines had been discontinued. Top speed for both was right at 150 mph with 0 to 60 mph in just under 7 seconds.

The 944 was possibly the most successful Porsche ever made, both in terms of its high production numbers, beautiful and functional design, and financial success. It may, in fact, be the car that actually saved the Porsche company. The money that it generated helped keep the company

Conversions

Some of the front-engine Porsches were converted to American V-8s by enterprising mechanics. This is an affliction which has been applied across the board to nearly every exotic marque that has ever reached U.S. shores. Ferrari, Aston Martin, Rolls Royce and Bentley, Jaguar, Austin Healey, and even Porsche have all been subject to conversions to American engines. Although many U.S.-made engines have been used, the engine of choice for conversions is usually a Chevrolet 350 V-8, a time-proven classic still available today. The 350 is compact, lightweight, and powerful, with a cast-iron block and cylinder heads. Many aftermarket companies have manufactured performance-enhancing products for this engine for literally decades, including, among other things, additional carburetors, generally as two four-barrel or three two-barrel configurations. Exhaust headers, racing cams, and valves are all readily available which enable this engine to produce plenty of torque and horsepower. Additionally, a Chevrolet 350 is understood by every mechanic anywhere in the US. Parts are available at any standard parts store, and its reliability is legendary.

Most American cities do not have a Porsche, Ferrari, or Rolls Royce dealer, even now. These exist mainly in larger major U.S. cities. While Porsche dealerships are rapidly expanding, this is more of a recent phenomenon. So there is much to be said for a conversion, especially in a case where the original engine has worn out and the cost of replacing or rebuilding it greatly exceeds the car's worth. Purists of all marques understandably shudder at the thought of bastardizing a great car.

The problem with conversions of all types is that the mechanic generally quits as soon as the car operates properly, neglecting to complete the job. It is therefore common to find a mechanical engine conversion but no heating or air conditioning. Be that as it may, there are a sufficient number of U.S. motorists, who, given the option of an original front engine Porsche or a properly performed 350 V-8 conversion, would choose the 350 over the original engine. This applies equally to the 944 or 928. With the cost of a rebuilt 928 fuel distributor at more than $750, while an entirely new and completely assembled 350 is available for less than $2,000, a conversion makes sense financially.

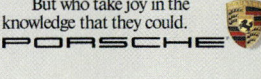

alive during the dark days at the end of the 1980s and the beginning of the 1990s.

Over the course of its 9-year run, the 944 was developed as much as possible within its basic configuration. All of these cars are every bit as desirable today as they were when first viewed by the public in 1981. As their prices continue to fall (for the time being), they represent possibly the best value in a pre-owned Porsche. They are less expensive to maintain than a 928, and yet in many ways represent the best of the 928's technological sophistication. As popular current car styles feature increasingly rounded edges (at the moment), the 944 seems even more attractive in comparison, and truly stands apart from the crowd. Creature comforts are most adequate even by today's high standards. And the 944's performance, across the model range is still more than anyone really needs in most circumstances. The 944 is a modern sports car which can be driven and enjoyed daily more than 25 years after its introduction.

A 1986 Turbo coupe shows off its racing form.
Porsche NA

959

The 911-based Porsche 959 is arguably the first true Porsche "supercar." That term is widely used today, and not without good reason, in light of the technical sophistication of modern cars in general, but at its introduction, the 959 was without equal in the automotive world.

The car made its first public appearance at the 1983 Frankfurt Auto Show as a design study for Porsche's Group B motorsport racing. For a car to be eligible for Group B competition (which was later cancelled), a manufacturer was required to make at least 200 street versions of a particular car. In the case of the 959, Porsche decided to make the car available to the public as a car that could be purchased by a select few who could afford it at nearly $250,000. Unfortunately, the car was never sold in the U.S. as a street-legal car because it failed to meet various U.S. government restrictions, despite Porsche's initial intention to make a version for the US.

Visually, the car is an exaggerated 911. The 911's classic lines are clearly obvious despite the 959's full-width rear spoiler, flattened headlights and front fenders, distinctive lower front treatment, and wider body sills. While the 959's appearance is undeniably aggressive and boldly suggests the speed and power lurking beneath its non-metallic skin, there is nothing visually that would indicate the high degree of technical sophistication beneath the surface.

The car is four-wheel drive full time. This is accomplished in the 959 by the use of a 928-type torque tube leading to a front differential with multiple-plate clutch in an oil-filled case. Front-to-rear torque was adjustable via a selector switch in four programmed modes from 40/60 to 20/80, depending on road conditions. An adjustable ground clearance could also be selected at 4.7, 5.9, and 7.1 inches, with the lower level for speeds over 75 mph. Aerodynamic properties supposedly resulted in zero lift. The drag coefficient was a respectable 0.31.

The body, despite its visual similarity to the 911, was a marvel of modern technology in its own right. The doors and hood were made of aluminum as with the 928, but the rest of the body was Kevlar-reinforced Fiberglas and deformable polyurethane.

The engine represented another technical milestone for a passenger car (if the 959 can seriously be called a passenger car)—an aluminum flat-six with an air-cooled block. The four-valve-per-cylinder (sodium-filled exhaust valves) heads, on the other hand, were water-cooled by twin radiators, one behind each rear wheel. Engine management was provided by a Bosch Motronic system, and twin KKK turbos were designed to act sequentially one for lower rpm and one for higher, reducing typical turbo lag.

The 959's magnesium alloy wheels featured tire pressure-loss sensors, a technical advance which would find its way to the later 928s. There was no provision for a spare tire in the 959 as wheels were fitted with run-flat tires that were good for 50 miles.

The limited production 959 was offered in two versions. The sport model lacked air conditioning, power windows and seats, back seats, and adjustable height control and weighed about 100 lbs. less than the fully equipped, "comfort" edition.

The 959 was successful for Porsche, though not necessarily in a financial sense, despite its extremely low production numbers estimated to be between 200 and 250, including prototypes. It received an incredible amount of press coverage during its time, as the technological work of art that it was, thus furthering the already prestigious Porsche name and serving notice to the automotive world that Porsche was on the cutting edge of future technology. The 959 in modified form also won the Paris-Dakar rally in 1984 and 1986. Most importantly, much of the technology that debuted with the 959 subsequently found its way into mainstream Porsche production. ABS brakes, tire-pressure sensors, all-wheel drive, and adjustable height control as found on the new Cayenne SUV all evolved from the 959.

The exotic 959 was officially clocked from 0 to 60 mph in 3.6 seconds.
Randy Leffingwell

959
Technical Specifications

Engine:	Horizontally opposed aluminum alloy six-cylinder	Engine management:	Bosch Motronic	Width:	72.5 in.
Displacement:	2850cc (173.9 cu. in.)	Fuel system:	Air-to-air intercooler, twin KKK two-stage turbochargers	Front wheels:	8 J x 17 in. Magnesium alloy
Compression ratio:	8.3:1	Transmission:	Six-speed manual	Rear wheels:	9 J x 17 in. Magnesium alloy
Horsepower:	450 bhp at 6500 rpm	Body:	Kevlar-reinforced fiberglass, aluminum	Calipers:	Four-piston
Torque:	369 ft.-lbs. at 5500 rpm	Drag coefficient:	0.31	Front brakes:	ABS, with 12.7-in. vented discs
Bore and stroke:	3.7 in. x 2.6 in. (95mm x 67mm)	Suspension:	Fully independent	Rear brakes:	ABS with 12-in. vented discs
		Wheelbase:	89.5 in.	0 to 60 mph:	3.6 sec.
		Length:	167.8 in.	Top speed:	197 mph

The U.S. government officially sanctioned one 959 for legal importation as a display car only for collector Otis Chandler's museum.
Randy Leffingwell

The 1988 959 used a six-speed transmission and all-wheel drive with settings for dry and wet pavement, snow and "difficult terrain needing traction."
Randy Leffingwell

The 1988 959 was powered by a six-cylinder engine that produced 450 hp.
Randy Leffingwell

The 959 was the first true Porsche supercar and was possibly more advanced and exotic for its time than the new V-10 Carrera GT is in relation to the present state of automotive technology. The 959 is extremely rare today and most owners keep them under lock and key the same way as one would a rare and valuable art work. It's doubtful that you are likely to encounter one under normal driving circumstances, and it's safe to say the 959 is possibly the most desirable Porsche ever made.

Many Americans who wanted to get behind the wheel of their 1988 Porsche 959 had to buy and keep their cars in Europe. The cars could not be legally imported to the U.S.
Randy Leffingwell

Among the features of the 959 was an electronically adjustable suspension system.
Randy Leffingwell

968

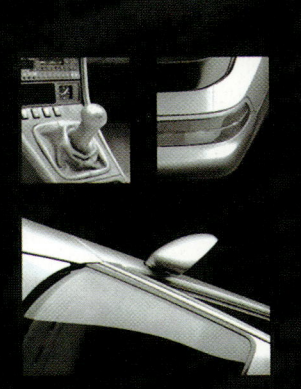

968 TIMELINE

1991
Sales of the new front-engine 968 begin (as a 1992 model)

1992
968 Club Sport introduced in the UK

1993
968 Turbo S offered

The 968, like the 912, 912 E, and subsequent 914 (all four-cylinder cars), was one of the few major Porsche production cars with a fairly brief run. It was in a sense the tail end of the front-engine experiment, and as such was the last in the line (for the moment) of front-engine sports cars, ceasing production at basically the same time as the remaining front-engine car, the 928.

With a decrease in sales for Porsche beginning in the early 1990s, the company was in need of something that would reinvigorate the image of Porsche. The 944, while extremely successful, was not particularly new or exciting for 1991. It was hoped at Porsche that the 968 would do as well as the 944 had, but it never reached the desired sales. When viewed together, or in sequence, the evolutionary pattern of 924, 944, 968 is clear, at least visually, and that might have been part of the problem, despite claims from Porsche that the 968 was 80 percent "new." It wasn't that the four-cylinder cars weren't wonderful cars, it was rather that they'd been out awhile and it was time for something new.

The profile of the three cars is very similar as all three had evolved from Harm Laagay's basic 924 design. On the other hand, from the front as well as the rear, the 968 is more similar visually to the 928. The exposed pop-up headlights in either the up or down position are virtually indistinguishable at first glance from those found on the more expensive 928. The rear end treatment on the 968, while similar to the 944 above the tail lights, more resembles the 928 S4 from the tail lights down, especially with the lights fitting flush within the rear bumper housing. Despite the visual similarities, the 968 was smaller, shorter, and narrower than the 928. The 968 debuted in August 1991 (as a 1992 model) as the replacement for the 944.

Porsche claimed to have "redefined" the sports car with the 968. That's probably a stretch, but it can be said that it

1995
Production of the 968 ceases

1994
968 Sport offered in UK market only

1991 968 coupe and cabriolet
Porsche NA

raised the level of what should be expected from any sports car. By the end of the 968's basically two-decade run, the concept of the sports car had changed forever. No longer would the buyer of any sports car tolerate unreliability, heating and ventilation systems which did not work, and convertible tops that leaked excessively. Across-the-board improvements involved new suspension dynamics, component shifts, improved steering, anti-lock brakes, advances in active and passive safety, and the concept of engine management.

The evolution of the modern sports car was effectively advanced by all of the Porsche front-engine cars, and each successive model was a substantial improvement over its predecessor. Standard features for the 968 included a rear window wiper, retractable halogen headlights, anti-theft wheel devices, cast-alloy wheels, electrically adjustable outside mirrors, power top (on the cabriolet), rear wing spoiler and electric sunroof (on the coupe), integrated fog lights, tinted glass, heated windshield washer nozzles, electrically adjustable seats, carpeted luggage area, and other refinements that would have been literally inconceivable in the 1950s or 1960s. The same can be said of the ongoing technical sophistication that reached its zenith with the 968's four valves per cylinder, Variocam variable timing, and electronic engine management. All of the four-cylinder front-engine cars are desirable today, and now much more affordable than they were at their introduction. It should also be mentioned that each of the series proved the viability of a water-cooled four-cylinder inline engine as a desirable power plant for a sports car. Few people would use the word "underpowered" when describing a 944 or 968, something that cannot be said for the more traditional air-cooled four-cylinder 914, 912, or 912E.

Engine

The 968's engine was made of an aluminum-alloy block, head, and pistons, and produced more torque at the time than any similarly sized and configured engine in the world. Engine modifications for the 968 included reduced exhaust backpressure by way of a redesigned catalytic converter and exhaust system, and lighter-weight crankshaft and

Porsche

connecting rods. It was still essentially the same 3-liter, four-valve-per-cylinder double-overhead-cam engine used in the 944S2, but the changes and upgrades resulted in 14 percent more horsepower and 9 percent more torque than on the earlier engine, while fuel consumption remained basically the same. The Porsche Variocam system came standard on the 968 and electronically determined ignition timing and fuel injection via the Bosch Motronic's computerized brain.

The 968's 3.0-liter inline four-cylinder engine is a visual and technical work of art, with its clean lines and matte finish. A comparison of the 924 or 944 engine compartment with that of the 968 clearly indicates attention to the visual removal, relocation, or disguise of pipes, wires, and hoses. The same attention was paid to the firewall, generally the site of brake booster, master cylinder, and wiper motor, all of which were cleaned up and covered by a removable plastic cover beginning with the 968. This is now a tradition at Porsche and no doubt a strong selling point. The de-cluttering of the engine compartment is a trend which is now followed by most high-end auto manufacturers, including Lamborghini, Rolls Royce, Mercedes, and Ferrari, among others. In the case of the 968, the engine compartment still retains the visual presence of the MacPherson suspension strut housing and covers, as found on the 944 and the earlier 924.

The engine was hand assembled at the Porsche plant in Zuffenhausen to extremely close tolerances, and each engine was bench tested for a full half-hour for fine tuning and break-in. In fact, the 968 was treated like an entirely new car by the Porsche engineers, despite its admitted descent from the popular 944S2. To this extent it was subject to the same rigorous and thorough testing that any new Porsche would receive.

Transmission

The 968 was equipped with a close-ratio six-speed manual transmission mounted behind the rear axle as with the 924 and 944. Much was made at the time of the 968's six forward gears and the high gear was not merely an "overdrive" for highway cruising, but in fact a full gear, which allowed maximum enjoyment of the engine at full throttle. The four-speed Tiptronic dual mode transmission was also offered on the 968 from the outset, providing the driver with the option of a clutchless manual or the convenience of an automatic transmission. As with all of the Tiptronic transmissions, there is the absence of the clutch pedal, which is considered by most motorists to be a plus in that shifting and operating a clutch at the same time can be inconvenient while talking on the phone, or drinking coffee, for example. Also, as a rule the torque converter in an automatic transmission seems to require less service than a strictly manual transmission which frequently needs the clutch plate

1991 968 coupe
Porsche NA

1991 968 cabriolet
Porsche NA

replaced, especially if the driver has a habit of riding the clutch more than necessary.

The absence of a clutch often felt strange (in the earlier dual mode transmissions), to someone used to a fully manual transmission. The clutch, in combination with the shifter and accelerator, always provided sort of a rhythm for any driver in tune with his car. For some reason, moving the shift lever manually without the clutch pedal didn't provide the same sense of driving, despite the physical operation of the shift lever. The placement and operation of the shift lever on the 968's optional Tiptronic was logical. By moving the lever to the right, the Tiptronic mode was engaged. With a slight forward motion a higher gear was attained. By moving the lever back, the transmission shifted to a lower gear. A backlit display located on the face of the tachometer visually indicates both mode and gear selection. Strangely, the steering wheel-mounted Tiptronic push button on the current Porsches has restored the sense of at-one-ment between the car and driver, despite the absence of the clutch, which in the case of the Tiptronic is likely gone forever.

The Tiptronic found on the 968 was a far cry from the earlier Porsche "Sportmatic" first used on the early 911. The Tiptronic was electronic in nature rather than mechanical, as was the Sportmatic, and allowed the positioning of the shift lever in either of two slots, one for the fully automatic, the other for the manual mode. Like the "Dual Gate" shift found on the GM cars, the transmission would only change gears in the manual mode when the shift lever was moved forward to a higher gear, or back for a lower gear. The lever movement was logical and a decided improvement over the earlier Sportmatic.

That Porsche continued the development of a clutchless manual transmission beyond the primitive Sportmatic was again primarily a result of racing considerations. With a traditional manual transmission, the engine rpms drop during the shifting process, Porsche engineers believed that it was possible for a driver to change gears at the appropriate time as fast as he could move the shift lever, without the drop in engine revolutions and subsequent temporary loss of power. For this to occur, the clutch had to be eliminated. The continued development centered around the 962C, a 600-horsepower racing car with a top speed of 225 mph. The result of the trials and experiments culminated in the Porsche Double Clutch Transmission, or PDK, which ultimately evolved into the Tiptronic. According to Porsche, the Tiptronic-equipped 968 was only 5 seconds slower than the manual six-speed (in the hands of professional test drivers) over the 14-mile Nurburgring circuit.

There were built-in mechanical and electric safety features standard with the 968's Tiptronic. In the U.S. market, federal regulations had mandated that every car sold in America have an anti-theft and safety feature in which a key could only be removed from the ignition if the transmission was in the "Park" position. Additionally, a car could not be shifted from to park to reverse unless there was pressure on the brake pedal. The idea in this instance was that if the brake were engaged the driver would be much less likely to automatically back over something or somebody as his foot would be on the brake to begin with. The transmission was also equipped with built-in protection against accidentally shifting into an inappropriate gear at the wrong time.

The six-speed manual transmission available in the 968 was developed at the Weissach plant and represented the culmination of 40 years of development, as well as being the first six-speed manual transmission offered on a Porsche road car. The shift pattern was as logical as possible

The famous Porsche phantom view shows the inner workings of the 1991 968 series.
Porsche NA

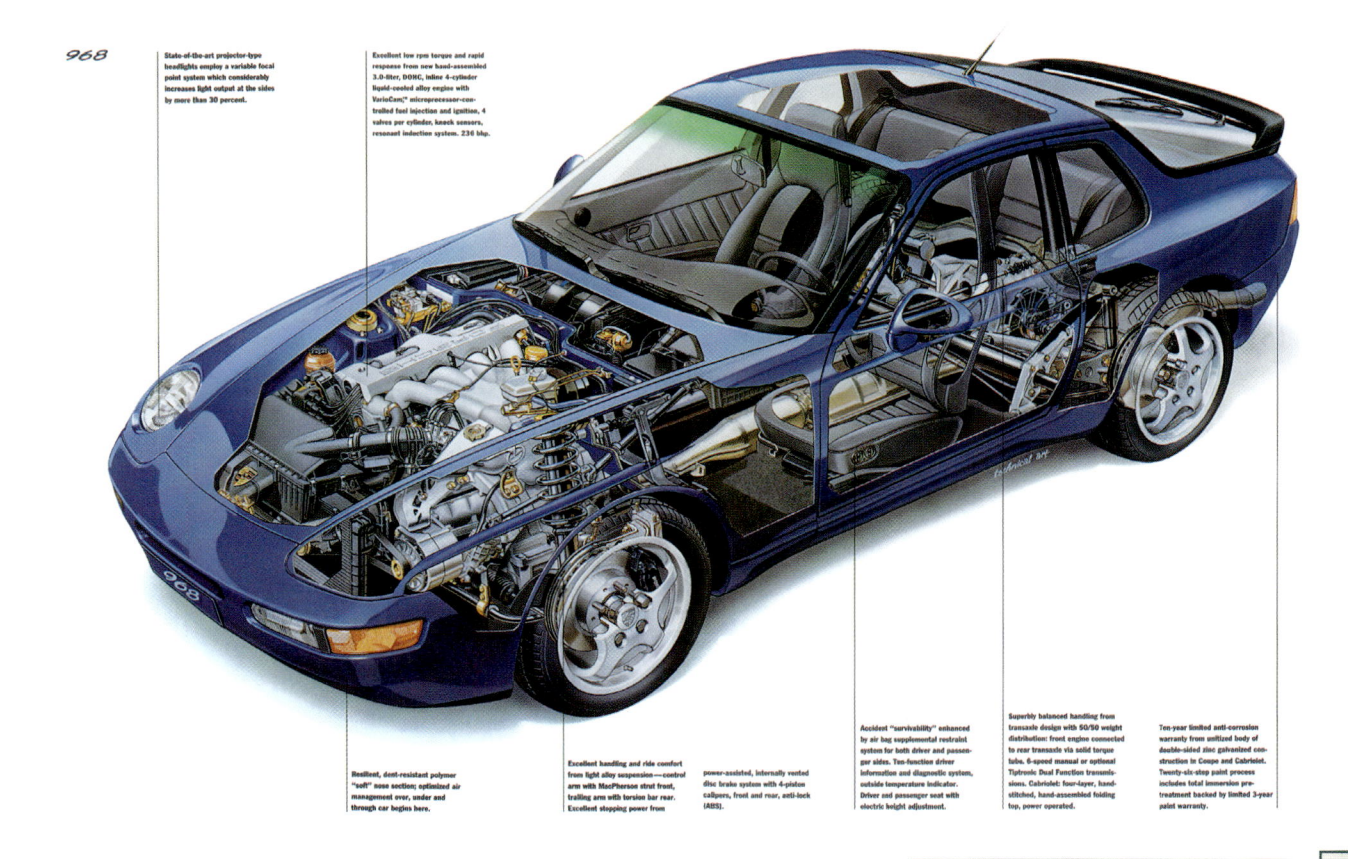

and the transmission allowed the car to hit freeway merging speeds with one shift, from first to second gear.

Drivetrain

Like its sisterships in the front-engine Porsche fleet (924, 928, 944), the 968 had a front engine and rear transaxle—a layout considered by many to be optimal with its 50/50 front to rear weight and balance ratio. This configuration was used on all of the front-engine cars produced by Porsche, with the engine and transaxle connected by a rigid torque tube that serves as a "spine" strengthening the car structurally. Unlike the 928, which had the transmission in front of the rear axles, the 924, 944, and 968 all had the transmissions behind the rear axles.

1991 968 cabriolet
Porsche NA

Body

The 968 was offered throughout its production run in both a 2 + 2 coupe and a two-seat roadster version known a Cabriolet (there was not a factory production 924 or 928 roadster in the front engine fleet). The 968 coupe was a true 2 + 2 with a back seat, but as with its predecessors, rear seating was minimal. The roadster's convertible top was designed to fold down and its mechanism covered with a tonneau cover as with most American convertibles, lacking the disappearing top now found on the Boxter, for example. Lowering the top is accomplished manually by unlatching two locks, and then electrically by pushing a button.

While both coupe and cabriolet versions are similar to the 944 and the 928S4, the coupe more resembled the higher priced 928 visually than it does the 944 from which it evolved. This is due in large measure to the similarity of profile, with the coupe having a rear wing and lower door sills similar to those of the later 928S4. The 968 also lacked the specific front and rear bumpers of the 944, and instead had a more aerodynamic deformable seamless polyurethane front bumper shell. The front chin spoiler of the 928 had been removed and replaced with an "air-dam" type front spoiler integrated within the more rounded front bumper beginning with the 1987 S4, and doubtless provided the inspiration for the similar treatment of the 968's front section. The result of the newer 928 inspired bumpers was a fluid integration of front and rear sections, blending with a visually sleeker, more aerodynamic looking body. The rear bumper was similar in appearance to that of the flagship 928, with bumper guards on each side of the license (in U.S. models). Tail lights were brought flush with the rest of the bumper as in the 928S4 (1987 and later. Engine cooling was accomplished via the central front air intake, and the lower louvers found beneath the front bumper. In fact, much attention was paid by the Porsche engineers to airflow under, over, and through the 968.

1991 968 interior
Porsche NA

Structural safety features included increased chassis rigidity from the torque tube as well as deformable crumple zones designed to deflect collision energy away from the passenger compartment. Airbags were offered as standard for both the driver and passenger.

The 968 can also be said to have a more subtle appearance than the 944 in that it lacks the rear window spoiler of the 944 as well as the tray-like appendage found beneath the rear bumper. The rear spoiler is lacking altogether on the 968 cabriolet, thus giving the stern an even less-cluttered appearance.

Optional exterior features available for the 968 included metallic paint, model designation deletion, headlight washers, and side protective strip deletion. The protective side door and fender strip found on all of the front-engine cars was considered an eyesore to some and a necessity to others. Each of the cars are seen with or without it.

Wheels

The 968 was the first of the front-engine cars not to be offered at some point with the 928 type "telephone dial" wheels. Instead, the 968 featured the pressure cast-alloy Carrera Cup wheels inspired by the 959. Standard wheels were cast alloy 7J x 16 front, and 8J x 16 rear. Standard tire sizes were 205/55ZR 16 front, and 255/50 ZR 16 rear. Optional cast-alloy wheels were available in a larger 7.5J x 17 front, and 9J x 17 rear which used corresponding 225/45ZR 17 front, and 255/40 17 rear.

1991 968 coupe
Porsche NA

Porsche

1992 968 coupe
Porsche NA

Brakes

The anti-lock brake system on the 968 consisted of four-piston fixed calipers on all four wheels. The calipers were made of lightweight aluminum alloy, for rapid heat dissipation. The internally vented brake discs were steel alloy, and the brake pads were asbestos free. One of the major problems associated with braking is brake fade due to heat. The Carrera Cup wheels of the 968, with their substantial open spaces, provided increased airflow and faster cooling. Front brakes were further cooled while the car is in motion by directed airflow through the air intake slits in the lower front bumper.

Interior

The interior of the 968 was largely a carryover of that found on the 944 beginning in 1985, prior to which the 944 and 924 dashboards and instrument pods were nearly identical, each having three large, recessed dials. The 968 instrument cluster, while not housed in a separate pod, as with the 928, was very similar in appearance to that of the 928. Instrumentation was more than adequate with a transistorized tachometer, oil pressure, fuel level, temperature gauges, a voltmeter, and speedometer. The emphasis for the 968 cabin was on ergonomics, this again derived from Porsche's extensive racing experience.

Despite the presence of a full back seat in the coupe, rear seating was minimal for rear passengers. Both rear seats, however, folded forward providing ample storage under the rear hatch. The electric sunroof on the coupe tilted open or lifted out altogether

The interior emphasis for the 968 was on practical and efficient luxury, with orthopedically designed reclining highback bucket seats and electric front seat height adjustment. The front center armrest was designed to

968
Technical Specifications (1992)

Engine:	Front-mounted, water-cooled, inline four-cylinder	Cabriolet:	3,240 lbs. (manual), 3,306 lbs. (automatic)	Standard wheels:	Cast-alloy front: 7J x 16, 205/55ZR 16 cast-alloy rear: 8J x 16, 225/50ZR 16
Displacement:	3.0 liters (182 cu. in.)	Front suspension:	MacPherson struts, aluminum alloy lower control arms, stabilizer bar	Options wheels:	Alloy front: 7.5J x 17, 225/45ZR 17 alloy rear: 9J x 17, 255/40 17
Bore & stroke:	4.09 x 3.46 in.	Rear:	Independent aluminum alloy, semi-trailing arms with one torsion bar per wheel, stabilizer bar	Acceleration:	0-60 mph: 6.3 seconds (manual) 0-60 mph: 7.7 seconds (automatic)
Horsepower:	236 @ 6200 rpm				
Torque:	225 ft.-lbs. @ 4100 rpm			Top speed:	156 mph (manual)
Compression ratio:	11.0:1			Top speed:	153 mph (automatic)
Valve train:	Double-overhead cam, 16 valves, hydraulic lifters, spur belt & chain drive, Variocam variable timing	Stabilizer bars:	Standard: 26.8mm front/ 16mm rear	Wheelbase:	94.5 in.
			Optional: 30.0mm front/ 20mm rear	Overall length:	170.9 in.
		Shocks:	Double-acting hydraulic (Sport Shocks Optional)	Width:	68.3 in.
				Height:	50.2 in.
Fuel system:	Electronic fuel injection			Track-front/rear:	58.0/57.4 in.
Battery:	12V/63 amp/hr	Brakes:	Front and rear power assisted, 4-piston aluminum alloy, fixed caliper, internally vented discs, ABS	Ground clearance:	4.9 in
Alternator:	115 amp			Curb Weight manual:	3,086 lbs. coupe 3,240 lbs. cabriolet
Ignition system:	Electronic, DME controlled			Curb weight Tiptronic:	3,152 lbs. coupe 3,306 lbs. cabriolet
Transmission:	6-speed manual	Disc:	11.73 front/11.77 in. rear (11.97/11.77 optional, coupe only)	Trunk room:	Seat up: 7.9 cu. ft., seat down: 19.1 cu. ft.
	4-speed Tiptronic Dual-Function				
Final drive (manual):	3.78:1	Steering type:	Rack & pinion, hydraulically assisted	Fuel fank:	19.6 gal.
Final drive (Tiptronic):	3.25:1			Engine oil:	7.4 qts.
Body:	Unitized steel (galvanized)	Steering ratio:	18.85:1	Transmission fluid:	2.9 qts. (7.4 Tiptronic)
Weight:	Coupe: 3,086 lbs. (manual), 3,152 lbs. (automatic)	Turns (lock to lock):	3.24	Engine coolant:	8.4 qts.
		Turning circle	35.27 ft.		

provide storage for cassettes and coins in addition to housing the shift lever, central door lock switch, outside mirror adjustment, convertible top switch, headlight adjustment switch, and analog quartz clock. Tinted glass with graduated windshield tint was effective at reducing glare. Other standard comfort and convenience features included one key central locking and alarm with LED warning lights, automatic temperature control air conditioning, electric power windows, cruise control with resume feature, door panel storage compartments, interior light with fade feature, and intermittent wiper with variable delay.

Optional interior and comfort features included an electric rear window defogger on the coupe, adjustable front lumbar seat support, full leather seats, leather interior trim, all cloth front and rear seats with matching cloth door panels, heated seats, full power seats, and ten speaker cassette AM-FM stereo (eight speakers on cabriolet).

Standard seating surfaces for the 968 consisted of leather bolsters with fabric surface inserts and optional leather seating surfaces. Most 968s destined for the American market arrived with the optional full leather.

Suspension

The suspension and handling benefited from association with the 928. Although none of the four-cylinder cars featured the famed Weissach rear axle of the 928, both the 944 and the 968 had power-assisted steering—a feature first found on the 928. Front suspension on the 968 was comprised of MacPherson struts with control arms, and semi-trailing arms with torsion bar springs at the rear.

Turbo S

As with the 924 and the 944, a Turbo model was offered by Porsche in addition to that of the normally aspirated inline four.

Sport

The Sport model was offered in 1994 and 1995 as a righthand-drive car in the UK market only, and was considerably cheaper than the standard 968, but still more expensive than the minimally-equipped Club Sport model, which was not offered in the U.S. It was slightly heavier (65 lbs.) than the Club Sport, but featured luxury features that the Club Sport lacked, including power windows and outside mirrors, an alarm system and a remote rear hatch release.

Conclusion

The 968 is one of the most beautiful and functional sports cars ever produced by Porsche or any other manufacturer. It represented the final step in the two-decade evolutionary spiral started with the 924 and followed by the 944. Despite its many exceptional qualities, it did not last long, with production halted in 1995, when the 928 also vanished.

In retrospect, it's strange to think that Porsche dropped two-thirds of its line of cars at one time. Sadly, the 968, the best of the three, four-cylinder cars, had the shortest manufacturing run of the bunch. Its demise, for the moment at least, marked the end of Porsche's production of water-cooled, four-cylinder, front engine, rear-wheel drive sports cars. And yet with Porsche, it seems that nothing is ever really final.

As far as value is concerned, the 968 is still generally more expensive than a comparable 924, 944, or even some earlier 928s. While the 968 is slightly more complex, and less readily available than the 924, or the 944, it represents a great value. As it ages, prices will decrease further, and its value for the money will continue to increase. Also, as time passes, the model year of any of the front engine cars becomes less important to a prospective buyer than overall condition and mileage of an individual car. As a rule, convertibles or cabriolet models are more desirable and expensive than the hardtop coupe versions, although some feel that the 968 convertible, especially with its top raised, suffers visually when compared to the more fluid lines of the coupe.

There are few who would prefer a 924 over either a 944 or a 968, but there are no doubt those who would prefer a 924 or 944 Turbo over a standard 944 or 968. All in all, the 968 represents the best and last of the inline four-cylinder front-engine Porsche cars, and their authenticity as "true Porsches" is no longer an issue except for the hardline traditionalist.

Boxster

Boxster TIMELINE

1992
Decision made for a new Porsche to augment the 911 line

1993
Boxster concept car debuts at Detroit Auto Show

1994
Testing of prototypes begins

By the time the production Porsche Boxster debuted in America in early 1997 the furor over what constituted a "true Porsche" had largely become irrelevant. The non-traditional front-engine 924, 928, 944, and 968 had forever blurred the lines of engine placement as a significant factor in determining what constitutes a Porsche. Interestingly enough, the phenomenal success of the mid-engine Boxster may be in some measure due to the earlier ancestry of its unlikely predecessor, the 914.

It was the mid-engine 914 that was the first major production Porsche of the modern era to dispense with the traditional behind-the-rear-axle engine. The 914, as the first to challenge traditional rear engine placement, took the heat and abuse for its effrontery from purists, but nevertheless managed to open the door for all of the front-engine cars that followed. That Porsche should return once again to a mid-engine configuration nearly 30 years later is not really that surprising. And unlike the 914, as some might now argue (and did at the time), the Boxster definitely "looks like a Porsche."

The Boxster, however, did not repeat the mistakes made with the earlier 914. The Boxster's power plant was not a standard four-cylinder Volkswagen engine with an optional (more expensive) six-cylinder Porsche engine, as was the case with the 914. Both the 914 and the Boxster are rear wheel-drive, mid-engine, two-seat sports cars with engine placement immediately behind the seat. In both cars the gearbox is located behind the engine between the rear wheels. Both cars have a nearly 50/50 weight balance, as well as horizontally opposed engines, and both cars offer front and rear cargo storage. This, however, is where the many obvious similarities end.

The heritage of the Boxster can be clearly traced back to the very first Porsche, Number 1, a mid-engine roadster unveiled in 1948 by Ferdinand and Ferry Porsche. The racing successes of this car, and indeed all of the mid-engine racing Porsches which followed, can be said to have culminated in the Porsche Boxster, a fabulous street machine built literally upon a 50-year foundation of technical knowledge gained on the race track.

If handling, performance, technical sophistication, safety, and the sheer thrill of driving are the most defining elements of Porsche, then the open Boxster carries the banner proudly into the future as the newest legendary sports car to enter the Porsche lineup. While Porsche has offered several open-top sports

1999
Boxster S introduced with 3.2-liter engine. Standard Boxster engine increased from 2.5-liter to 2.7-liter

2005
Front and rear bumpers redesigned and side intakes enlarged for

1997
Boxster reaches dealer showrooms with 2.5-liter engine

2003
Slightly redesigned front bumper. Addition of retractable rear spoiler. Glass window replaces plastic rear window on convertible top

1997 Boxster
Porsche NA

cars to the buying public in recent years, such as the 911 cabriolet (1983-present), 944S2 cabriolet (1991-1992), 968 cabriolet(1992-1995), it is arguably the Boxster which best embodies the original Porsche concept. In that sense the Boxster may actually be the best production Porsche sports car ever manufactured.

The Boxster, originally known as Project 986, was designed to replace the front-engine 968 at a time when Porsche sales overall were at a critically low phase. By the 1990s many famous automotive names had already either ceased to exist or had been absorbed by major automotive conglomerates like Ford, Chrysler, or General Motors. Numerous motoring enthusiasts and publications wondered both privately and publicly whether a similar fate might await Porsche, an undeniably important but small-time player in the automotive world, at least in terms of sheer sales volume. Porsche total sales in the U.S. for 1993 were not quite 3,700, in comparison to 1986 when Porsche North America sold more than 30,000 cars.

There were, according to Porsche NA's publicity director essentially three reasons for the reduction of Porsche sales in the U.S.: the 1987 stock market decline; the U.S. dollar dropped significantly against the Deutschmark; and Porsche raised prices significantly to compensate. All of these factors had a disastrous effect on the high-end car market, especially for sports cars. And further, there wasn't really anything new or exciting on the horizon for Porsche. The product line had been static between 1989 and 1993. Porsche had to do something to increase sales as soon as possible. Equally as significant was that Porsche was making three separate cars (911, 968, 928), which shared no common parts whatsoever—an expensive proposition for any company, but especially so for a relatively small company like Porsche.

Porsche

The decision was made in 1992 to create a new Porsche designed from the ground up, which would be known as the 986. It would be developed simultaneously with the new 911 model known as the 996, and the two models would share 40 percent of their parts, thus significantly reducing manufacturing costs.

The original Boxster show car designed primarily by Grant Larson (exterior), and Stefan Stark (interior) debuted at the Detroit Auto Show in January, 1993 initially as a concept car, and was not at the time of its presentation the car actually under development. It was merely one of several designs under consideration. The response of the press would hopefully help determine whether it was worthy of further pursuit. According to Porsche NA's Bob Carlson, he was given the task of presenting a car to the press which he'd actually not even seen. The prototype had merely been described to him in conversations over the phone between the U.S. and Germany. The response of the assembled press corps was overwhelmingly positive. The concept car was presented in traditional German racing silver with red seats and interior trim. It was at once simple, elegant, and exotic, with its rounded edges and fluid lines.

1997 Boxster
Porsche NA

1998 Boxster
Porsche NA

Unlike most concept cars, the Boxster concept car did not continue long on the show circuit as most concept show cars do. Instead, attention was focused intently on getting an actual version into production and onto dealer sales and showroom floors as soon as possible. The response to the concept car had been so overwhelmingly favorable that there was an almost unanimous feeling on the part of everyone who'd seen the car that, if it could be put into production as presented in Detroit, it represented the future of Porsche. This perception on the part of the automotive press and public who had seen the car, was equally matched at Porsche by the urgent desire that the car should be created and marketed as soon as possible.

The similarities between the Boxster concept car and the actual production model are very obvious visually, but the concept car actually had no engine. It was merely a rolling body/chassis only. In the actual production version the front air intakes had to be enlarged to provide increased airflow to the dual radiators for the now water-cooled flat six-cylinder "boxer" engine. The production version was over an inch longer, nearly 20 inches wider, and a full 2 inches taller than the original concept car. Other physical differences included extending the lower span of the doors for easier entry and exit, and raising the side air intake scoops. There were changes to the interior as well. The aluminum inside door panels of the show car were replaced with less-expensive, easier-to-manufacture door panels that were able to match the buyer's interior color selections.

A primary consideration for the 986 from the beginning was easy brand identification, something which the long running 911 clearly possessed. The new Boxster should look like a Porsche, and indeed it

Porsche

does. There is no mistaking the Boxster for something else. From the front the similarities between the 911 and Boxster are obvious. The headlights, for example, are almost identical in appearance, and unlike those of the early 911s were finally integrated aerodynamically into the front fenders rather than standing out obtrusively on the front fenders, as they had until the early 1990s. The 986/Boxster was developed simultaneously in many respects along with the new 911, known in its early project stages as the 996, and this explains their similarities in appearance.

Another extremely important consideration for the Boxster from the very beginning was its price. The 911 would remain in the Porsche lineup and again return to its former flagship status. The Boxster, as a second line, would offer something new and exciting to potential customers, but it needed to be affordable. The sum of $40,000 became the target price for the new mid-engine Porsche. This amount was roughly the entry-level cost of the retiring 968 coupe (25 percent higher for the 968 roadster).

Most importantly, the Boxster would be something entirely new from Porsche—something truly exotic, desirable and, above all else, Porsche.

1999 Boxster
Porsche NA

2001 Boxster
Porsche NA

Engine

With its mid-ships configuration (and consequent front to rear weight ratio), low center of gravity, and basic overall design, the engine is perhaps the most significant single component of the Boxster. The term "Boxer," as applicable to automotive engines, refers to the opposed flat placement of horizontal cylinders on either side of a central crankshaft as well as to the reciprocal "punch-counter punch" of the pistons. Opposed engines are not a new idea, and have been used by manufacturers from Porsche to Tucker to Ferrari.

But why a flat six? If the Boxster was to be a "clean sheet," that is, an all-new car, then why not, as in the case of the 928, consider other options? A V-8, as with the 928, was more engine than a small open roadster needed. It would also not fit within the allotted space. Furthermore, its additional expense would have increased the cost both to the manufacturer and to the consumer, and pushed it beyond the desired base price of $40,000 US. The vertical four-cylinder engines of the front engine cars, while adequate were not particularly exciting by 1992, and the flat four-cylinder engines had the negative associations (to some) associated with the 912, 912 E and 914. The flat six was considered to be the optimal choice for several reasons. One important advantage of a flat engine, is its lower center of gravity. Generally speaking, the lower the overall center of gravity in a car, the better it handles. A vertical inline engine, even a four-cylinder, would be too tall for the car's desired exterior profile. Additionally, the flat six was traditionally associated with Porsche.

If the Boxster was to be really successful it should have adequate power and performance from the outset. In retrospect, the decision to use a six-cylinder engine on all model Boxsters as standard was certainly the right one.

The all aluminum alloy engine is equipped with dual overhead cams, four valves per cylinder, as well as dry sump lubrication typically found in racing cars. The initial standard Boxster 2.7-liter engine produces 217 horsepower at 6400 rpm and 192 ft.-lbs. of torque at 4750 rpm. The Boxster's aluminum engine is also water-cooled, a first for a production Porsche flat six. Water travels through individual channels within the engine to each cylinder and cylinder head allowing the engine to run at a uniform temperature, cooling both heads and cylinders simultaneously. Porsche had become accustomed to the manufacture of water-cooled inline four-cylinder production engines in the 924, 944, and 968, but a water-cooled flat-six engine for a mid-engine car offered a new set of problems for Porsche.

2001 Boxster (top) and Boxter S (bottom)
Porsche NA

Part of the problem for any rear or mid-engine car is the noise level (outside the car) generated by the proximity of engine, exhaust, and drivetrain in one area. The noise problem is also a significant consideration for passengers in any car where the engine is positioned immediately behind the seat and close to the ears. Although noise tends to travel backward as the car moves forward, the engine is actually much closer to passengers in a mid-engine car than in a front-engine car. While the familiar sound of the earlier air-cooled mid and rear engines was comforting to Porsche traditionalists, noise levels which were previously acceptable in the U.S. market in particular, were becoming less so by the 1990s. A water-cooled engine for the Boxster had to be quieter, as well as more efficient.

The placement of the radiator became a main consideration: Where and how could a radiator be positioned to function efficiently within a small sports car while at the same time not interfering with the car's

Boxster

2001 Boxster S
Porsche NA

desired aerodynamics and overall appearance? It was a problem that had been successfully faced earlier by other manufacturers of mid-engine sports cars, such as the six-cylinder Maserati Merak and its eight-cylinder sister, the Bora. Lamborghini had also addressed the problem with its Miura and Countach, as had Ford with its early 1970s mid-engine, eight-cylinder Pantera. None of these cars, however, with the exception of the Countach, used four valves per cylinder, which would generate more heat and require even more efficient cooling.

Porsche had dealt successfully with the problem of radiator placement in the front engine cars by placing the radiator in front of the engine in the usual manner. But Porsche cars do not have traditional vertical grilles. Ultimately, the decision was made to use two radiators in the front of the car, one on each side in front of each wheel. The air passing through the grill opening on each side of the lower front bumper would provide the necessary ventilation through the radiator for effective cooling. A third radiator was decided upon solely for use with the air conditioning system.

The engine's dry sump lubrication system known as "integrated dry sump lubrication" differs from standard dry sump lubrication in that instead of having an external radiator for cooling oil, often located some distance from the engine, the oil is kept in a separate tank in the engine, near the crankshaft, but separated from it, thus elimi-nating lengthy connecting hoses and the possibility of oil leaks. Oil lines are also cast directly into the block and cylinder heads, eliminating the need for drilling after casting, thus saving both time and extra expense in manufacturing. Temperature maintenance of engine oil is accomplished through the car's cooling system.

The Boxster engine's computerized Motronic ME7.2 digital management system oversees and operates every aspect of the Boxster's engine from Porsche's patented VarioCam variable valve timing, to ignition, induction, fuel supply, temperature monitoring, and even to individual knock sensors for each cylinder. Sensors throughout the engine send a constant stream of information to the Motronic's computer processor which instantly responds to changing conditions. An example is the Boxster's exhaust system which features two exhaust manifolds, one for each cylinder head. Sensors within the exhaust instantly read the exhaust composition, report to the processor separately, allowing it to instantly adjust the air-fuel mixture for maximum performance and minimum emissions. That such technological sophistication exists along with other aspects of the Boxster's operating systems would have been inconceivable 30 years ago in the days of its 914 predecessor.

2002 Boxster
Porsche NA

The ultimate question for most Boxster enthusiasts is "Will there ever be a Boxster Turbo?" The overwhelming desire to have as much speed and power available, whether or not it is ever used, seems to be an important consideration for many Porsche owners. So the question of a Boxster turbo has come up often in conversations between Porsche owners and enthusiasts. A factory production model for general public consumption is doubtful, not that such a car wouldn't likely be a commercial success. It is simply unlikely that the Boxster will ever be developed beyond the

2002 Boxster S
Porsche NA

Boxster 183

"Like the 356 of the Fifties, the Boxster shows that sports car greatness isn't about speed alone. It's a measure of how much fun you can have, how alert the car is to your demands, and how rigorously it has been developed and engineered. Strip away the style, the badges, and the hype, and what you're looking at in the Boxster is a car that redefines the breed."
~ *Automobile*

A 2002 Boxster takes to the road in this Porsche ad.
Porsche NA

911, which remains the Porsche top of the line, a position it will probably keep. The fact is that many people consider the Boxster's mid-engine layout to be inherently superior in every way to the traditional engine-behind-the-rear-axle 911 platform. This being the case, the Boxster's basic design in theory at least, allows its development, but more especially its performance, to potentially reach or even exceed that of its more expensive older brother, the flagship 911. This is understandably not a turn of events which would be desirable to Porsche with what passes for its "entry-level" car. Be that as it may, great minds think alike and an aftermarket twin-turbo conversion for the Boxster S producing a claim of 400 hp is now available through U.S. company Aerocorp.

The 2002 Porsche Boxster flat-six engine
Porsche NA

Porsche

The Aerocorp Boxster S Twin-Turbo is in production now and is available, but in limited numbers. Estimated production will be in the neighborhood of 15 cars a year. Aerocorp can deliver the car as a turnkey finished product or you can send your own Boxster S into their facilities for the modifications. The complete upgrades including body, brake, wheel, and engine modifications are about $30,000 in addition to the approximate $52,000 for the stock car. Another project which will be available for 930 Turbo owners from Aerocorp is a bolt-on replacement for the original oil-consuming stock turbo. The simple bolt-on turbo kit retails at this time for around $4,000 and includes the turbo, a muffler, and all necessary mounting hardware. The Boxster S Twin-Turbo is available through First Choice Auto Sales in East Avon, New York.

Brakes

The Boxster uses a computerized ABS braking system which features a vacuum brake booster for power assisted stopping. The standard three-channel system uses four-wheel vented discs. By three-channel, it is meant that there are three brake lines leaving the hydraulic unit, an individual brake line for each of the front wheels, with one line going to the rear which basically splits and feeds each of the rear wheels separately. The hydraulic unit is located in the Boxster's front trunk with the master cylinder and brake booster positioned along the forward part of what would normally be called the firewall in a front engine car. Basic components of the system include the brake booster and master cylinder, a computerized control unit, which is located near the brake booster, and individual ABS speed sensors within each wheel hub, which send information to the computerized control unit. Individual four-piston monoblock calipers are located on each wheel, at the rear of the front wheels, and in front of each rear wheel.

The Boxster S brake system is distinguished visually from the standard Boxster by the presence of bright red calipers clearly visible through the open wheels.

Apart from the pleasing visual effects, there are also real differences between the standard system and that of the S. For one thing, the S has larger discs (see technical specifications below), which are also drilled for more efficient cooling and dissipation of water vapor.

The Bosch ABS 5.3 traction control system was optional initially on both the standard and S versions. By 2003, both versions offered ABS 5.3 as standard, but with the Porsche Stability Management (PSM) still optional in both models. What the PSM does is provide instant braking as necessary to individual wheels.

Body

The Boxster's basic body-chassis unit is made of rigid double galvanized steel in order to inhibit the formation of rust. The body is reinforced throughout with specifically placed bars and supports that, in the event of a collision, are designed to deconstruct in a specific manner to protect the passenger cabin. This is especially important in dissipating the energy which might otherwise be transferred directly to the car's occupants. The fuel tank is securely housed in front of the firewall, ahead of the passenger compartment.

While a rollover is extremely unlikely in the Boxster due to its width, low center of gravity and excellent balance, inherent safety provisions have been made to protect passengers. The windshield pillars are reinforced by steel tubes, which in combination with the braced free-standing roll bar located behind the seats, provide an effective roll cage for the occupants.

The decision having been made from the outset that the Boxster was to be an open roadster, the problem of creating a functioning top which would be easy to operate while not detracting from the car's appearance in either up or down position became a major consideration. Porsche's solution was an automatic power convertible soft top with an optional detachable hard top (now approximately $3,000). The average sports car owner today

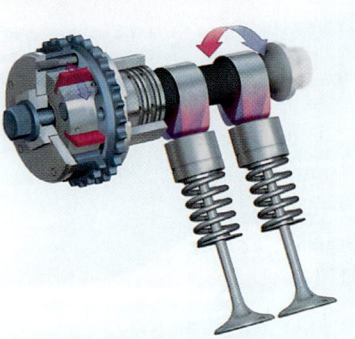

VarioCam:
Variable valve timing.
Constant gratification.

Every detail of the Boxster's hand-built engine has once again been re-examined and optimized for even greater power and efficiency. Both Boxster powerplants feature the latest evolution of VarioCam, our patented variable valve timing system that automatically adjusts the intake valve timing for maximum performance at every speed.

The introduction of a new VarioCam system delivers even more torque in the lower rev band while lowering emissions in the process. Using a rotary vane adjuster on the intake camshaft, this inventive piece of engineering works in concert with the Motronic engine management system and adapts to changing throttle inputs by adjusting the overlaps between intake and exhaust valve openings in mere fractions of a second. Essentially, VarioCam offers the benefits of two optimized Porsche engines fused into one. At lower engine speeds it advances the timing works to optimize idling for reduced fuel consumption and lower emissions.

As engine revs increase, the dynamics instantly shift: timing is adjusted for no-holds barred performance and an all-out assault on your adrenal glands.

1. Oil scavenge pump
2. VarioCam
3. Hydraulic tappets
4. Crankshaft bearing bridge
5. Resonance valve
6. Resonance induction system
7. Water channel
8. Intake valves
9. Intake camshaft
10. Single-spark ignition coils
11. Valve springs
12. Water pump
13. Lokasil-coated bores
14. Aluminum pistons
15. Crankshaft
16. Combustion chamber
17. Air-conditioning compressor
18. Oil scavenge pump
19. Drive belt for ancillaries
20. Forged connecting rods
21. Power-steering pump
22. Oil-pressure pump (obscured)

• 28 •

The impressive elements of the 2002 Boxster can be seen in this brochure page.
Porsche NA

expects a power top, and is not inclined to tolerate the inconveniences usually associated with sports car ownership in the past. And women, an increasingly larger percentage of sports car owners, are not inclined to fool with a manually operated top at all. The Boxster, like its competitors, has solved this problem permanently, with a simple electric power top. The top can be automatically raised from or lowered beneath a rear deck panel with the simple touch of a finger in a mere twelve seconds. This incredible convenience and ease of operation end forever the question of "Is it worth the time and trouble to put the top down?" Or the familiar, "What if it rains?"

The optional detachable aluminum top weighs a minimal 55 lbs. and yet provides an excellent seal against rushing air. The Boxster S is immediately visually discernible from the standard Boxster by the subtle exterior nuances of a central, third air duct in front, and twin exhaust pipes mounted side by side at the center of the stern. Other exterior differences include 17-inch wheels, and the desirable "S" designation in gold script on the rear deck lid. The "S" features a larger 3.2-liter flat six-cylinder engine boasting 250 hp at 6250 rpm with 225 ft.-lbs. of torque at 4500 rpm, as well as a six-speed manual transmission.

Options

As with all current model Porsches there are a wide array of options available to help the buyer design the car to suit his or her particular

Porsche

individual tastes. These are available for both the standard Boxster and the Boxster S.

Exterior colors: The Boxster was introduced in four standard exterior colors of Black, Guards Red, Speed Yellow, and Bizzaritz White, with six optional metallic colors of Ocean Blue Metallic, Zenith Blue Metallic, Rain Forest Green Metallic, Arena Red Metallic, Arctic Silver Metallic, and Black Metallic.

Additional exterior options include headlight washers, wind deflector, roof transport system, and a black tonneau cover. Perhaps the most desirable exterior option is a detachable hard top for winter use in inhospitable climates. It is available in any exterior color to match the body.

Interior leather color selections are: Black, Metropole Blue, Graphite Grey, Savanna Beige, with "Special Leather" selections of Boxster Red, and Nephrite Green. Matching textured carpet selections are available in the same colors.

Interior trim selections were initially offered in three packages: Carbon Package I, and Carbon Package II, Dark Burr Maple Packages I and II, Leather Packages I and II. These options allow the buyer to custom design the interior according to individual tastes. What these various interior packages include are parts of the instrument panel, speaker covers, door

2002 Boxster S
Porsche NA

Boxster

handle covers, gear shift knob, hand brake grip, door sills, floor mats, and interior lighting.

The convertible top is available in Black, Graphite Grey, and Metropole Blue.

The Aerokit option includes front and rear spoilers and aerodynamic left and right rocker panel covers.

1997 Boxster

The 1997 Boxster was offered with only one engine, a 2.5-liter (2480cc) six-cylinder, water-cooled, horizontally opposed engine, with aluminum alloy block, heads, and pistons. The valve train consisted of dual overhead camshafts, and four valves per cylinder, with electronic fuel injection. A five-speed manual transmission was standard.

The 2002 Boxster was available with an optional burr maple wood interior.
Porsche NA

Burr maple wood: Distinctive design. Timeless appeal.

Comfort within a Porsche is derived through an interior designed specifically around what you deem as necessary to pursue your passion for driving. Naturally, the ability to customize your driving environment is an integral part of this philosophy.

Nothing creates a sense of warmth and prestige more convincingly than rare, beautifully crafted wood. Like Porsche automobiles themselves, wood grows more refined with age. Precisely cut and exquisitely finished, dark burr maple lends an ambiance of stately elegance to the interior's modern-day shape and layout.

Individual wood trim pieces along the dashboard and center console are complemented by additional accent pieces trimmed in leather or painted to match the interior color. The gearshift and handbrake are wrapped in polished maple and highlighted with striking aluminum-look inlays. Each piece of wood inlaid throughout the cockpit is hand-finished for a deep luster and precise fit.

From the careful selection of the world's finest native stocks to the extensive finishing processes, the Boxster wood interior is imbued with old-world craftsmanship that upholds a Porsche tradition – quite simply, to create works of art. Objects of pure beauty that are treasured by their owner as well as their artist.

Boxster Technical Specifications (1999)

Engine:	2.7-liter, mid-placed, flat, horizontally opposed six-cylinder.
Valve train:	Dual overhead camshafts, four valves per cylinder with Variocam variable timing system
Induction:	Two-stage resonant induction
Displacement:	2.7 liters (2687cc)
Horsepower:	217 hp @ 6400 rpm
Torque:	192 ft.-lbs. @ 4750 rpm.
Bore:	85.5mm (3.37 in.)
Stroke:	78mm (2.83 in.)
Compression ratio:	11.0:1
Engine management:	Motronic ME 7.2 system
Front suspension:	Independent MacPherson struts with aluminum control arms and stabilizer bar
Rear suspension:	Independent Macpherson struts with aluminum control arms and stabilizer bar; toe angle control
Steering:	Hydraulically assisted force-sensitive rack and pinion
Steering wheel turns:	2.98 lock-to-lock
Turning circle:	35.8 ft. (10.9 m)
Brakes:	4-wheel ventilated discs with 4-piston fixed monobloc calipers, ABS
Disc diameter:	11.7 in. (298mm) front, 11.5 in. (292mm) rea
Standard wheels:	Cast alloy 6 J x 16 front, 7 J x 16 rear
Optional wheels:	7 J x 17 or 7.5 J x 18 front, 8.5 J x 17 or 9J x 18 rear
Standard tires:	205/55 ZR 16 front, 225/50 ZR 16 rear
Optional tires:	205/50 ZR 17 or 225/40 ZR 18 front, 255/40 ZR 17 or 265/35 ZR 18 rear
Transmission:	5-speed manual or optional 5-speed Tiptronic S dual mode
Curb weight:	2,778 lbs. manual, 2,888 lbs. Tiptronic S
Length:	171.0 in. (4340mm)
Height:	50.8 in. (1290mm)
Wheelbase:	95.1 in (2415mm)
Ground clearance:	4.1 in (104mm)
Track (with 16-in. wheels):	57.5-in. (1465mm) front, 60.2-in. (1528mm) rear
Cargo area volume:	9.1 cu. ft. (260 liters)
Fuel tank capacity:	16.9 gal. (64 liters)
0-62 mph:	6.6 sec. manual, 7.4 sec. Tiptronic S
Top speed:	155 mph manual, 152 mph Tiptronic S
Fuel economy:	20/28 manual, 17/25 Tiptronic S

2003 Boxster
Porsche NA

Boxster

Boxster S Technical Specifications (1999)

Engine:	Mid-mounted, water-cooled, horizontally opposed six-cylinder
Valve train:	Dual overhead camshafts, four valves per cylinder with Variocam variable timing
Induction:	Two-stage resonant induction.
Displacement:	3.2 liters (3179cc)
Horsepower:	250 @ 6250 rpm
Torque:	225 ft.-lbs. @ 4500 rpm
Bore/stroke:	93mm/78 mm
Compression ratio:	11.0:1
Engine management:	Motronic ME 7.2 system
Front suspension:	Independent MacPherson struts with aluminum control arms and stabilizer bar; toe angle control
Rear suspension:	Independent MacPherson struts with aluminum control arms and stabilizer bar
Steering:	Hydraulically assisted force-sensitive rack and pinion
Steering turns:	2.98 lock to lock
Turning circle:	35.8 ft. (10.9 m)
Brakes:	4-wheel cross-drilled ventilated discs with 4-piston monobloc calipers
Disc diameter:	12.52 in (318mm) front, 11.77 in (299 mm) rear
Standard wheels:	Cast alloy 7 J x 17 front, 8.5 J x 17 rear
Optional wheels:	Cast alloy 7.5 J x 18 front, 9 J x 18 rear
Standard tires:	205/50 ZR17 front, 255/40 ZR17 rear
Optional tires:	225/40 ZR 18 front, 265/35 ZR 18 rear
Transmission:	6-speed manual or optional 5-speed Tiptronic S dual mode
Curb weight:	2,855 lbs. manual, 2,943 lbs. Tiptronic S
Length:	171 in. (4340mm)
Width:	70.1 in. (1780mm)
Height:	50.8 in. (1290mm)
Wheelbase:	95.1 in. (2415mm)
Ground clearance:	4.1 in. (104mm)
Track (with 17-in. wheels):	57.3 in. (1455mm) front, 59.4 in. (1508mm) rear
Cargo area:	9.1 cu. ft. (260 ltr.)
Fuel tank:	16.9 gal. (64 ltr.)
0-62 mph	5.9 sec. manual, 6.5 sec. Tiptronic S
Top speed	162 mph manual, 158 mph Tiptronic S
Fuel economy	18/26 manual, 17/25 Tiptronic S

2003 Boxster S
Porsche NA

Porsche

1998 Boxster

There were no significant changes in either overall dimensions or engine displacement between 1997 and 1998.

1999 Boxster

The Boxster remained basically the same for 1999, except that the engine size on the standard model was increased from the initial 2.5-liter engine to a larger 2.7-liter engine that produced approximately 220 bhp. What was significant was the introduction of the Boxster S. While there was little visually to distinguish the standard Boxster from the new Boxster S, other than the S logo, twin exhaust pipes, and 1-inch larger wheels, the new S sported a larger 3.2-liter (195-cu. in.) 246-bhp engine.

2003 Boxster

Changes were minimal for 2003. Exterior differences included slightly redesigned front bumper and side air scoops, and more significantly, a glass rear window for the convertible top. At around $43,000, The base price remained fairly close to Porsche's initial 1997 target price of $40,000. Options including 17- or 18-inch wheels, interior selections, and performance options such as a $1,200 Stability Management system can run the price up to nearly $60,000 for the Boxster S—a hefty amount for a two-seat sports car.

2004 Boxster
Porsche NA

Boxster S Technical Specifications (2003)

Engine:	Mid-mounted, water-cooled, horizontally opposed six-cylinder
Valve train:	Dual overhead camshafts, four valves per cylinder with VarioCam variable timing
Induction:	Two-stage resonant induction
Displacement:	3.2 liters (3179 cc)
Horsepower:	258 @ 6200 rpm (SAE)
Torque:	229 ft.-lbs. @ 4600 rpm (SAE)
Bore/stroke:	93.0mm /78.0mm
Compression ratio:	11.0:1
Engine management:	Motronic ME 7.8 system
Front suspension:	Independent MacPherson struts with aluminum control arms and stabilizer bar
Rear suspension:	Independent MacPherson struts with aluminum control arms and stabilizer bar; toe-angle control
Steering:	Hydraulically assisted force-sensitive rack and pinion
Turning circle:	35.8 ft. (10.9 m)
Brakes:	4-wheel ventillated and cross-drilled discs with 4-piston fixed monobloc calipers (red), ABS 5.3
Disc diameter:	12.53 in (318mm) front, 11.78 in (299mm) rear
Standard wheels:	Cast alloy 7 J x 17 front, 8.5 J x 17 rear
Optional wheels:	Cast alloy 7.5 J x 18 front, 9 J x 18 rear
Standard tires:	205/50 ZR17 front, 255/40 ZR 17 rear
Optional tires:	225/40 ZR18 front, 265/35 ZR18 rear
Transmission:	6-speed manual or optional 5-speed Tiptronic S Dual mode automatic
Curb weight:	2,910 lbs. (manual), 2,998 lbs. (Tiptronic S)
Length:	170.0 in. (4320mm)
Width:	70.1 in. (1780mm)
Height:	50.8 in. (1290mm)
Wheelbase:	95.1 in. (2415mm)
Cargo volume:	9.2 cu. ft. (260 ltr.)
Fuel tank capacity:	16.9 gal. (64 ltr.)
0 to 62 mph:	5.7 sec. (manual), 6.4 sec. (Tiptronic S)
Top speed:	164 mph (manual), 160 mph (Tiptronic S)
Fuel economy:	18/26 mpg (manual), 17/26 mpg (Tiptronic S)

2004 Boxster S
Porsche NA

Porsche

2004 Boxster S Special Edition
Porsche NA

2004 Boxster

It's been more than 10 years since the Boxster debuted at the Detroit Auto Show (1993) and yet there was no indication that the car has aged at all. Except for the increased engine size from 2.5 to 2.7 liters in the standard Boxster, and optional larger wheels, the differences between the 1997 and 2004 were truly minimal. The car is immediately recognizable as a Porsche and has established itself as one of the best handling, most technologically advanced, and most exhilarating cars of any kind to drive. Prices have increased steadily, though not excessively in the car's run (so far), from an initial price for the standard model of just under $40,000 to approximately $51,000. The S which debuted in 1999 as a more expensive car than the standard Boxster has increased in price along with its less expensive sister, and now, fully equipped is nearly $60,000, certainly not an "entry-level" Porsche, but substantially less expensive than the current 911.

2005 Boxster

For 2005, both models received significant styling changes, more powerful engines, numerous handling enhancements, and greater safety features.

These next-generation Boxsters have more refined exterior styling that is highlighted by larger front and side air intakes, new head and front lamp treatments, more aggressive doorsills, and larger side widows.

While the size of the Boxster's 2.7-liter and the Boxster S's 3.2-liter flat-six cylinder engines remain unchanged, both have significant horsepower increases. The Boxster jumps from 225 to 240 horsepower (SAE), while the Boxster S grows from 258 to 280 horsepower (SAE) and is the most powerful engine ever in the Boxster model line. The result is a top track speed of 159 mph for the Boxster and 166 mph for the Boxster S. The Boxster races from 0 to 60 mph in 5.9 seconds, while the Boxster S achieves it in 5.2 seconds.

2005 Boxster
Porsche NA

2005 Boxster S
Porsche NA

2005 Boxster
Dan Lyons

2005 Boxster
Dan Lyons

Conclusion

The decision to recreate the thrill of the original 550 Porsche Spyder in an updated version has proved to have been an exceptionally successful one, and has gone a long way towards helping Porsche reclaim its share of the luxury sports car market. That the Boxster has changed little since its inception shows that Porsche refined the concept fairly extensively prior to the car's release to the public, even given the comparatively short time span between the concept car's debut and the production of the actual car.

Usual modifications involve increased engine size, the addition or redesign of spoilers, and different wheel and tire sizes. Today, the Boxster is much the same car as originally produced. It is immediately recognizable as a Porsche and remains highly desirable as a car to own in terms of its prestige, but more importantly it captures the thrill of top down driving in an open sports car as few others can. The Boxster is so revered and enjoyed by its owners that it's likely that given the choice between the more expensive current 911 and a Boxster S if the prices were equal, many would actually choose the Boxster over the 911.

The Boxster continues to adhere closely to the original Porsche design, yet with all the refinements of modern automotive technology. In considering the Boxster, one cannot help but imagine that Ferdinand Porsche would have been thrilled that his original Porsche concept is alive and doing very well half a century later.

Cayenne

Cayenne TIMELINE

1998
Porsche announces that it will build an SUV

2000
New Porsche Complex at Liepzig completed, testing of Cayenne begins

Cayenne represents Porsche's first giant step away from sports cars into previously uncharted territory, and in 2003 became its third line along with the evergreen 911 and the highly popular Boxster. While the car had been rumored for some time before being formally announced in 1998, the actual press debut of the Cayenne took place on September 25, on the eve of the 2002 Paris Auto Show.

The new vehicle had been in development since 1997 when the decision at Porsche had been made to compete in the evolving SUV arena, the fastest growing segment of the automotive market. While that particular niche had been expanding rapidly, especially in the U.S., it was felt that Porsche could peel off a substantial part of the upper end of that field by offering the proven prestige and reputation of the Porsche name to a method of transportation not yet associated with the Porsche name.

The model designation of a new car by a specific name, rather than with a number, also represented a major departure from established tradition at Porsche. All Porsche cars from the 356 to the current version of the 911 have always been identified with numbers rather than names. Even the popular Boxster has a numerical designation (986). The Cayenne originally received the internal designation "E1," but the new SUV was named in honor of a popular red pepper known around the world for its bold and spicy character.

The Cayenne was developed and built at the new Porsche plant in the German city of Leipzig. While the Weissach research and develop center is traditional in appearance, this can hardly be said of the Leipzig plant which opened on August 20, 2002. The most prominent feature of this sprawling complex is the huge multi-story Customer Center, which in shape resembles a traditionally cut diamond, or the top section of a cone. It is a far cry from the small shop in the Austrian city of Gmund, where the first car to bear the Porsche name was designed and built by Ferdinand Porsche and a few associates. But rather than building a new plant in the U.S. to produce its SUV, as Mercedes had done in Alabama, and BMW, in South Carolina, the Cayenne would remain a true German car, designed, constructed, and assembled in Germany.

With such a huge abundance of sport utility vehicles available already, why would any company risk the cost of introducing yet another one into an already over-saturated market? A company like Chrysler, Ford, or General

2002
Cayenne S and Turbo introduced to the world in September at the Paris Auto Show

2003
Six-cylinder Cayenne debuts

Motors can risk a potential failure with much greater ease than an independent company like Porsche, both because it has more money and because it has a wider range of other vehicles to compensate for any possibility of lagging sales in one area. Besides, Porsche has already successfully established itself as one of the premier makers of sports cars, exclusively. It would seem, on the surface, from a standpoint of pure logic, that the risk involved would not justify the expense or possible damage to the company's already well respected reputation as a maker of sports cars exclusively. It was also extremely unlikely that the Cayenne would threaten the Cadillac Escalade, Lincoln Navigator, or other large American luxury SUV since these cars already own a large portion of the upscale SUV market in the U.S., presumably a target market for Porsche. The BMW, the Mercedes, and the Range Rover, all of which are excellent cars and have enjoyed phenomenal success, would seem to already command the upper end of the imported SUV market in the U.S., and likely elsewhere as well.

It would appear that the market was already thoroughly saturated, from the lowest rung of the entry level SUV ladder to the most expensive and luxurious SUV. It was into this vast and eclectic automotive gumbo that the Cayenne was introduced.

Porsche decided that despite the wide array of existing SUVs in all categories, there was nothing on the market comparable to what Porsche intended to build, that is a car which is at once a luxury SUV, and all that entails, as well as a true off-road vehicle able to handle any terrain, no

2002 Cayenne Turbo
Porsche NA

2002 Cayenne S
Porsche NA

matter how hostile. And then the Cayenne would be a sports car, despite its size, a car which would outperform any of its so-called competitors.

The development of the Cayenne was to be an expensive, from-the-ground-up, multi-year project requiring millions of dollars. More than that, it was a bold leap of faith into a market with which Porsche was totally unfamiliar. While Mercedes is known primarily for its cars in the U.S., it is also a major player in the world market in other forms of transportation, including its trucks, which are well known for their durability and reliability. That Mercedes should offer an SUV was to be expected, given its popularity in the U.S. market. It was an entirely different undertaking for Porsche however, a company known solely for sports cars, but the risk was minimized by an agreement with Volkswagen.

While mutually beneficial arrangements between Porsche and Volkswagen were long- standing on a project-to-project basis (see 914 and 924 chapters), this arrangement would be different than either of those involving the 914 or the 924. The agreement concerning the SUV would enable Porsche and Volkswagen to each sell a similar car under different names. The Porsche Cayenne would be the most expensive version, at an entry-level price of about $50,000. The Volkswagen version, named the Touareg, would be somewhat less expensive than the Porsche Cayenne at a base price of $36,000, but still above the normal price range of any Volkswagen ever made. As it turned out, the two cars are very similar in appearance, especially when seen from either the side or the rear, but the Porsche Cayenne has a much more attractive front section than the Volkswagen version which has an oversized badge with "VW" lettering. While the Cayenne is equipped with a Porsche engine the, Touareg has an Audi 4.2 liter A-8 engine. It shares the six-speed Tiptronic transmission with the Cayenne, and also has an optional air suspension.

Cayenne 199

The Cayenne has benefited extensively from a number of sports car developments. Among them are the Cayenne's water-cooled 4.5-liter V-8, reminiscent of the all aluminum 4.5-liter V-8 originally found in the 1977 928, although the four-valve engines did not appear in the 928 until 1985. The Cayenne's full-time all-wheel drive is itself a direct descendent of the specially built all-wheel-drive 911 that won the Paris-Dakar rally in 1984. And the fully independent rear suspension of the Cayenne was preceded and heavily influenced by the 928's famed multi-link "Weissach axle," a development which revolutionized all previously held concepts of what a sports car's rear suspension should, or even could be.

The body of the Cayenne is state of the art in every way and was designed and drawn mainly on computers, rather than with individual sketches as has been traditional since the dawn of the automobile design. The modern computers allow each designer, exterior, interior, and mechanical, to access the same program so their efforts are coordinated. The high state of design technology enabled the body drawing to be rotated and seen from any angle, providing an accurate preview of the car's actual appearance.

For Porsche, the Cayenne needed to have Porsche brand identification with the Boxster and the current 911, some feature or features common to other Porsche models which immediately identified it as being a Porsche, and not merely another SUV. To this end, there had to be some visual similarities. This was accomplished to a large degree by the use of a headlight assembly, which is very similar in appearance to that of both the Boxster and the modern 911. Placing the traditional Porsche Crest midway between the lights further identifies the Cayenne as a Porsche. The large one-piece front bumper with its broad air intakes on either side of a horizontal center mounted intake increases the familial recognition even further.

2002 Cayenne *Porsche NA*

The rear of the car received dual exhausts, indicating that this was not simply another mild mannered SUV, but something far more formidable. The use of visually distinctive larger than usual alloy wheels also contributes to the impression that the Cayenne is not any ordinary SUV. As far as the Cayenne's profile, its large rear seating and storage areas clearly do not resemble that of any other Porsche, and ultimately the Cayenne, while certainly a Porsche, is clearly an SUV. But structurally, beneath the surface, the Cayenne is again much more than it seems at first glance.

Safety features

In modern motoring today, the concept of automotive safety is addressed in terms of "passive" and "active." Passive safety refers to built-in design features that are an intrinsic part of the car's basic design which, while not actively involved in the day-to-day operation of a vehicle, are there should they become necessary. In the case of the Cayenne, these elements include dual front and side air bags and dual side-curtain air bags. Porsche was, in fact, the first company to install front driver and passenger airbags on all its cars. But the air bag system used for the front passengers in the Cayenne, in keeping with the ultra high-tech nature of the entire car, features a two-stage mode that enables the sensor to instantly detect the severity of an impact and determine the appropriate level of deployment response. In addition to the front airbags, and the side curtain air bags providing front and rear head protection, there are additional airbags integrated into each of the Cayenne's front seats.

The basic structure of the Cayenne has been engineered with both comfort and safety in mind. Front and rear deformation zones are engineered into the basic "three-box" body design structure of the car so that in the event of a collision, energy is absorbed by the front and rear sections of the car, rather than transmitted directly to the occupants.

The term "active safety" refers to components of a car's standard operating systems that contribute to the avoidance of an accident in the first place. The Cayenne's all-wheel drive is the best possible arrangement for maximum traction on all road surface conditions. But the all-wheel drive found in the Cayenne is different than the system found in some 911 models for several reasons. In the first place, the engine is in the front, rather than at the rear of the car—a significant consideration in an uphill climb, especially given the uneven terrain likely to be encountered in an off-road adventure. This is the optimal and thus traditional layout for most SUVs and, in the case of the Cayenne, provides a 53/47 front-to-rear ratio, thus placing slightly more weight on the front axles. This allows the maximum effective balance of weight on uphill slopes, on or off road.

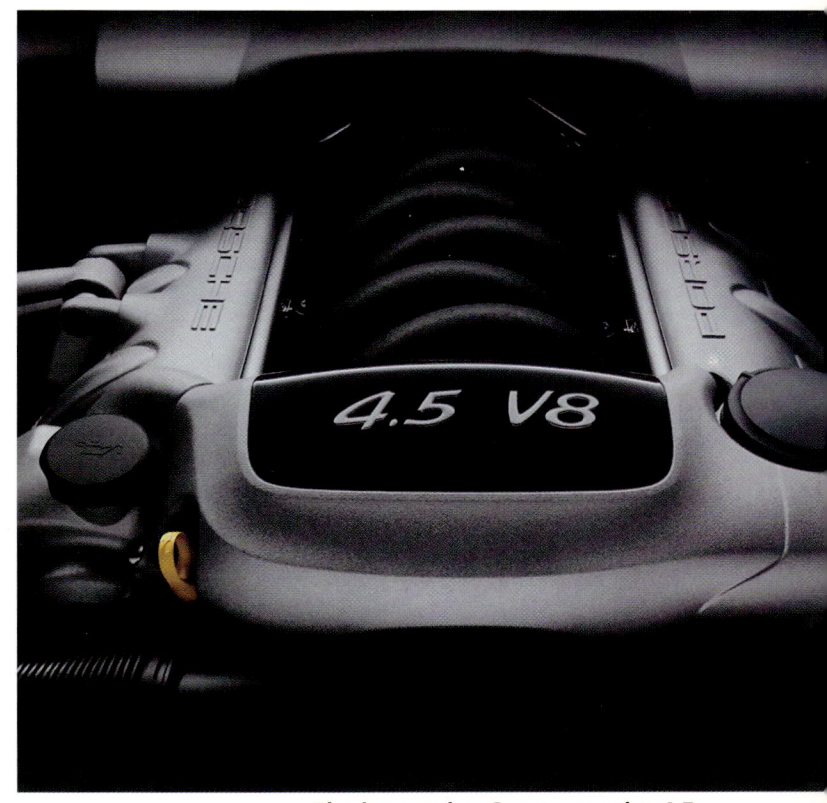

The impressive Cayenne series 4.5-liter V-8 engine.
Porsche NA

Cayenne

In the case of the Cayenne, the Porsche Traction Management (PTM) system works in conjunction with the Antilock Braking System (ABS) and determines where traction is most needed in specific circumstances. Generally, that is under normal circumstances, approximately 62 percent of power is directed to the rear wheels with the remaining 38 percent going to the front wheels. The PTM system can instantly alter that equation should circumstances require, moving as much or as little traction as necessary to either front or rear. While this sounds simple enough in theory, there are several components involved in PTM's operation. The delivery of torque to the front and rear wheels is handled by a lockable center differential.

Transmission

The six-cylinder Cayenne comes standard with the six-speed Tiptronic transmission that offers the driver the option of fully automatic or manual push-button shifting, although a fully manual six-speed was originally planned as an alternative. The normal driving range is found in the first five gears, with top speed reached in fifth gear. The sixth gear reduces engine speed to around 3800 rpm on the Cayenne S and 4,200 rpm on the Cayenne Turbo at speeds of 140 mph. The basic components of the drivetrain are the engine, transmission, transfer case, front and rear differentials. The transmission contains a torque converter that converts the lower speeds of the engine into more rpm at the driveshaft for more power in initial start-up.

What differentiates the Cayenne from other competitors is its highly sophisticated computerized electronics. The combination of the transfer case, front and rear differentials in conjunction with anti-lock brakes and

2002 Cayenne S
Porsche NA

2002 Cayenne S
Porsche NA

Porsche Traction Management immediately anticipate any road situation and respond accordingly, assuring the driver maximum traction on all surface conditions on or off road. A special feature of the Tiptronic S transmission is its "Hill Holder" mode, which automatically prevents the car from rolling backward on steep slopes.

Suspension and chassis

While independent front suspensions have been common in rear wheel drive trucks, their application to four-wheel drive SUVs is a fairly recent development. The same can be said of the independent rear suspension. For an off-road vehicle to be capable of handling extreme conditions and terrain, an independent rear suspension is a necessity.

The visual similarity of the Cayenne's multi-link rear suspension to that of the earlier 928's is apparent, but in the Cayenne, the lower aluminum wishbones generally found in Porsche sports cars have been replaced by more durable steel for off-roading. The rear suspension itself is mounted to a steel subframe and then to the Cayenne's body via heavy bushings which soften the ride, rather than bolting directly to the body as with the 928, even though the 928 also had bushings to dampen vibrations.

The front suspension is of a double-wishbone type, also fully independent, a complete departure from the steering employed in any SUV with a rigid live front axle, as with the earlier Jeep Wagoneers. It is contained within a rigid subframe, which like the rear suspension, also bolts to the underside of the car. Also, as with the rear suspension, coil springs surrounding shock absorbers are the standard issue for the Cayenne, but an air suspension, standard on the Turbo, is available as an option on the Cayenne S as well. The technical sophistication of the

A 2002 Porsche Cayenne S interior includes the in-dash computer, known as the Porsche Communications Management option.
Porsche NA

self-leveling air suspension is a marvel in its own right. The driver is able to select a desired height setting from inside the cabin, which the car's suspension automatically maintains at all speeds, regardless of the weight or persons in the car, keeping it steady and balanced in all circumstances.

A total of six different settings are available with the Turbo's standard air suspension. The first off-pavement position raises the car 2.2 inches above the normal level, providing a maximum ground clearance of 10.7 inches, while a second off-pavement setting raises the car 1 inch above normal, to a maximum ground clearance of 9.6 inches. At the normal setting, ground clearance is 8.5 inches. There are three low level settings, the first 1.1 inches below normal gives a maximum ground clearance of 7.5 inches. A special low level setting drops the car's height to 1.5 inches below normal, providing a maximum ground clearance of 6.2 inches. The lowest, or loading level, setting drops the overall height to a maximum ground clearance of 6.2 inches, that is, 2.4 inches below the normal level. This last setting can only be achieved manually with the car at rest.

A 2002 Porsche Cayenne Turbo is ready for some off-road action.
Porsche NA

Porsche

The Porsche Active Suspension Management system is standard on the Turbo and optional on the Cayenne S when equipped with optional air suspension. It allows the driver to select one of three chassis setups: comfort, normal, and sport. The PASM, which is active at all times in one of the three selected modes, constantly monitors and filters data from a number of sources, evaluates it, and makes ongoing adjustments as necessary, to maintain the selected setting. As if this weren't sophisticated enough, the PASM monitors the operator's driving style constantly and automatically switches to an appropriate mode should the driver suddenly alter his driving style or road conditions change rapidly.

The 2002 Porsche Cayenne has made it to the top of the SUV mountain.
Porsche NA

Brakes

The Cayenne's state-of-the-art four-channel braking system was designed to accommodate its high-speed potential, large towing capacity, and off-road capability. The four wheel disc brakes are internally vented with pad wear sensors on all four wheels. At the front are fixed six-piston monobloc aluminum brake calipers, thus providing maximum gripping of the discs. Front brakes are cooled by air specifically directed to them via air intakes, as well as air circulating through the open spaces of the Cayenne's large wheels. At the rear are similar four-piston monobloc aluminum calipers. The brake lines themselves are protected from puncture by rocks in off road situations. Unlike the brakes on the 911 and the Boxster S, however, the discs of the Cayenne have not been drilled for heat and water vapor dissipation in consideration of its off-road use, where dirt and other debris could be likely to get stuck in the discs. Instead, additional cooling is achieved for the front brakes by specifically directed airflow through the side intakes in the front bumper. As with brake calipers on most high end cars now, the calipers themselves are painted bright red on the Turbo, and finished in titanium on the S.

Options

Beyond the optional air suspension and Porsche Active Suspension Management, for the Cayenne S, most of the options are appearance oriented, and include interior and comfort selections such as Dark Walnut or Light Olive wood, or aluminum interior trim, a roof rack, fire

Cayenne

2003 Cayenne
Porsche NA

extinguisher, side window sunshade, side running boards, and a covered outside spare tire.

All three Cayenne models come in one of three standard exterior colors: are Black, Dark Sea Blue, and Sand White. There are eight optional colors in metallic finish which are: Prosecco Metallic, Jarama Beige Metallic, Titanium Metallic, Crystal Silver Metallic, Basalt Black Metallic, Lapis Blue Metallic, Dark Teal Metallic, and Carmon Red Metallic. Interior leather selections are available in solid colors Black and Palm Green, as well as in two-tone interior color combinations consisting of Havanna/Sand Beige, and Stone Grey/Steel Grey.

Engine

The aluminum 4.5-liter V-8 offered in the Cayenne S is the second aluminum 90-degree V-8 offered by the Porsche company in a passenger car. The first was the 4.5 liter V-8 used in the front engine 928, a car many feel to have been the best closed sports GT coupe in the world. Like the 928's engine, the block of the Cayenne's is cast in two parts with the crankshaft housed longitudinally between the upper and lower sections. Additionally, the cylinders are made from an aluminum silicon alloy, and are therefore linerless, saving both weight and the extra time and expense of cast iron cylinder liners.

As is generally the case with all Porsche engines, the basic design of the Cayenne's V-8 allows the likely increase in displacement in future models, a Porsche tradition which also occurred with the 928 which started out at 4.5 liters in 1977 but increased to 4.7, then to 5, and ultimately to a 5.4-liter size.

2003 Cayenne S.
Porsche NA

The six-cylinder Cayenne

The six-cylinder version of the Cayenne is a new addition to the line, previously existing in eight-cylinder turbocharged or

206 Porsche

Cayenne S Technical Specifications

Engine:	Front-mounted, water-cooled V-8 with alloy block, cylinder heads and pistons	**Compression ratio:**	11.5:1	**Tires:**	255/55 R 18
Displacement:	4.5 liter (4,511cc)	**Engine management:**	Motronic ME 7.7.1 system	**Transmission:**	6-speed Tiptronic S
Valve train:	Dual overhead camshafts, four valves per cylinder	**Body:**	Unitized steel with subframes	**Ground clearance (Min):**	7.6 in.
Valve timing:	Variocam variable valve timing system	**Front suspension:**	Fully independent double wishbone	**Curb weight:**	4,949 lbs.
Induction:	Resonance tube induction	**Rear suspension:**	Fully independent multi-link	**Length:**	188.3 in. (4783mm)
Horsepower:	340 @ 6000 rpm (SAE)	**Steering:**	Rack and pinion (power assisted)	**Width:**	75.9 in. (1928mm)
Torque (max):	310 ft.-lbs. @ 5500 rpm	**Turning circle:**	39.04 ft. (11.9 m)	**Height:**	66.9 in. (1699mm)
Bore/stroke:	3.66 in/3.27 in (93.0 mm/83.0mm)	**Front brakes:**	Six-piston aluminum fixed calipers	**Wheelbase:**	112.4 in. (2855mm)
		Rear brakes:	Four-piston aluminum fixed caliper	**Maximum load:**	1,797 lbs.
		Wheels:	8 J x 18	**Towing load:**	7,716 lbs.
				Fuel tank capacity:	26.2 gal. (100 ltr.)
				0-62 mph:	7.2 sec.
				Top track speed:	Approx. 150 mph

normally aspirated versions only. Like the other two members of the Cayenne family, the six offers the same state of the art features, including the optional Porsche Traction Management system, a two-speed transfer case, and full-time all wheel drive, as well as the optional Porsche Active Suspension Management system. Except for the smaller engine, the V-6 version is basically identical to the Cayenne S.

The engine block of the Cayenne six-cylinder engine is cast iron, a total departure from the alloy blocks which had become so successful and popular. The heads, however, in keeping with tradition, are aluminum and contain four valves per cylinder. Like the Boxster and the current model 911, the Cayenne's 3.2-liter, water-cooled engine has variable valve timing, which in conjunction with 3.2's variable length intake manifold, provides a broader torque range, with 229 ft.-lbs. of torque available from 2500 rpm to 5000 rpm. The six-cylinder engine is rated at 247 horsepower.

Cayenne Turbo

The Cayenne S and Turbo (list price about $95,000) are probably the most sophisticated machines of their type on this planet. *Car and Driver* magazine tested the Cayenne Turbo and

2003 Cayenne Turbo
Porsche NA

**Cayenne V-6
Technical Specifications**

Engine:	Front-mounted, water-cooled V-6 with cast-iron block, alloy cylinder heads and pistons, and four valves per cylinder.
Displacement:	3.2 liters
Horsepower:	247 @ 6000 rpm (SAE)
Engine management:	Motronic ME 7.7.1 system
Acceleration (Tiptronic S):	0-62 mph 9.7 sec.
Top speed:	133 mph (214 km/h)
Fuel economy:	15/19
Drivetrain:	Front engine with six-speed Tiptronic dual mode automatic transmission
Front suspension:	Fully independent double wishbone
Rear suspension:	Fully independent multi-link
Brakes:	Ventilated discs front and rear
Wheels:	Cast alloy: 75 J x 17
Wheelbase:	112.4 in (2855mm)
Curb weight:	Tiptronic S: 4,784 lbs. (2170 kg)
Gross vehicle weight rating:	6,493 lbs. (2945 kg)

found it had acceleration of 0 to 60 in 5.0 seconds and a top speed of 161 mph.

Special delivery

For those fortunate enough to spare both the time and money necessary, Porsche offers an exceptional European delivery program for the Cayenne. Customers picking up their Cayenne at the new Porsche factory in the German city of Leipzig, where it is built, can visit the customer center for an introduction as well as a film presentation, followed by a tour of the factory. On-board instruction is provided by an expert Porsche instructor who will acquaint buyers with every nuance of the Cayenne's many features, as well as its on and off road abilities. New Cayenne owners can take their vehicle on 2.5-mile test track and 3.7-mile off-road circuit consisting of 15 separate training courses.

Conclusion

For one who likes analog, that is, things that are purely mechanical rather than computerized, the Cayenne's vast amount of electronic circuitry and computerization might be intimidating. And while the on-board diagnostic system (OBD II) is an amazing piece of wizardry to the technophile, it is a frightening consideration to some, given the fact that a light which comes on will require a trip to the Porsche dealer's service department (the only place that has the test equipment) and at least several hundred dollars to have it turned off. But that having been said, given the Cayenne's inherent quality of design and construction, its substantial weight (which most owners will consider an asset), its unequalled technological sophistication, its obvious luxury and comfort,

2004 Cayenne (above)
Porsche NA

2003 Cayenne (left)
Porsche NA

incredible off-road capability, and its breathtaking performance, the Cayenne in either its S or Turbo configuration is undoubtedly the best SUV ever offered by any manufacturer at any price. At this stage, its commercial success as an investment for the Porsche company remains to be seen. It's only been on the market for a couple of years, and it's still too early to tell. But for the lucky number who can afford a Cayenne, it will be well worth the money, whether or not it's ever taken off the road.

2004 Cayenne S
Porsche NA

Cayenne Turbo Technical Specifications

Engine:	Front-mounted, water-cooled, twin turbocharged V-8 with alloy block, cylinder heads and pistons
Valve train:	Four overhead camshafts, four valves per cylinder
Valve timing:	Variocam variable timing
Induction:	Resonance-tube
Torque (max):	460 ft.-lbs. @ 4750 rpm
Bore/stroke:	3.66 in/3.27 in (93mm/83mm)
Compression ratio:	9.5:1
Engine management:	Motronic ME 7.7.1 system
Curb weight:	5,192 lbs.
Length:	188.4 in. (4785mm)
Width:	75.9 in. (1928mm)
Height:	66.9 in. (1699mm)
Wheelbase:	112.4 in. (2855mm)
Maximum load:	1,598 lbs.
Towing load:	7,716 lbs.
Fuel tank capacity:	26.2 gal. (100 ltr.)

2004 Cayenne Turbo
Porsche NA

Cayenne

Carrera GT

The Carrera GT debuted at the Paris Auto Show in 2000 as an open roadster. It featured a 216-cid (5.5-liter) mid-engine 68-degree V-10 that produced 558 bhp and 435 ft.-lbs. of torque. The engine is all alloy with dry sump lubrication, titanium connecting rods, and forged aluminum pistons moving within a Nikasil aluminum and silicon lining similar to that found on the 928's aluminum block. The fuel tank is positioned behind the driver but in front of the engine.

This concept car made the transition from one-off after the announcement of its production at the Detroit Auto Show in January 2002. Production would be limited to between 1,000 and 1,500 cars at a cost of approximately $450,000 each, with sales starting at the end of the following year. One wonders at the introduction of a V-10 in a Porsche since Porsche is generally associated with flat-six engines. The successful Dodge Viper features a V-10, but otherwise, the generally accepted supercar power plant is a 12 cylinder.

The Carrera GT is obviously a Porsche, but its futuristic, if not fantastic appearance indicates that it is much more than either a Boxster or a 911. It was developed by Porsche's Motorsport crew in Weissach from what would have been the LeMans 2000 prototype that was dropped due to development of the Cayenne and construction of the new Cayenne plant at Leipzig. As with all Porsche external features, the scoops and air exits are all functional. Air coming through the front bumper at each outside end is directed toward the 14.96-inch six-piston caliper front brake discs, and then, passing around them, exits behind the front wheel at the trailing edge of the front fender. Rear scoops on each side provide constant airflow to help control engine as well as rear brake temperature. As with the Carrera, a rear spoiler, in this case a wing, deploys, this time at speeds in excess of 75 mph to reduce rear end lift.

Perhaps the most interesting aspect of this car from a technical standpoint is the car's aluminum and carbon fiber frame which, with the body panels removed, resembles some futuristic robotic machine. Like the Boxster the windshield frame is reinforced, and there are unobtrusive integral rollbars located behind the passenger compartment. A removable roof panel allows full access to the sun.

The cockpit is ultra hi-tech and equally futuristic as well might be expected from the most exotic Porsche road car ever offered for sale. A rear-mounted six-speed manual transmission is operated by a shift lever placed high in the center console, within easy reach of the steering wheel.

While the very rare 959 supercar was in its day the ultimate Porsche 911, the new Carrera GT replaces it now as the most exotic Porsche ever built.

Carrera GT Technical Specifications

Engine:	5.7-liter mid-mounted longitudinal, water-cooled, V-10, four-valves per cylinder
Lubrication:	Dry sump
Engine management:	Bosch Motronic 7.1.1
Horsepower:	612 hp (SAE) at 8000 rpm
Torque:	435 ft.-lbs. (SAE) at 5750 rpm
Engine weight:	472 lbs.
Compression:	12.0:1
Type:	Six-speed manual transmission
Clutch:	6.65-in.-diameter ceramic composite
0 to 62 mph:	3.9 seconds
Top speed:	205 mph
Maximum engine speed:	8400 rpm
Brakes:	Power assisted dual circuit four wheel, 14.96 x 1.34-in. ceramic
Wheels:	Five-spoke forged magnesium
Front wheel:	19 x 9.5J
Rear wheel:	20 x 12.5J
Front tires:	265/30R19
Rear:	335/30R20
Weight:	3,043 lbs.
Height:	45.9 in.
Width:	75.6 in.
Length:	179.4 in.
Wheelbase:	107.5 in.

2004 Carrera GT

Porsche

2003 Carrera GT
Porsche NA

2004 Carrera GT engine

Every design element visible on the 2004 Porsche Carrera GT suggests speed.
Porsche NA

Porsche

2004 Carrera GT interior

2004 Carrera GT

Carrera GT 215

Porsche Price Guide

Vehicle Condition Scale

6	5	4	3	2	1
Parts car: May or may not be running, but is weathered, wrecked and/or stripped to the point of being useful primarily for parts.	**Restorable:** Needs complete restoration of body, chassis and interior. May or may not be running, but isn't weathered, wrecked or stripped to the point of being useful only for parts.	**Good:** A driveable vehicle needing no or only minor work to be functional. Also, a deteriorated restoration or a very poor amateur restoration. All components may need restoration to be "excellent," but the car is mostly useable "as is."	**Very Good:** Complete operable original or older restoration. Also, a very good amateur restoration, all presentable and serviceable inside and out. Plus, a combination of well-done restoration and good operable components or a partially restored car with all parts necessary to compete and/or valuable NOS parts.	**Fine:** Well-restored or a combination of superior restoration and excellent original parts. Also, extremely well-maintained original vehicle showing minimal wear.	**Excellent:** Restored to current maximum professional standards of quality in every area, or perfect original with components operating and apearing as new. A 95-plus point show car that is not driven.

	6	5	4	3	2	1
1950 Model 356, 1100cc, 40 hp						
Cpe	1,500	4,550	7,600	15,200	26,600	38,000
1951 Model 356, 1100cc, 40 hp						
Cpe	900	2,750	4,600	9,200	16,100	23,000
Cabr	1,200	3,600	6,000	12,000	21,000	30,000
1952 Model 356, 1100cc, 40 hp						
Cpe	900	2,750	4,600	9,200	16,100	23,000
Cabr	1,440	4,320	7,200	14,400	25,200	36,000
1953 Model 356, 40 hp						
Cpe	900	2,750	4,600	9,200	16,100	23,000
Cabr	1,440	4,320	7,200	14,400	25,200	36,000
1954 Model 356, 1.5 liter, 55 hp						
Spds	2,700	8,050	13,400	26,800	46,900	67,000
Cpe	1,000	3,000	5,000	10,000	17,500	25,000
Cabr	1,450	4,300	7,200	14,400	25,200	36,000
1954 Model 356, Super, 1.5 liter,						
Spds	2,800	8,400	14,000	28,000	49,000	70,000
Cpe	1,100	3,350	5,600	11,200	19,600	28,000
Cabr	1,550	4,700	7,800	15,600	27,300	39,000
1955 Model 356, 4-cyl., 55 hp						
Spds	2,700	8,050	13,400	26,800	46,900	67,000
Cpe	1,000	3,000	5,000	10,000	17,500	25,000
Cabr	1,550	4,700	7,800	15,600	27,300	39,000
1955 Model 356, Super, 1.5 liter, 70 hp						
Spds	3,100	9,250	15,400	30,800	53,900	77,000
Cpe	1,050	3,100	5,200	10,400	18,200	26,000
Cabr	1,650	4,900	8,200	16,400	28,700	41,000

	6	5	4	3	2	1
1956 Model 356A, Normal, 1.6 liter, 60 hp						
Spds	2,550	7,700	12,800	25,600	44,800	64,000
Cpe	1,100	3,250	5,400	10,800	18,900	27,000
Cabr	1,550	4,700	7,800	15,600	27,300	39,000
1956 Model 356A, Super, 1.6 liter, 75 hp						
Spds	3,100	9,250	15,400	30,800	53,900	77,000
Cpe	1,100	3,350	5,600	11,200	19,600	28,000
Cabr	1,700	5,150	8,600	17,200	30,100	43,000
1956 Model 356A, Carrera, 1.5 liter, 100 hp						
Spds	5,700	17,000	28,400	56,800	99,500	142,000
Cpe	2,650	7,900	13,200	26,400	46,200	66,000
Cabr	2,900	8,650	14,400	28,800	50,400	72,000
1957 Model 356A, Normal, 1.6 liter, 60 hp						
Spds	2,600	7,800	13,000	26,000	45,500	65,000
Cpe	1,100	3,350	5,600	11,200	19,600	28,000
Cabr	1,550	4,700	7,800	15,600	27,300	39,000
1957 Model 356A, Super, 1.6 liter, 75 hp						
Spds	3,500	10,400	17,400	34,800	61,000	87,000
Cpe	1,100	3,350	5,600	11,200	19,600	28,000
Cabr	1,700	5,150	8,600	17,200	30,100	43,000
1957 Model 356A, Carrera, 1.5 liter, 100 hp						
Spds	5,700	17,000	28,400	56,800	99,500	142,000
Cpe	2,650	7,900	13,200	26,400	46,200	66,000
Cabr	2,900	8,650	14,400	28,800	50,400	72,000
1958 Model 356A, Normal, 1.6 liter, 60 hp						
Spds	2,600	7,800	13,000	26,000	45,500	65,000
Cpe	1,100	3,250	5,400	10,800	18,900	27,000
Cabr	1,550	4,700	7,800	15,600	27,300	39,000
HT	1,250	3,700	6,200	12,400	21,700	31,000

	6	5	4	3	2	1
1958 Model 356A, Super, 1.6 liter, 75 hp						
Spds	3,500	10,400	17,400	34,800	61,000	87,000
Cpe	1,100	3,350	5,600	11,200	19,600	28,000
HT	1,750	5,300	8,800	17,600	30,800	44,000
Cabr	1,700	5,150	8,600	17,200	30,100	43,000
1958 Model 356A, Carrera, 1.5 liter, 100 hp						
Spds	5,700	17,000	28,400	56,800	99,500	142,000
Cpe	2,650	7,900	13,200	26,400	46,200	66,000
HT	2,650	7,900	13,200	26,400	46,200	66,000
Cabr	3,700	11,000	18,400	36,800	64,500	92,000
1959 Model 356A, Normal, 60 hp						
Cpe	950	2,900	4,800	9,600	16,800	24,000
Cpe/HT	1,150	3,500	5,800	11,600	20,300	29,000
Conv D	1,200	3,600	6,000	12,000	21,000	30,000
Cabr	1,250	3,700	6,200	12,400	21,700	31,000
1959 Model 356A, Super, 75 hp						
Cpe	1,100	3,350	5,600	11,200	19,600	28,000
Cpe/HT	1,250	3,700	6,200	12,400	21,700	31,000
Conv D	1,300	3,850	6,400	12,800	22,400	32,000
Cabr	1,300	3,950	6,600	13,200	23,100	33,000

	6	5	4	3	2	1
1959 Model 356A, Carrera, 1.6 liter, 105 hp						
Cpe	2,650	7,900	13,200	26,400	46,200	66,000
Cpe/HT	2,650	7,900	13,200	26,400	46,200	66,000
Cabr	3,700	11,000	18,400	36,800	64,500	92,000
1960 Model 356B, Normal, 1.6 liter, 60 hp						
Cpe	1,100	3,250	5,400	10,800	18,900	27,000
HT	1,250	3,700	6,200	12,400	21,700	31,000
Rds	1,450	4,300	7,200	14,400	25,200	36,000
Cabr	1,500	4,450	7,400	14,800	25,900	37,000
1960 Model 356B, Super, 1.6 liter, 75 hp						
Cpe	1,100	3,350	5,600	11,200	19,600	28,000
HT	1,300	3,850	6,400	12,800	22,400	32,000
Rds	1,500	4,450	7,400	14,800	25,900	37,000
Cabr	1,500	4,550	7,600	15,200	26,600	38,000
1960 Model 356B, Super 90, 1.6 liter, 90 hp						
Cpe	1,200	3,600	6,000	12,000	21,000	30,000
HT	1,350	4,100	6,800	13,600	23,800	34,000
Rds	1,550	4,700	7,800	15,600	27,300	39,000
Cabr	1,600	4,800	8,000	16,000	28,000	40,000

2004 Carrera 4S

Price Guide 217

	6	5	4	3	2	1
1961 Model 356B, Normal, 1.6 liter, 60 hp						
Cpe	1,100	3,250	5,400	10,800	18,900	27,000
HT	1,250	3,700	6,200	12,400	21,700	31,000
Rds	1,450	4,300	7,200	14,400	25,200	36,000
Cabr	1,500	4,450	7,400	14,800	25,900	37,000
1961 Model 356B, Super 90, 1.6 liter, 90 hp						
Cpe	1,150	3,500	5,800	11,600	20,300	29,000
HT	1,300	3,950	6,600	13,200	23,100	33,000
Rds	1,550	4,700	7,800	15,600	27,300	39,000
Cabr	1,600	4,800	8,000	16,000	28,000	40,000
1961 Model 356B, Carrera, 2.0 liter, 130 hp						
Cpe	3,300	9,850	16,400	32,800	57,400	82,000
Rds	3,700	11,000	18,400	36,800	64,500	92,000
Cabr	4,900	14,600	24,400	48,800	85,500	122,000
1962 Model 356B, Normal, 1.6 liter, 60 hp						
Cpe	1,100	3,250	5,400	10,800	18,900	27,000
HT	1,250	3,700	6,200	12,400	21,700	31,000
1962 Model 356B, Super 90, 1.6 liter, 90 hp						
Cpe	1,100	3,350	5,600	11,200	19,600	28,000
HT	1,300	3,850	6,400	12,800	22,400	32,000
Rds	1,500	4,450	7,400	14,800	25,900	37,000
Cabr	1,500	4,550	7,600	15,200	26,600	38,000
1962 Model 356B, Carrera 2, 2.0 liter, 130 hp						
Cpe	3,300	9,850	16,400	32,800	57,400	82,000
Rds	3,700	11,000	18,400	36,800	64,500	92,000
Cabr	4,900	14,600	24,400	48,800	85,500	122,000
1963 Model 356C, Standard, 1.6 liter, 75 hp						
Cpe	950	2,900	4,800	9,600	16,800	24,000
Cabr	1,300	3,850	6,400	12,800	22,400	32,000
1963 Model 356C, SC, 1.6 liter, 95 hp						
Cpe	1,050	3,100	5,200	10,400	18,200	26,000
Cabr	1,300	3,950	6,600	13,200	23,100	33,000
1963 Model 356C, Carrera 2, 2.0 liter, 130 hp						
Cpe	3,300	9,850	16,400	32,800	57,400	82,000
Cabr	4,900	14,600	24,400	48,800	85,500	122,000
1964 Model 356C, Normal, 1.6 liter, 75 hp						
Cpe	950	2,900	4,800	9,600	16,800	24,000
Cabr	1,300	3,850	6,400	12,800	22,400	32,000
1964 Model 356C, SC, 1.6 liter, 95 hp						
Cpe	1,050	3,100	5,200	10,400	18,200	26,000
Cabr	1,350	4,100	6,800	13,600	23,800	34,000
1964 Model 356C, Carrera 2, 2.0 liter, 130 hp						
Cpe	3,300	9,850	16,400	32,800	57,400	82,000
Cabr	4,900	14,600	24,400	48,800	85,500	122,000
1965 Model 356C, 1.6 liter, 75 hp						
Cpe	1,000	3,000	5,000	10,000	17,500	25,000
Cabr	1,300	3,850	6,400	12,800	22,400	32,000

	6	5	4	3	2	1
1965 Model 356SC, 1.6 liter, 95 hp						
Cpe	1,050	3,100	5,200	10,400	18,200	26,000
Cabr	1,300	3,950	6,600	13,200	23,100	33,000
1966 Model 912, 4-cyl., 90 hp						
Cpe	900	2,750	4,600	9,200	16,100	23,000
1966 Model 911, 6-cyl., 130 hp						
Cpe	1,000	3,000	5,000	10,000	17,500	25,000
1967 Model 912, 4-cyl., 90 hp						
Cpe	900	2,750	4,600	9,200	16,100	23,000
Targa	1,000	3,000	5,000	10,000	17,500	25,000
1967 Model 911, 6-cyl., 110 hp						
Cpe	1,000	3,000	5,000	10,000	17,500	25,000
Targa	1,100	3,250	5,400	10,800	18,900	27,000
1967 Model 911S, 6-cyl., 160 hp						
Cpe	1,150	3,500	5,800	11,600	20,300	29,000
Targa	1,200	3,600	6,000	12,000	21,000	30,000
1968 Model 912, 4-cyl., 90 hp						
Cpe	950	2,900	4,800	9,600	16,800	24,000
Targa	1,050	3,100	5,200	10,400	18,200	26,000
1968 Model 911, 6-cyl., 130 hp						
Cpe	1,100	3,250	5,400	10,800	18,900	27,000
Targa	1,100	3,350	5,600	11,200	19,600	28,000
1968 Model 911L, 6-cyl., 130 hp						
Cpe	1,100	3,350	5,600	11,200	19,600	28,000
Targa	1,150	3,500	5,800	11,600	20,300	29,000
1968 Model 911S, 6-cyl., 160 hp						
Cpe	1,200	3,600	6,000	12,000	21,000	30,000
Targa	1,300	3,850	6,400	12,800	22,400	32,000
1969 Model 912, 4-cyl., 90 hp						
Cpe	950	2,900	4,800	9,600	16,800	24,000
Targa	1,000	3,000	5,000	10,000	17,500	25,000
1969 Model 911T, 6-cyl., 110 hp						
Cpe	1,100	3,250	5,400	10,800	18,900	27,000
Targa	1,150	3,500	5,800	11,600	20,300	29,000
1969 Model 911E, 6-cyl., 140 hp						
Cpe	1,100	3,250	5,400	10,800	18,900	27,000
Targa	1,150	3,500	5,800	11,600	20,300	29,000
1969 Model 911S, 6-cyl., 170 hp						
Cpe	1,200	3,600	6,000	12,000	21,000	30,000
Targa	1,300	3,850	6,400	12,800	22,400	32,000
1970 Model 914, 4-cyl., 1.7 liter, 80 hp						
Cpe/Targa	900	2,650	4,400	8,800	15,400	22,000
1970 Model 914/6, 6-cyl., 2.0 liter, 110 hp						
Cpe/Targa	950	2,900	4,800	9,600	16,800	24,000

	6	5	4	3	2	1
1970 Model 911T, 6-cyl., 125 hp						
Cpe	1,000	3,000	5,000	10,000	17,500	25,000
Targa	1,100	3,250	5,400	10,800	18,900	27,000
1970 Model 911E, 6-cyl., 155 hp						
Cpe	1,050	3,100	5,200	10,400	18,200	26,000
Targa	1,100	3,350	5,600	11,200	19,600	28,000
1970 Model 911S, 6-cyl., 180 hp						
Cpe	1,200	3,600	6,000	12,000	21,000	30,000
Targa	1,300	3,950	6,600	13,200	23,100	33,000
1971 Model 914, 4-cyl., 1.7 liter, 80 hp						
Cpe/Targa	900	2,650	4,400	8,800	15,400	22,000
1971 Model 914/6, 6-cyl., 2.0 liter, 110 hp						
Cpe/Targa	950	2,900	4,800	9,600	16,800	24,000
1971 Model 911T, 6-cyl., 125 hp						
Cpe	1,000	3,000	5,000	10,000	17,500	25,000
Targa	1,100	3,250	5,400	10,800	18,900	27,000
1971 Model 911E, 6-cyl., 155 hp						
Cpe	1,050	3,100	5,200	10,400	18,200	26,000
Targa	1,100	3,350	5,600	11,200	19,600	28,000
1971 Model 911S, 6-cyl., 180 hp						
Cpe	1,300	3,850	6,400	12,800	22,400	32,000
Targa	1,400	4,200	7,000	14,000	24,500	35,000
1972 Model 914, 4-cyl., 1.7 liter, 80 hp						
Cpe/Targa	900	2,650	4,400	8,800	15,400	22,000
1972 Model 911T, 6-cyl., 130 hp						
Cpe	1,000	3,000	5,000	10,000	17,500	25,000
Targa	1,100	3,250	5,400	10,800	18,900	27,000
1972 Model 911E, 6-cyl., 165 hp						
Cpe	950	2,900	4,800	9,600	16,800	24,000
Targa	1,100	3,250	5,400	10,800	18,900	27,000
1972 Model 911S, 6-cyl., 190 hp						
Cpe	1,200	3,600	6,000	12,000	21,000	30,000
Targa	1,300	3,950	6,600	13,200	23,100	33,000
1973 Model 914, 4-cyl., 1.8 liter, 76 hp						
Cpe/Targa	900	2,650	4,400	8,800	15,400	22,000
1973 Model 914, 4-cyl., 2.0 liter, 95 hp						
Cpe/Targa	950	2,900	4,800	9,600	16,800	24,000
1973 Model 911T, 6-cyl., 140 hp						
Cpe	1,050	3,100	5,200	10,400	18,200	26,000
Targa	1,100	3,350	5,600	11,200	19,600	28,000
1973 Model 911E, 6-cyl., 165 hp						
Cpe	1,050	3,100	5,200	10,400	18,200	26,000
Targa	1,100	3,350	5,600	11,200	19,600	28,000

	6	5	4	3	2	1
1973 Model 911S, 6-cyl., 190 hp						
Cpe	1,200	3,600	6,000	12,000	21,000	30,000
Targa	1,300	3,950	6,600	13,200	23,100	33,000
1974 Model 914, 4-cyl., 1.8 liter, 76 hp						
Cpe/Targa	900	2,650	4,400	8,800	15,400	22,000
1974 Model 914, 4-cyl., 2 liter, 95 hp						
Cpe/Targa	950	2,900	4,800	9,600	16,800	24,000
1974 Model 911, 6-cyl., 150 hp						
Cpe	1,100	3,250	5,400	10,800	18,900	27,000
Targa	1,150	3,500	5,800	11,600	20,300	29,000
1974 Model 911S, 6-cyl., 175 hp						
Cpe	1,150	3,500	5,800	11,600	20,300	29,000
Targa	1,250	3,700	6,200	12,400	21,700	31,000
1974 Model 911 Carrera, 6-cyl., 175 hp						
Cpe	1,350	4,100	6,800	13,600	23,800	34,000
Targa	1,450	4,300	7,200	14,400	25,200	36,000
NOTE: Add 10 percent for RS. Add 20 percent for RSR.						
1975 Model 914, 4-cyl., 1.8 liter, 76 hp						
Cpe/Targa	750	2,300	3,800	7,600	13,300	19,000
1975 Model 914, 4-cyl., 2 liter, 95 hp						
Cpe/Targa	800	2,400	4,000	8,000	14,000	20,000
1975 Model 911S, 6-cyl., 175 hp						
Cpe	1,100	3,350	5,600	11,200	19,600	28,000
Targa	1,150	3,500	5,800	11,600	20,300	29,000
1975 Model 911 Carrera, 6-cyl., 210 hp						
Cpe	1,300	3,950	6,600	13,200	23,100	33,000
Targa	1,400	4,200	7,000	14,000	24,500	35,000
1976 Model 914, 4-cyl., 2 liter, 95 hp						
Cpe/Targa	800	2,400	4,000	8,000	14,000	20,000
1976 Model 912E, 4-cyl., 90 hp						
Cpe	1,000	3,000	5,000	10,000	17,500	25,000
1976 Model 911S, 6-cyl., 165 hp						
Cpe	1,100	3,350	5,600	11,200	19,600	28,000
Cpe 3.0	1,750	5,200	8,700	17,400	30,400	43,500
Targa	1,200	3,600	6,000	12,000	21,000	30,000
1976 Model 930, Turbo & Turbo Carrera						
Cpe	1,700	5,050	8,400	16,800	29,400	42,000
1977 Model 924, 4-cyl., 95 hp						
Cpe	800	2,400	4,000	8,000	14,000	20,000
1977 Model 911S, 6-cyl., 165 hp						
Cpe	1,050	3,100	5,200	10,400	18,200	26,000
Targa	1,100	3,350	5,600	11,200	19,600	28,000
Targa 3.0 (200 hp)	1,750	5,200	8,700	17,400	30,400	43,500

	6	5	4	3	2	1
1977 Model 930 Turbo, 6-cyl., 245 hp						
Cpe	1,700	5,050	8,400	16,800	29,400	42,000
1978 Model 924						
Cpe	800	2,400	4,000	8,000	14,000	20,000
1978 Model 911SC						
Cpe	1,100	3,250	5,400	10,800	18,900	27,000
Cpe Targa	1,100	3,350	5,600	11,200	19,600	28,000
1978 Model 928						
Cpe	1,200	3,600	6,000	12,000	21,000	30,000
1978 Model 930						
Cpe	1,700	5,050	8,400	16,800	29,400	42,000
1979 Model 924						
Cpe	750	2,300	3,800	7,600	13,300	19,000
1979 Model 911SC						
Cpe	1,050	3,100	5,200	10,400	18,200	26,000
Targa	1,100	3,350	5,600	11,200	19,600	28,000
1979 Model 930						
Cpe	1,650	4,900	8,200	16,400	28,700	41,000
1979 Model 928						
Cpe	1,700	5,050	8,400	16,800	29,400	42,000

	6	5	4	3	2	1
1980 Model 924						
Cpe	750	2,300	3,800	7,600	13,300	19,000
Cpe Turbo	900	2,650	4,400	8,800	15,400	22,000
1980 Model 911SC						
Cpe	1,100	3,350	5,600	11,200	19,600	28,000
Cpe Targa	1,150	3,500	5,800	11,600	20,300	29,000
1980 Model 928						
Cpe	1,250	3,700	6,200	12,400	21,700	31,000
1981 Model 924						
Cpe	700	2,150	3,600	7,200	12,600	18,000
Cpe Turbo	800	2,400	4,000	8,000	14,000	20,000
1981 Model 911SC						
Cpe	1,100	3,250	5,400	10,800	18,900	27,000
Cpe Targa	1,100	3,350	5,600	11,200	19,600	28,000
1981 Model 928						
Cpe	1,300	3,850	6,400	12,800	22,400	32,000

1997 Boxster

Porsche

	6	5	4	3	2	1
1982 Model 924						
Cpe	700	2,050	3,400	6,800	11,900	17,000
Cpe Turbo	750	2,300	3,800	7,600	13,300	19,000
1982 Model 911SC						
Cpe	1,000	3,000	5,000	10,000	17,500	25,000
Cpe Targa	1,050	3,100	5,200	10,400	18,200	26,000
1982 Model 928						
Cpe	1,300	3,850	6,400	12,800	22,400	32,000
1983 Model 944						
Cpe	700	2,050	3,400	6,800	11,900	17,000
1983 Model 911SC						
Cpe	1,000	3,000	5,000	10,000	17,500	25,000
Cpe Targa	1,050	3,100	5,200	10,400	18,200	26,000
Conv	1,100	3,350	5,600	11,200	19,600	28,000
1983 Model 928						
Cpe	1,350	4,100	6,800	13,600	23,800	34,000
1984 Model 944						
2d Cpe	700	2,050	3,400	6,800	11,900	17,000
1984 Model 911						
2d Cpe	1,000	3,000	5,000	10,000	17,500	25,000
2d Cpe Targa	1,100	3,350	5,600	11,200	19,600	28,000
2d Conv	1,250	3,700	6,200	12,400	21,700	31,000
1984 Model 928S						
Cpe	1,350	4,100	6,800	13,600	23,800	34,000
1985 Model 944						
2d Cpe	700	2,150	3,600	7,200	12,600	18,000
1985 Model 911						
Carrera 2d Cpe	1,100	3,250	5,400	10,800	18,900	27,000
Carrera 2d Conv	1,300	3,950	6,600	13,200	23,100	33,000
Targa 2d Cpe	1,200	3,600	6,000	12,000	21,000	30,000
1985 Model 928S						
2d Cpe	1,400	4,200	7,000	14,000	24,500	35,000
1986 Model 944						
2d Cpe	750	2,300	3,800	7,600	13,300	19,000
Turbo 2d Cpe	800	2,400	4,000	8,000	14,000	20,000
1986 Model 911 Carrera						
2d Cpe	1,450	4,300	7,200	14,400	25,200	36,000
2d Conv	1,700	5,050	8,400	16,800	29,400	42,000
2d Cpe Targa	1,500	4,550	7,600	15,200	26,600	38,000
2d Cpe Turbo	2,050	6,100	10,200	20,400	35,700	51,000

	6	5	4	3	2	1
1986 Model 928S						
2d Cpe	1,400	4,200	7,000	14,000	24,500	35,000
1987 Model 924S						
2d Cpe	750	2,300	3,800	7,600	13,300	19,000
1987 Model 928S4						
2d Cpe	2,000	6,000	10,000	20,000	35,000	50,000
1987 Model 944						
2d Cpe	900	2,650	4,400	8,800	15,400	22,000
2d Cpe Turbo	950	2,900	4,800	9,600	16,800	24,000
1987 Model 944S						
2d Cpe	900	2,750	4,600	9,200	16,100	23,000
1987 Model 911 Carrera						
2d Cpe	1,450	4,300	7,200	14,400	25,200	36,000
2d Cpe Targa	1,500	4,550	7,600	15,200	26,600	38,000
2d Conv	1,700	5,050	8,400	16,800	29,400	42,000
2d Turbo	2,050	6,100	10,200	20,400	35,700	51,000
1988 Porsche						
2d 924S Cpe	900	2,650	4,400	8,800	15,400	22,000
2d 944 Cpe	950	2,900	4,800	9,600	16,800	24,000
2d 944S Cpe	1,000	3,000	5,000	10,000	17,500	25,000
2d 944 Cpe Turbo	1,050	3,100	5,200	10,400	18,200	26,000
2d 911 Cpe Carrera	1,700	5,150	8,600	17,200	30,100	43,000
2d 911 Cpe Targa	1,750	5,300	8,800	17,600	30,800	44,000
2d 911 Conv	1,900	5,650	9,400	18,800	32,900	47,000
2d 928S4 Cpe	1,300	3,950	6,600	13,200	23,100	33,000
2d 911 Turbo Conv	2,450	7,300	12,200	24,400	42,700	61,000
1989 Model 944						
2d Cpe	1,000	3,000	5,000	10,000	17,500	25,000
2d Cpe (Turbo)	1,100	3,250	5,400	10,800	18,900	27,000
2d S2 Cpe	1,150	3,500	5,800	11,600	20,300	29,000
2d S2 Conv	1,400	4,200	7,000	14,000	24,500	35,000

Price Guide | **221**

	6	5	4	3	2	1
1989 Model 911						
2d Carrera	1,600	4,800	8,000	16,000	28,000	40,000
2d Targa	1,650	4,900	8,200	16,400	28,700	41,000
2d Conv	1,900	5,750	9,600	19,200	33,600	48,000
2d Conv Turbo	2,450	7,300	12,200	24,400	42,700	61,000
1989 Model 928						
2d Cpe	1,300	3,950	6,600	13,200	23,100	33,000
1990 Model 944S						
2d Cpe	950	2,900	4,800	9,600	16,800	24,000
2d Conv	1,100	3,250	5,400	10,800	18,900	27,000

	6	5	4	3	2	1
1990 Model 911						
2d Carrera Cpe 2P	1,500	4,550	7,600	15,200	26,600	38,000
2d Targa Cpe 2P	1,550	4,700	7,800	15,600	27,300	39,000
2d Carrera Conv 2P	1,850	5,500	9,200	18,400	32,200	46,000
2d Carrera Cpe 4P	1,700	5,050	8,400	16,800	29,400	42,000
2d Targa Cpe 4P	1,700	5,150	8,600	17,200	30,100	43,000
2d Carrera Conv 4P	1,900	5,750	9,600	19,200	33,600	48,000
1990 Model 928S						
2d Cpe	1,300	3,850	6,400	12,800	22,400	32,000
1991 Model 944S						
2d Cpe 2P	1,000	3,000	5,000	10,000	17,500	25,000
2d Conv 2P	1,100	3,350	5,600	11,200	19,600	28,000

2004 Cayenne

Porsche

	6	5	4	3	2	1
1991 Model 911						
2d Carrera 2P	1,650	4,900	8,200	16,400	28,700	41,000
2d Carrera Targa 2P	1,700	5,050	8,400	16,800	29,400	42,000
2d Carrera Conv 2P	1,900	5,750	9,600	19,200	33,600	48,000
2d Carrera 4P	1,800	5,400	9,000	18,000	31,500	45,000
2d Carrera Targa 4P	1,850	5,500	9,200	18,400	32,200	46,000
2d Carrera Conv 4P	2,050	6,100	10,200	20,400	35,700	51,000
2d Turbo Cpe	2,150	6,500	10,800	21,600	37,800	54,000
1991 Model 928S						
2d Cpe 4P	1,250	3,700	6,200	12,400	21,700	31,000
1992 968, 4-cyl.						
2d Cpe	1,200	3,600	6,000	12,000	21,000	30,000
2d Conv	1,400	4,200	7,000	14,000	24,500	35,000

	6	5	4	3	2	1
1992 911, 6-cyl.						
2d Cpe 2P	1,850	5,500	9,200	18,400	32,200	46,000
2d Targa Cpe 2P	1,900	5,650	9,400	18,800	32,900	47,000
2d Conv 2P	2,050	6,100	10,200	20,400	35,700	51,000
2d Cpe 4P	1,900	5,750	9,600	19,200	33,600	48,000
2d Targa Cpe 4P	1,950	5,900	9,800	19,600	34,300	49,000
2d Conv 4P	2,150	6,500	10,800	21,600	37,800	54,000
2d Turbo Cpe	2,450	7,300	12,200	24,400	42,700	61,000
1993 968, 4-cyl.						
2d Cpe	1,250	3,700	6,200	12,400	21,700	31,000
2d Conv	1,450	4,300	7,200	14,400	25,200	36,000

2004 911 Turbo

Price Guide

	6	5	4	3	2	1
1993 911, 6-cyl.						
2d Carrera 2	1,900	5,750	9,600	19,200	33,600	48,000
2d Carrera Targa	2,100	6,250	10,400	20,800	36,400	52,000
2d Carrera Cabrio	2,150	6,500	10,800	21,600	37,800	54,000
2d Carrera 4	2,250	6,700	11,200	22,400	39,200	56,000
2d Carrera Turbo	2,700	8,050	13,400	26,800	46,900	67,000
1993 928 GTS, V-8						
2d Cpe	2,100	6,250	10,400	20,800	36,400	52,000
1994 968, 4-cyl.						
2d Cpe	900	2,650	4,400	8,800	15,400	22,000
2d Conv	1,100	3,250	5,400	10,800	18,900	27,000
1994 911, 6-cyl.						
2d Cpe Carrera 2	1,600	4,800	8,000	16,000	28,000	40,000
2d Cpe Carrera 2 Targa	1,700	5,050	8,400	16,800	29,400	42,000
2d Cpe Carrera 2 Conv	1,750	5,300	8,800	17,600	30,800	44,000
2d Cpe Carrera 4	1,700	5,050	8,400	16,800	29,400	42,000
2d Cpe Carrera 4 Targa	1,700	5,150	8,600	17,200	30,100	43,000
2d Cpe Carrera 4 Conv	1,900	5,650	9,400	18,800	32,900	47,000
1994 928 GTS, V-8						
2d Cpe	1,500	4,450	7,400	14,800	25,900	37,000
1995 968, 4-cyl.						
2d Cpe	900	2,650	4,400	8,800	15,400	22,000
2d Conv	1,100	3,250	5,400	10,800	18,900	27,000
1995 911, 6-cyl.						
2d Cpe Carrera 2	1,600	4,800	8,000	16,000	28,000	40,000
2d Cpe Carrera 2 Conv	1,750	5,300	8,800	17,600	30,800	44,000
2d Cpe Carrera 4	1,700	5,050	8,400	16,800	29,400	42,000
2d Cpe Carrera 4 Conv	1,900	5,650	9,400	18,800	32,900	47,000

	6	5	4	3	2	1
1995 928GTS, V-8						
2d Cpe	1,500	4,450	7,400	14,800	25,900	37,000
1996 911, 6-cyl.						
2d Cpe Carrera 2	1,500	4,550	7,600	15,200	26,600	38,000
2d Cpe Carrera 2 Conv	1,700	5,050	8,400	16,800	29,400	42,000
2d Cpe Carrera 4	1,600	4,800	8,000	16,000	28,000	40,000
2d Cpe Carrera 4S	1,700	5,150	8,600	17,200	30,100	43,000
2d Cpe Carrera 4 Conv	1,800	5,400	9,000	18,000	31,500	45,000
2d Targa Cpe	1,650	4,900	8,200	16,400	28,700	41,000
2d Turbo Cpe 4x4	3,000	9,000	15,000	30,000	52,500	75,000
1997 911, 6-cyl.						
2d Cpe Carrera 2	1,520	4,560	7,600	15,200	26,600	38,000
2d Cpe Carrera 2 Conv	1,680	5,040	8,400	16,800	29,400	42,000
2d Cpe Carrera 4	1,600	4,800	8,000	16,000	28,000	40,000
2d Cpe Carrera 4S	1,720	5,160	8,600	17,200	30,100	43,000
2d Cpe Carrera 4 Conv	1,800	5,400	9,000	18,000	31,500	45,000
2d Targa Cpe	1,640	4,920	8,200	16,400	28,700	41,000
2d Turbo Cpe 4x4	3,000	9,000	15,000	30,000	52,500	75,000
1997 Boxster, 6-cyl.						
2d Conv	880	2,640	4,400	8,800	15,400	22,000

NOTE: Add 5 percent for detachable HT.